D0952049

The Uncivil War

The Rise of Hate, Violence, and Terrorism in America

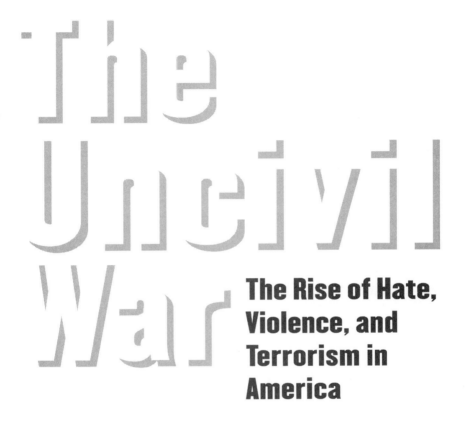

The Uncivil War

The Rise of Hate, Violence, and Terrorism in America

Stephen Singular
New York Times Bestselling Author

NEW MILLENNIUM PRESS
Beverly Hills

Design: Susie Dotan
Typeface: Body - Journal Text, Titles - Folio Bold Condensed, Future Bold
Condensed

Copyright ©2001 by Stephen Singular
All rights reserved. No part of this book may be produced or transmitted in any
form or by any means, electronic or mechanical, including photocopying, recording, or by any information storage and retrieval system without permission in
writing from the publisher.

Library of Congress Cataloging-in-Publication Data

Singular, Stephen
    The uncivil war: the rise of hate, violence, and terrorism in America / Stephen
Singular
        p.cm.
    Includes index.
    ISBN: 1-893224-19-9 (hc.)
    1. Violence—United States. 2. Terrorism—United States. 3. Hate—United States. 4.
United States—Social conditions—1980- I. Title.

HN90.V5 S48 2001
303.6'0973—dc21

00-42383

New Millennium Press
A Division of NMWorldMedia, Inc.
301 N. Canon Drive
Suite 214
Beverly Hills, CA 90210

Printed in the United States of America

to Y.

CONCORDIA UNIVERSITY LIBRARY
PORTLAND, OR 97211

> "WHOEVER CHASES MONSTERS SHOULD SEE TO IT THAT IN THE PROCESS HE DOES NOT BECOME A MONSTER HIMSELF"

Rafael Perez, former LAPD officer, at his sentencing for stealing cocaine from a police evidence room

PROLOGUE

On a cloudy afternoon in late June 1984, I drove over to the Denver townhouse where Alan Berg had recently been murdered. The place was deserted and the air was heavy and quiet, eerily peaceful, like the ominous still moments before a violent spring storm. The yellow police tape had been removed from around Berg's home, so I got out of the car and walked up to the driveway where he'd stepped from his Volkswagen at 9:30 the previous Monday night. A dozen rounds of gunfire had shattered his lean torso and bearded face, instantly killing him. Traces of dried blood were still on the pavement near my feet.

Several bullets had passed through him and splintered his gray garage door, leaving holes in the wood. I studied the marks from a distance but felt the urge to come closer. I approached the door gingerly, then reached out and put my fingers in the fresh bullet holes. The feel of the rough wood made the murder real to me, and I realized, in the strange way of such things, that Berg truly was dead and that his grating, searching, funny, intelligent voice had been silenced forever. A radio talk show host in Denver, he'd once simultaneously won awards for being the most liked and most disliked media personality in the city. His words were like an irritant that could become addictive. His death would resonate throughout the community and far beyond it for years to come. I missed him, and slipping my fingertips into these holes was my way of saying goodbye.

On a cold, damp evening in April 1999, I drove out to Columbine High School in southwestern Denver, not far from my home. This time I was not alone at the crime scene, and it was not at all quiet or peaceful. I stood next to a chain-link fence near the facility and watched hundreds upon hundreds of teenagers and adults kneel down in the spring mud and burst into tears, grabbing onto one another for support or clutching the fence and swaying as they wailed out their anguish. Several days earlier two Columbine students, Eric Harris and Dylan Klebold, had walked into this suburban school and opened fire with shotguns and semi-automatic weapons, wounding twenty-three students and killing twelve teenagers, one teacher, and themselves.

I raised my hand and touched the chilly metal fence, looking around at the mourners. A man was crying and holding a basketball; he leaned over and set it down gently in the mud. A woman mumbled a prayer and placed a yellow rose in a square hole in the fence. No one said anything or made eye contact with anyone else, as if the shame of what had happened at

Columbine was too deep to be put into words or even glances. The emotion of the moment was overwhelming horror and surprise. These were our kids who'd done this, the ones we thought we knew. We could no longer pretend that as a community or a society we were innocent or better than any other group of people.

The blood that flowed across our television screens at night was usually spilled in faraway places like Kosovo in the former Yugoslavia, where Serbs had conducted a war of "ethnic cleansing" and you could expect such madness. But now something similar had happened in a very respectable Denver suburb, and, grief-stricken, we wandered around in the biting April air with our mouths open and utter bewilderment on our faces: How can this be? Why are our children killing one another?

These two events — Alan Berg's murder and the carnage at Columbine High — were separated by fifteen years and fifteen times as many bodies. But they were also, I dimly sensed on that first visit to the school, closely connected. In 1984, it had taken time to grasp why Berg had been gunned down in his driveway. In 1999, months also passed before any substantial information leaked out about Harris and Klebold — information that revealed their deeper purpose for unleashing this horrific attack on their fellow students. Only time could unravel the strands of violence that had led to Berg's demise and the massacre inside the walls of Columbine.

The strands were in many ways the same.

At first local authorities believed that Berg, who'd enjoyed arguing on the air with callers and hanging up on them, had been killed by a lone angry radio listener. Early in the investigation, Don Mulnix, the chief of the detective division, had been asked about suspects in the case. Looking at the Denver phone book, he replied, "There are at least two million suspects. Anybody within the sound of his voice might have had a motive for killing him."

Berg's death seemed to be a single, random act of violence, but the police eventually learned that there was nothing random about it. The holes in his garage door had been made by a .45-caliber MAC-10 machine pistol with a silencer. The weapon had been fired by Bruce Pierce, a neo-Nazi in his late twenties who belonged to the Order, a small band of terrorists from the American Northwest (their name came from a blood-soaked, anti-Semitic novel by William Pierce titled *The Turner Diaries*). Berg had been killed because he was Jewish and outspoken, and because he'd tangled with David Lane, one of the Order's founders, on his talk show.

This death was the first political assassination in Denver's history. Four months to the day after the crime, the firearm that slayed Berg was discovered in an Idaho farmhouse holding a huge arsenal — guns, ammunition, and explosives — and a room decorated as a shrine to Adolf Hitler. The Order had hoped to start a white-power revolution that would eliminate minorities, homosexuals, feminists, liberals, and other enemies. Berg was its first target. His murder was intended as a test run for killing more prominent Jews later on.

Berg's shooting was a classic "environmental" homicide. Long before Bruce Pierce unloaded his weapon into the talk show host, Reverend Richard Butler and his racist followers were preaching hatred of Jews and other minorities at the Aryan Nations church in the northwest woods of Idaho. The church attracted bigots from all over the country, and the Order emerged from its congregation. After Berg's death, Butler and his minions were quick to point out that they hadn't violated any laws, did not advocate physical violence against anyone, and were merely exercising their constitutional rights of free speech and freedom of religion.

Butler may not have broken any laws, but he'd done something just as dangerous. From his pulpit he'd encouraged feelings of hatred toward others, eventually attracting people to his compound who would one day normalize those feelings by picking up guns and firing them at human beings. The hate generated at the Aryan Nations church eventually hardened into murder because the environment supported it.

Who pulled the trigger that ended Berg's life was almost incidental. When it was time for blood to flow, a killer arrived and the bullets began to fly.

Before Columbine, the country had seen numerous school

shootings — in Mississippi, Arkansas, and Oregon, among other places — but Columbine was special, or at least especially horrifying. Harris and Klebold had engineered the most deadly school shooting in the nation's history, but from the boys' perspective, it was a colossal bust. They'd built ninety-five bombs and planted most of them around Columbine. Some of the explosives were intended to detonate inside the school cafeteria at 11:20 a.m., during the height of lunch hour. Hundreds of kids would die while eating. When those who survived came running outside to escape the fireballs and mayhem, Harris and Klebold would gun them down one by one. The bombs and bullets could easily kill 500 people, maybe more. However, when the explosives failed to go off and the plan went awry, the young men entered the school and began shooting, ending their own lives after taking thirteen others.

The purpose of this bloodbath, as revealed on a videotape discovered after the killers' deaths, closely resembled the Order's. Harris and Klebold had wanted to "kick-start a revolution" against their enemies: "niggers, spics, Jews, gays, fucking whites...humanity." They were motivated by extreme hatred and, like the members of the Order, Adolf Hitler was one of their heroes. Their day of infamy at the school — April 20, 1999 — was the Fuhrer's 110th birthday.

Initially, the Columbine massacre was widely viewed as a killing spree by a couple of late adolescent boys who had given in to their random violent impulses. The aching question — Why would they would do such a thing? — hung in the air and lingered there long after all the wilted flowers honoring the dead at the school had been scooped up and hauled away. Why would two intelligent young men from solid middle-class families (Klebold drove a BMW, after all) have chosen to engage in mass murder and destroy themselves in the process? How could this have occurred in the upwardly mobile suburb of Littleton, Colorado? How could it have taken place at a good institution like Columbine High School? What was the message the boys were sending — the point of the event?

Like the Berg murder, Columbine was anything but a random act of violence. It was much more carefully planned than the 1984 assassination and designed to be the single largest act of domestic terrorism in the history of the United States, one that would have dwarfed the 1995 bombing of the Alfred P. Murrah federal building in Oklahoma City, which ended 168 lives. Two key differences separate the perpetrators of these criminal deeds. Timothy McVeigh, the convicted killer in the Oklahoma City bombing, who'd also used *The Turner Diaries* as a blueprint for his destruction, did not know his victims. The Columbine shooters were acquainted with some of theirs. More significantly, the teenagers chose to die with their victims. They believed so strongly in their cause that they made no attempt to hide their involvement or get away with their crimes.

A month earlier, the boys had made a detailed video outlining exactly what they were going to do and how they would die in the process. They sacrificed themselves for their convictions, just as Middle Eastern terrorists had been doing for a long time. This kind of commitment is very rare in the annals of American homicide; almost every killer tries not to get caught and to avoid death while slaying others. But this was not homicide, which was why the event seemed so confusing and impenetrable. This was war — a war that had been building and spreading throughout the country for the past couple of decades, a war that like any other produced tributes and memorials to the dead.

In the spring of 1999, people from all over the Denver area gathered flowers or handwritten tributes to the murdered students and placed them near Columbine, expressing their shock and sorrow and trying to make sense of the tragedy. Lately, such massive bouquets had begun showing up all around the nation, in the wake of other school shootings, in workplace and domestic killings, and at locations of similar acts of violence — none of which was driven by monetary or personal gain, but by the emotion of hatred. The adult world, symbolized by all the men and women who stood out in the mud and wept at Columbine, did not begin to comprehend why this was happening, nor did they understand what role they were playing in the spreading madness.

At the close of twentieth century, a great catharsis was unfolding across the land, a venting of pure rage that was leaving the dead strewn everywhere. This force, this movement, this warning, which flourished directly below the veneer of American society, was rising up and killing people. In the midst of widespread peace abroad and unparalleled prosperity at home, some of our neighbors and their children had decided to shoot as many others as they pleased.

The uncivil war had begun.

Like the Berg murder, the slaughter inside Columbine High School was a classic environmental crime, but this time the toxic environment was not limited to a handful of people preaching hatred in hidden enclaves in the Northwest woods. Now it had permeated the tree-lined, manicured lawns of suburban America.

A very dark evolution can be found in the fifteen years that separate the murder of Alan Berg from the deaths at Columbine. Those who killed Berg lived on the fringes. They held obviously fanatical beliefs. They were young, angry, uneducated, and unsuccessful working-class white men. Their prospects in life were poor, and they clung to their racism and hatred as a kind of life raft, something to give them an identity and make them feel important. Their terrorism came out of their own limited circumstances. By contrast, Harris and Klebold seemed to have everything to live for and all the privileges one could want: money, family support, friends, and educational opportunities. But they also had bottomless reservoirs of hurt and rage — and their terrorism evolved in Eric Harris's well-furnished, suburban bedroom.

Between 1984 and 1999, domestic terrorism, in many different forms and guises, moved from the edges of our society directly into the mainstream — from the back woods of Idaho to the heart of Middle America, from the public expression of unexamined feelings of anger and contempt for others to the actual act of pulling a trigger or detonating a bomb. And it did so because the nation's political, social, and economic climate supported this change. The events at Columbine are the result of the cultural environment we have created, nurtured, pandered to, protected, rewarded, and greatly expanded since the murder of Alan Berg — a culture of judgment, blame, division, hate, and meanness that saturates the Internet, our political landscape, our religions, our legal system, our urban police departments, and most especially, our media. We are all soldiers in this war.

To experience the prevailing emotional atmosphere of America at the beginning of the new millennium, all one has to do is click onto a hate-filled website or tune in an AM radio station or a cable-TV talk show and listen to hosts, guests, and callers rip apart people they've never met and know virtually nothing about. Under the constitutional rights of the First Amendment, they are free to proclaim their hatred of anyone and everyone, free to accuse them of all manner of evil or criminal behavior — rape or child molestation or murder — regardless of the truth. The producers of these shows prod guests and callers to engage in this demonizing because it makes for more heated programming, which in turns yields better ratings. The nineties experienced a bull market in public hatred, and along the way talk shows overruled the principles of fairness and balance in the law upon which our nation was built. The consequences have been disastrous.

In grotesque ways, we are learning — or failing to learn — one of the oldest and saddest historical lessons of all: a society that violates or destroys its ideals and underlying principles will eventually descend into violence. What Harris and Klebold did was truly shocking, but equally shocking was the number of similar plans for bloodshed made in the first few weeks following Columbine. According to the National Safety Center, 3,000 other high school students across the country — 3,000! — concocted bomb threats or violent schemes that were intended to result in death. As a journalist reporting on the disaster's aftermath for a national magazine told me, "If I hear one more teenager say that he or she understands why those two kids did what they did, I'm going to scream."

Our legal, political, and journalistic principles are being publicly shattered one by one as our children gun each other down and as domestic terrorism moves from the extremes of our society to the boys next door. America is now fighting a very uncivil war, and everyone is losing. The battle is not being covered by the media, except in scattered fragments, and there is no recognition that all of us are engaged in the combat.

This war is subtle and difficult to see as a whole. Most violence in America is viewed as individual acts of madness — not as the outcome of a collective social process. There is no time for the media to try to search for or identify any deeper connections beneath the steady flow of blood because they're out covering the next ghastly round of murders.

Moreover, the foundation of this war's battlefield is largely not in the external world that journalists normally explore. It's inside of human beings, in our emotions and private distortions, and that's a far more difficult territory to penetrate and uncover. It's much easier to look for villains to blame and for solutions that exist outside of us.

Looking back to the slaying of Alan Berg, the Order's assassination of the talk show host seems almost quaint compared to the plans Harris and Klebold had for Columbine, yet it remains relevant. The same basic dynamics that killed Berg are currently shaping our nation and its children in dangerous ways, and too many of us are downloading the hatred in our culture and converting it into emotional and verbal abuse — or murder. An understanding of those dynamics can illuminate what we are all now facing. How we came to this place of laying flowers near where our kids or coworkers have died in mass shootings is not a short or simple story. The violence afflicting us is neither mysterious nor random, but its origins are something we have not yet chosen to confront.

In April of 1999, it was genuinely horrifying to visit

Columbine, look at the crime scene, and listen to people weep on the cold school grounds — and to realize that the children of my generation, whose ideals about curing society of hatred, fear, and racism had brought about the political and cultural revolutions of the 1960s, were committing acts of savagery in defiance of these very ideals. You could not escape the conclusion that something had gone very wrong.

This book is a starting place for identifying that wrong, for understanding its causes, and, hopefully, for ending it.

THE ROOTS OF RAGE

1

The Aryan Nations compound in northern Idaho is surrounded by a chain-link fence and holds a watchtower, armed guards, a rifle range, German shepherds, and Doberman pinschers. On a wooden shed two words are painted in red and blue letters: "Whites Only." The organization's world headquarters, twenty acres of land near the Coeur d'Alene National Forest, is known by its inhabitants as the "Heavenly Reich." Hitler had lost the Second World War, committing suicide near its conclusion, but his ideas on racial hatred still rule here.

The brutality of the beliefs expressed inside the compound, which also contains a church and an elementary school, makes a startling contrast to the beauty of the hills, evergreens, and lakes of the Northwest woods, a landscape that local people call "God's Country." The natural setting conjures up freedom and solitude, but the armed guards and chain-link fence ensure that nothing different or new can enter these grounds. The world is divided into what lies outside this compound and what lives within — into "us versus them."

Reverend Richard Butler preaches that Jews are not the Chosen People of the Old Testament but wicked impostors who'd been born from the coupling of Eve and Satan. The real Chosen People, Butler declares in his sermons, are just like him. They're the Anglo-Saxons and Scandinavians who came from England, Ireland, Scotland, Germany, Sweden, Norway, and the United States. Jews, African-Americans, and other minorities, Butler insists from his pulpit, are inferior or less than inferior. In fact, blacks are subhuman and referred to as "mud people."

The worst thing a white person can do, according to Butler, is marry someone with black skin and have children. Mixing the races is the essence of evil. At the Aryan Nations school, young children are taught the four "R's": readin', ritin', rithmetic, and race. They're taught that whites are superior to all others, the "law bearers of the world." They're taught to hate. The state of Idaho requires no accreditation for this "Christian Academy," so the kids inside the Aryan Nations classrooms learn about white supremacy without any influence from the outside world.

The Aryan Nations religion began in nineteenth-century England but found its home in America during the post-war years in Southern California. In 1946, Wesley Swift started the Anglo-Saxon Christian Congregation in Los Angeles, a city well-known for its racial prejudice (until the 1960s, real estate covenants prevented African-Americans and other minority groups from living in many sections of the metropolis). When Swift died in 1970, two new leaders came forward to spread his message. William Potter Gale had served under General Douglas MacArthur and directed anti-Japanese operations in the Philippines. Following the war, he ran his own paramilitary group, the California Rangers, wrote tracts on conducting guerilla warfare, and preached anti-Semitic sermons in churches and over the radio. He taught his followers that America was involved in a holy war, a death struggle between the white Christian population and minorities — a fight for the soul of the nation.

The other new white supremacist leader, Richard Butler, studied aeronautical engineering at Los Angeles City College and was an Air Force instructor in World War II. He then worked at Lockheed before opening his own lucrative airplane parts business. After he and Gale clashed over who should carry on Swift's legacy, Butler took his vision and moved north. He settled just outside Hayden Lake in Kootenai County, Idaho, which had 1,200 square miles and a population of 60,000. Only fifty residents were Jewish and only twenty were African-American. Kootenai County was an excellent location for a fishing or hiking expedition, but for some it was also the perfect spot to escape the growing complexities of modern American life and cities like Los Angeles.

You could buy twenty pristine wooded acres and pretend

that the rest of the world did not exist. You could establish your own rules, your own religious and educational guidelines. You could start your own society from scratch if the larger one beyond the forest was changing in ways you could not tolerate or accept. There were many people out there who looked and acted, felt and thought, differently from you, and rather than adapt to the incredible diversity of America and join with others in a unified community, you could retreat and turn inward. If you had the money, you could even break away and build your own little kingdom. You could become the god of this new realm, dictating exactly who could inhabit your land and what they could read or believe in or worship. You could force them to be just like you — or to get off your property.

Inside his church, Butler made the men wear blue poplin jackets, blue ties, and white shirts. He made the women don blue or white blouses and skirts. He told all mothers and fathers that white children were to be exceedingly well behaved. On the shoulders of their uniforms, the men wore the Aryan Nations insignia, featuring two crosses, a shield, a crown, and a double-edged sword. During celebrations or rituals, they used the one-armed Nazi salute made famous by Hitler and cried out "Hail Victory!" They ran the Aryan Nations printing press and sent out tracts to prisons and other venues about how white men should think; how white women should not work outside the home and how they should conduct themselves within the home; how white children should be raised; and how all Aryan

Nations warriors should prepare themselves for the upcoming battle against their enemies.

When the sun went down, the men gathered in the darkness at the compound and, shoulder to shoulder, burned large crosses that sent flames high into the sky. They chanted slogans in the firelight, with loaded guns in their hands and mounting violence in their words. They railed against the "other" — the black other, the Jewish other, the Hispanic other, the Asian other, the homosexual other, the liberal other, the feminist other, the white other who did not accept their views, or any other human being who did not fit Butler's iron-fisted view of what people had to be.

The heavyset Butler had flat, narrow, dull-looking eyes. The monotone of his voice and the hard lines of his face told you that he did not acknowledge either social or personal complexity. He did not question his own assumptions. He did not have time for self-doubt or skepticism. He did not want to know about others, about the secrets, ambiguities, subtleties, and ironies that make up the texture and fabric of human life. He did not want to hear any evidence about race or religion that did not fit his own preconceptions. He did not want his world disturbed. His eyes told you that he was certain he knew the truth. Anyone who disagreed with him was not merely wrong, but his enemy.

Because he was right, Butler had no compunction about attacking others, and his message could not have been more clear: individual differences were not to be celebrated as part of God's limitless imagination and creativity, but to be feared and despised and destroyed. Individual preferences at the most private levels of human behavior were to be denied or obliterated altogether. Sexual issues in particular — the sexual behavior of men and women regarding intercourse and abortion — were to be controlled or stopped absolutely. There was only one way to live, Richard Butler's way.

Butler mailed out Aryan Nations literature to white inmates in jails across America because he liked to recruit among the poor, the dispossessed, and the incarcerated. After being set free, some of the ex-prisoners came north to visit the man behind the pamphlets. A few took up Butler's beliefs, which he now called the Identity Christian religion and movement. He was God's chosen person, he told the newcomers, and so were his worshippers, those young men who traveled to the compound from all over the Northwest and beyond.

He brought in David Lane from Denver, who'd argued on the radio with Alan Berg. He brought in Bruce Pierce from Kentucky, a troubled, volatile high school dropout who came to Butler looking for political guidance and a spiritual teacher. He brought in Bob Mathews from Arizona, a rabblerouser with charismatic qualities, a hothead who was tired of all the windy speeches about white power and Identity Christianity, who believed in action and was itching for it to begin.

This trio of men listened to Butler's ideas. They read and

studied *The Turner Diaries* by William Pierce, a physicist who'd begun his career at the Los Alamos National Laboratory in New Mexico. In the 1960s, Pierce became a professor at the University of Oregon but soon left academia and went to work for George Lincoln Rockwell, the head of the American Nazi Party. *The Turner Diaries* was published in 1978 and eventually sold 350,000 copies, establishing itself as *the* classic of hate fiction and fantasy.

In the novel, a handful of white men form a hardcore group of revolutionaries called the Order, who are committed to bloodshed and to changing the ethnic face of America. They execute Jews, blacks, homosexuals, women, and many others, eliminating 60 million of their fellow citizens before their victory is complete. They use hatchets, guns, and bombs (a photocopied segment of this book — detailing how white supremacists blow up a government building — was found in the vehicle driven by Timothy McVeigh following his arrest for the 1995 Oklahoma City bombing).

While William Pierce and Richard Butler engaged in violent rhetoric, Butler in particular did not want anyone breaking the law on his property. Chanting anti-Semitic slogans was one thing. Killing people, Butler contended, at least in public, was something else. He disavowed any connection to the illegal behavior and hate crimes that were being committed all around him.

It wasn't his fault that in 1983, a decade after his arrival in

Idaho, the state's Human Rights Commission reported that racial harassment over the past three years had increased by 550 percent. He wasn't responsible for those painted swastikas that were showing up in Kootenai County or for the words "JEW SWINE" that appeared on a Hayden Lake restaurant owned by sixty-two-year-old Sid Rosen. Butler wasn't to blame when Connie Fort, a local white woman married to a black man, began receiving hate mail and death threats. He couldn't be held accountable for the disappearing line between emotional violence and bloodletting.

In 1979 in Greensboro, North Carolina, Ku Klux Klan members opened fire on white left-wing demonstrators, leaving five of them dead. In 1981, Henry Francis Hays, the Exalted Cyclops of a klavern in Mobile, Alabama, beat and hung a black teenager. That same year Louis Beam, a former Grand Dragon of the KKK, attacked Vietnamese refugees and burned their fishing boats off the coast of the Texas. Also in 1981, Joseph Paul Franklin was convicted of a Salt Lake City sniper attack that killed two black youths. In 1982, Frank Spisak gunned down two more black men in Cleveland and killed a third, whom he mistakenly believed was Jewish.

In 1983, Gordon Kahl, a member of the anti-government group Posse Comitatus, killed two U.S. marshals who came to his home to arrest him for tax violations. And in 1984, the year of Berg's death, Richard Butler held a World Congress for Aryan soldiers at his compound, where the talk now focused on specific strategies for domestic terrorism. The warriors learned how to bomb bridges and put gas in urban sewers (ignite the fuel and you can bring a major city to a halt). They laid plans for a nationwide computer system that would link white supremacists everywhere — a secret, electronic network of plotted violence and rage. The network would soon be online and carry the names and addresses of many Aryan Nations enemies.

The era of high-tech hatred had arrived — and the terrorists were ready to strike.

Nineteen eighty-four, the year made famous by George Orwell's chilling novel, turned out to be the year of the Order. Its members, a score of men and one woman, committed 240 crimes, counterfeited untold thousands of dollars, stole more than $4 million, killed five people, and forced the federal government to launch the largest-ever investigation into domestic terrorism. The tragedy of 1984 was not, as Orwell had foreseen, that the government tried to take away the rights of American citizens or turn them into automatons, but that a handful of racists set out to kill individuals and destroy democracy.

All of the Order's members were eventually incarcerated or killed. Bob Mathews died in a shootout with authorities on Whidbey Island, north of Seattle. David Lane was arrested in Winston-Salem, North Carolina, and Bruce Pierce was taken into custody in Rossville, Georgia. About half of the group cooperated with the government and testified against the other half in a 1985 federal trial in Seattle. The defendants were prosecuted under the 1970 Racketeer Influenced and Corrupt Organization (RICO) law, which had been designed to go after organized crime. Each of the defendants was found guilty and given a lengthy sentence.

The distinguishing trait in the saga of the Order was that the social, political, and legal systems handling these crimes acted appropriately. Various police departments across the country and the FBI ran good investigations and solved the cases. Prosecutors and defense attorneys behaved with intelligence and decorum. The Seattle trial, under the stern hand of Judge Walter McGovern, dealt efficiently and fairly with the defendants. The media covered the story with restraint and objectivity, respecting the rights of the accused and the months-long, tedious courtroom proceeding that ended with the incarceration of dangerous people. Finally, the public let the legal system do its work without interference. When the trial was over, the event had meaning and clarity: a small but deadly cancer had been defeated. One could take some comfort and pride in the way our society had responded to a true menace.

All of that would change soon enough.

2

The men who killed Alan Berg believed they were starting a white power revolution, but they were really just acting out their individual pathologies based on fear, hurt or anger. Those pathologies might have many names, but they all had one thing in common: they defined the world as "us versus them." In the eyes of the Order, "we" were good and right, while "they" were bad and wrong. All Jews were guilty of something because they were Jewish. All African-Americans were criminals or had criminal tendencies because they were black. Asians, Hispanics, homosexuals, feminists, other minorities, and Caucasians who embraced tolerance were despised because they were different.

Members of the Order saw evil in "the other" — in anyone perceived as being different — and once they'd identified the enemy, they were free to destroy him. When their religious beliefs and racial fanaticism collided with their emotional disturbances, all hell broke loose.

After the group's demise, many people analyzed the Order from a political perspective. The men had presented themselves as white radicals, yet their politics made no sense. They ranted against a federal government that they felt was trying to ruin them personally and choke off their freedom, but they were deeply anti-freedom in their positions against abortion, sexual preferences, and other forms of private behavior. They all were working class men who'd struggled to earn a living, yet they had no plans for redistributing wealth to help people like themselves. They were simply afraid that a black person or a woman would take away their jobs (and much more fearful that black men would sleep with and marry white women). They had no strategy for how to improve society — only to purge it.

Their rage centered not on conventional political issues but on what people intrinsically *are:* white or black, Jew or Gentile, gay or straight. The Order was threatened, to the point of committing murder, by innate human differences.

Each of the leaders had his own pathology that was rooted in his past. David Lane had grown up very poor and was abandoned by his father. His boyhood diet had been so bad that he'd contracted rickets, and he once confessed to a friend that in order to survive, he'd eaten rats. In adulthood, his hands still ached so much from his old illness that he often couldn't engage in one of his favorite activities: hustling people and winning bets on the golf course. Each time he swung the club and felt pain shiver through him, he blamed someone else for his condition. His anger cost him two marriages. The more he succumbed to his emotional instability, the more his political and racist ideas consumed him.

Sometimes at night he would listen to the Alan Berg show to feed his hatred of Jews. Or he would go to nightclubs and seek out Jewish women as dance partners, not telling them who he was or how he felt about them. He was intimately involved with his own rage. His problems, which over the years became a global, political philosophy, were intensely personal.

So were Bob Mathews's. With dark hair and a dark complexion, he was once described as "looking like a Mexican." The remark infuriated him. Another time a co-worker at the Pend Oreville lead and zinc mine in northeastern Washington taped a pinup of a naked black woman to his locker. Mathews was ready to fight. He desired to be whiter than he was, and because of this he hated people who were not the color he wanted to be.

To compensate, he created a fantasy world based on his racist ideas. Mathews enjoyed sitting around with his buddies and recalling the ancient Norse and Viking sagas, the great tales of courage and strength about the northern warriors in distant times. He wanted to be a Scandinavian god. More than anything, he wanted to be a hero who could clean up the confusion and the complexity, the mess of modern life. He believed that if he died in battle, fighting against his racial enemies, he would be whisked off by the Valkyries — the handmaidens of Odin, the supreme being of Norse mythology — and laid to rest in the great hall of immortality in Valhalla. For this honor, he was willing to die in a shootout with the FBI.

Mathews and Lane shared a common vision: They passionately felt that something was wrong with America and believed they could fix it. All around them they saw a pervasive spiritual disease that was eroding the country's moral foundation. Mathews viewed himself as one of our nation's Founding Fathers, recast for the late twentieth century, when all of society was engulfed in rapid change and rapid decline. Lane compared himself to Thomas Jefferson, a true patriot who only wanted to help the United States become a better place to live. The two men spent months and years thinking and writing about building a purified white America, while ignoring that the disease they perceived everywhere lived inside of them. One piece of that disease was narcissism — not self-love but self-obsession.

"It is too simple," Norman Mailer wrote of Henry Miller in *Genius and Lust*, "to think of the narcissist as someone in love with himself. One can detest oneself intimately and be a narcissist. What characterizes narcissism is the fundamental relation. It is with oneself."

Mathews and Lane were primarily involved with their own unseen, unexamined demons. The flesh-and-blood lives of African-Americans or Jews or homosexuals may not have existed for them and nothing may have mattered except their own hateful feelings, but they were not assassins.

Bruce Pierce was. A native of Frankfort, Kentucky, and a high school dropout, Pierce had married after quitting school, had soon fathered a child, and had gotten divorced in 1979. In the next several years, he remarried, had more children, and came to Aryan Nations searching for others who shared his views. A number of Order members liked to debate issues and discuss their philosophy, but not Pierce, who was a large man with a strong, intimidating physical presence. He liked action. He liked going into the woods with his guns and shooting at six-pointed stars, at pictures of former Israeli prime minister Menachem Begin, at other photos of prominent Jews, and at caricatured images of African-Americans. Pierce always had trouble at home, with his wife and kids, or when he tried to hold a job, but he found satisfaction and relief in discharging his weapons and pretending that he was a white Aryan warrior. Yet he was soon bored with firing at cut-out figures of his enemies and wanted to take his idea of revolution to another, more tangible level. Mathews and Lane were intellectuals compared to Pierce, who had to have an outlet for his rage.

He was totally armed and totally violent. More than any other member of the Order, he was also clearly mentally ill and removed from the emotional consequences of his actions. The older he got, the more desensitized, disturbed, and dangerous he became. He had a lifelong inability to fit in with any group of people, except the haters who made up the Order, and in time he broke away from them too, fleeing across the country with his arsenal in tow. He was alone when arrested — and involved with no one but himself. After observing Pierce for several months, Neil Halprin, a defense lawyer at the RICO trial in Seattle, remarked: "Bruce Pierce is psychotic. If ever there was a man who should enter a plea of not guilty by reason of insanity, it is Bruce Pierce."

Alan Berg's killer had been drawn to Aryan Nations because

that organization took away all of his doubts and answered all of his questions. It made clear who his real enemies were. The constant background noise of anti-Semitism at Butler's compound, the steady flow of words and emotions laced with anger, the normalizing of hate, and the growing drumbeat of violence that surrounded him had taken root in Pierce's mind. They had become so much a part of his damaged psyche that by June 18, 1984, he was more than ready to open fire at the first available breathing Jewish target. When Berg stepped from his Volkswagen that evening, Pierce aimed the MAC-10 at his upper body and pulled the trigger.

The social tragedy was complete. The demonizing of human beings had joined with deep psychological turmoil, and blood had spilled on the pavement. Richard Butler had given Pierce a reason to kill. Mathews and Lane had told him where Berg lived and when he was expected home. All Pierce had to do was wait for him in his driveway.

That night at Berg's townhouse, two significant things occurred that would echo across America and disturb its future in bigger and bloodier ways for years to come. The first was that a hate group had stopped talking and started acting. Committed to criminal behavior, the Order had taken its anti-Semitic and anti-African-American bigotry to the level of physical violence. Other domestic terrorists would soon follow.

Second, Berg's murder signaled (or should have signaled) the end of innocence for the talk show media. Until now, the radio talk program — TV talk shows had not yet become so popular — was nothing more than a kind of old-fashioned telephone connection for the lonely, the bored, the opinionated, or for anyone looking to get on the air and make a statement.

Bob McWilliams, one of Berg's first on-air employers, summed up that point of view shortly after the murder when he said, "Talk radio is so successful because of the sense of community people get out of it. We live in an era that is so impersonal, so mechanical, and so remote that people love to get on the country party line and talk with Aunt Jessie and raise a little bit of hell. It's a throwback to the old country store and whittling and yakking about this and that. People just sort of like it."

Berg's own definition of the medium was delivered on CBS's *60 Minutes* a few months before his demise. "It's the last neighborhood in town," he said. "People don't talk to each other anymore. Talk radio is the last place for them to hear human voices. So many people are isolated today. They don't have a chance to communicate."

Before Berg's death, few people paid attention to the power of the talk show. It was, after all, just entertainment and carried no other meaning or importance. Few questioned what effect the medium might be having on callers and listeners. If Berg's murder did not change this view, it did cause some observers to address these issues and to wonder about the larger ramifications.

Ken Hamblin, a talk show host who'd worked with Berg at his last station, confessed that he'd been naive before the killing. "We were just very innocent," he said. "We didn't understand what was out there."

"We didn't know the impact we were having," said Judy Wegener, a colleague of Berg's at another Denver station. "We didn't know if we were talking to thousands of people or five. When I started on the radio, I used my own name on the air. I had no idea how vulnerable I was making myself. People called me up and made kidnapping threats on my children. At first, Alan and I were playing at something on the radio and having a good time. Then the times got nastier and the people got nastier and it got scarier. It got to be a bigger game, just heating up and heating up."

In 1984, the game abruptly ended for Berg, but the violence behind his death was just the beginning of a wave of hatred and bloodshed — a wave that was building and filtering out beyond the fringes and into the mainstream institutions that held together the fabric of our society.

In a sense William Potter Gale, Richard Butler's rival for the control of the white power movement, had been right. A holy war was coming to America, a war for the soul (or the future) of the country, but it wasn't really a war between the religions or the races or between the sexes or even specific groups of people. It was broader and deeper — yet more hidden — than that. It was a war that existed within individuals and it would be fought not over public policy issues, but over personal differences and personal emotions. It was as intimate as David Lane's hatred of Jews and Bob Mathews's detestation of the color of his own skin.

Alan Berg's voice had once reached thirty-eight states plus parts of Canada and Mexico, and following his assassination, Denver and the Rocky Mountain region showed a great outpouring of feeling for the slain talk show host. Listeners brought flowers and hand-scrawled messages to the crime scene. They wrote poems to honor him. They called up his old radio station and cried on the air while remembering him. A few days after the killing, Denverites drove home from work with dimmed lights as a tribute to a voice now silenced forever. The informal wake for Berg lasted nearly a week and culminated on a Sunday afternoon, when two thousand mourners showed up at Temple Emanuel to grieve the untimely end of someone who'd been known as "the man you love to hate."

No one could have predicted this spontaneous eruption of warmth for somebody whom most listeners had never met and many others did not like. In death, Berg's role in the local media was finally revealed. He got under people's skin. He crawled inside their minds and their emotions. He let them feel. He made them think. At times he was overbearing but he was never complacent, and he jarred people out of their own complacency. He wasn't, as widely advertised, just a loudmouth on the radio, but a provocateur, and he'd had a far larger effect on the community than anyone would have imagined, shaping and coloring parts of an entire metropolitan area. It took his murder to bring the startling realization to the surface: Berg had mattered.

In every modern scientific discipline, discoveries have been made that echo the phenomenon surrounding the life and the assassination of Alan Berg. Nothing exists in isolation. Everything is connected to everything else, even if the connections are not visible. The globe functions like a single living cell and the cliché has become this: a butterfly flapping its wings in Atlanta affects the weather in Singapore. Though an exaggeration, the statement holds an essential truth: We are part of a greater whole and our actions have consequences far beyond what we can trace or fully see. We are affecting and changing the lives of others all the time. Alan Berg saw himself as a failure in life and had no concept of the impact he was having on listeners. He would have been shocked to discover that someone thought he was important enough, or threatening enough, to murder, and even more shocked by the size of the gathering for his memorial service.

Berg's demise demonstrated just how threatening he was, but it also showed something more: Words and feelings are forces that alter our physical reality. They are far more significant than we often realize. And because we now have the technology to amplify words and emotions in ways that were not possible in the past, as well as the ability to broadcast them to millions of people at once, our relationship with these forces is no longer the same. Talk radio and talk television are not, as Berg's old boss once suggested, just a couple of folks chatting it up over the back fence. They are among the most potent mechanisms shaping our consciousness, our thoughts, our actions, and our society today. How we use them can change the way we live — or die.

When the car was invented a century ago, we could travel faster than horses could run — and we could smash into things with far more damaging consequences. One could not drive an automobile with the same mindset as that with which one rode a horse. The new technology had created more possibility for good — and bad. It took an awareness of the danger of vehicles and a commitment to the requirements of public safety to bring the automobile into society without mass destruction. That process has never been fully completed: Car accidents still kill around one hundred Americans each day.

We're now living with a set of unprecedented new electronic technologies, yet we're bringing the same level of self-awareness and emotional behaviors to them that we use when speaking to a neighbor or only to ourselves. We act as if our broadcast thoughts and feelings have no social consequences, when in fact our individual power, as the 1990s clearly demonstrated, has been immeasurably increased.

<u>3</u>

The 1990s began with a rush of optimism. Media trendsetters predicted that the new decade would be somewhat of a re-run of the 1960s — just as the sixties, with its expanding social awareness and widespread protests, had conjured up America's politically active thirties. Every three decades or so, according to this assumption, the country was ready for something startlingly new. The nineties would be a time for altruism and change, for a direction away from the cash-driven, materialistic eighties. The baby-boomer generation, which had made a lot of money over the last decade, now wanted to add meaning to their lives.

Volunteerism to help the less fortunate at schools, churches, and homeless shelters was gaining popularity. The moment had come to fulfill the social promises of the sixties and give something back to the world. The spirit of that earlier tumultuous decade could be revitalized, but everything would be better now because the boomers were no longer distracted by violent war protests, drug use, sexual liberation, and other excesses of youth. They were older and far more mature.

As with many other media speculations, this one held pieces of the truth but neglected deeper political and social realities. While baby boomers had been raising families and gathering wealth, other things had been occurring in America, most notably on the religious right. In 1979, the Reverend Jerry

Falwell of the Thomas Road Baptist Church in Lynchburg, Virginia, founded a lobbying and political action group called the Moral Majority, which launched an aggressive nationwide campaign supporting the practice of Christianity in public schools and opposing abortion, homosexuality, and other activities it deemed immoral. Anyone who did not embrace Falwell's view of religion, education, or sexual behavior was, by definition, wrong about both God and country. Falwell had clout, resources, and a very focused game plan. Every Sunday evening during his evangelical TV show, sixty-two telephone operators were standing by to take donations. Fundamentalist Christianity was now being presented to a mass audience as primetime entertainment — and it worked brilliantly.

The Moral Majority soon had 6.5 million members and lots of money. Its leader, like many others, perceived a vast spiritual void in the country and had all the answers to fill it. In the aftermath of the sixties, many Americans were afraid of social change, afraid of relaxed codes of sexual conduct, and afraid of the future, but now someone was speaking directly to them and addressing their fears. Someone was there to call for a return to a time when the nation was not so diverse or complex. Falwell kept the phones ringing.

He was only the most visible and successful of the new breed of religious/political activists who were using the airwaves to recruit among the population. By the mid-eighties, Fundamentalist Christianity was a major growth industry. One thousand of America's 9,642 radio stations and 200 local TV outlets were broadcasting the evangelical message (those numbers would roughly double in the next decade). The 1985 Nielsen ratings reported that 16.3 million of the nation's 80 million households tuned in to Reverend Pat Robertson's "700 Club" at least once a month, and Jimmy Swaggart, Robert Schuller, Jim Bakker, Oral Roberts, Rex Humbard, and several other ministers also reached multi-millions of viewers on a regular basis. The Christian Broadcasting Network of Virginia Beach, Virginia estimated that more than half of all Americans who owned a television set watched at least one of the sixty nationally syndicated religious shows each month. They also contributed more than half a billion dollars to support the teachings and political agenda of the Christian right.

The airwaves were only one front in this nationwide religious campaign. From coast to coast, Fundamentalists built and ran 10,000 classrooms for pre-school children and thousands more elementary schools. The latter taught a program called Accelerated Christian Education, which paralleled the teachings in the Bible (as interpreted by the evangelists) and avoided what many regarded as a humanist curriculum. In politics, Pat Robertson talked about running for president; he would do so in 1988. In Washington, D.C., the American Coalition for Traditional Values, made up of a variety of Christian groups, lobbied hard for a federal quota system that would assure that at least 25 percent of U.S. government employees shared its faith.

During the sixties, the political left had risen in America because it had found meaning in struggling for the civil rights movement and against the Vietnam War. In the seventies and eighties, the religious right emerged with its own version of meaningful politics. This meaning wasn't about making people equal or about ending racism or social injustice at home or about changing worn-out foreign policies abroad or even about balancing the budget. It wasn't about public policies at all, at least as they'd been defined in the past. It was about personal behavior and about defining yourself politically through your intimate relationship with Jesus Christ and God. The religious right appropriated morality for itself and enlisted Jesus on its political ticket. It made Christ a mouthpiece for an absolute agenda about private human affairs.

Jerry Falwell, like the men in the Order, deeply believed that something was wrong with America, and he wanted to help his country by doing the right things for it. He wanted to be a hero and straighten up a misguided nation. Compared to Richard Butler and his Aryan Nations followers, Falwell and his cohorts were eminently presentable and respectable, but they had also devised an ironclad political plan to accompany their evangelical message. They wanted to impose their standards and fears on the most individual aspects of human behavior.

They wanted to dictate what should be done to the minds and spirits of all young children in schools; to tell women what they could and could not do with their own bodies; to dictate what should and should not be allowed between partners in their own bedrooms. The religious right was fundamentally consumed with people's sexuality — and determined to do something about it. While posing as anti-government conservatives, members of the movement wanted government to control the most private aspects of Americans' lives. This was a radical departure from our historical past. It was also where the first battles of the new civil war were now being fought.

The U.S. Constitution, written at the end of the eighteenth century, designated that church and state were to be kept separate. The Founding Fathers understood that some issues deserved public attention, whereas others were deeply personal, and concerned only one's own body or soul. The great American experiment with government was great precisely because it institutionalized the concept that people were free to worship as they pleased, to live as they pleased, and to explore their own sensuality, within the limits of the law. The men who established the nation were not content to assume that future generations would always hold these beliefs or protect these rights, so they built them into the country's founding principles. They respected differences and they respected privacy. Part of their lasting wisdom was the conviction that the government of a free people had no business regulating intimate behavior — including that of its own leaders. Men like Thomas Jefferson and Alexander Hamilton were public figures with complicated and well-concealed private lives.

In 1973, in Roe vs. Wade, the Supreme Court ruled that the issue in granting a woman the legal right to choose (or not choose) to have an abortion was not a moral issue. It was a matter of privacy. Not allowing her to make this decision for herself was a violation of her constitutional right to a private life.

Jerry Falwell and his compatriots sought to abolish the distinctions between private and public lives. They had no difficulty obliterating the lines that separated church from state, no trouble tossing away the rights to privacy. They did not believe in freedom and did not want others to explore it. It wasn't enough that they chose not to engage in certain kinds of behavior. It wasn't enough that their set of answers be sufficient for themselves; they wanted their dogma to be universal. They were committed to controlling in others what made them most uncomfortable about human life — or within themselves. Their reaction to the spiritual and sexual experimentation of the sixties and seventies was a full-scale retreat from the notion that adult Americans had the right to choose their own beliefs and lifestyles. Falwell and his brothers would tell children how to think and men and women how to breed.

With God on their side, Fundamentalists marched into the future as frontline Christian soldiers. While the baby boomers were raising kids or going into therapy or getting rich in the marketplace, those who sought spiritual guidance and political power were embracing Falwell's essential message. That message was quickly taking hold and becoming integrated into the lives of many, many people. It was far nicer than the Aryan Nations message, of course. There was no talk of "mud people," no overt anti-Semitism (except for an occasional slip of the Falwellian tongue), and no call for physical violence against anyone else. Imposing emotional or verbal or intellectual violence on your fellow citizens didn't really count, because those things weren't considered damaging.

Bob Mathews, David Lane, and Bruce Pierce had sought to hurt others, but the evangelicals wanted to have just the opposite effect. As a group, the TV preachers were sincere and decent enough men who did not consciously intend to cause harm. But as the nation would discover throughout the nineties, you don't have to intend harm to create it. You only have to be unaware of the effect you are having on other human beings and on the society at large. You can be an unconscious terrorist just as easily as a conscious one.

The evangelicals' words were bitterly judgmental, exclusive, and divisive.

One religious group wore the mantle of moral superiority and charged all other groups with sins and crimes against God. The first group found the others guilty on every count and sentenced them to a life term of damnation in the eyes of Jerry Falwell. The evangelicals and their followers knew the mind of God, and everyone who thought differently from them was wrong. They knew that what God had intended for aging, white, male, heterosexual, Fundamentalist Christians who lived in fear of diversity was what He'd intended for all.

This was narcissism on a colossal scale.

As defined by the *American Heritage Dictionary*, narcissism is: "An arresting of development at, or a regression to, the infantile stage of development in which one's own body is the object of erotic interest." But who wanted to suggest that men like Falwell were not true spiritual leaders? That they were merely projecting their own un-confronted, un-healed, and unconscious wounds on an entire nation of people desperately looking for political meaning and religious guidance? That preachers who could dismiss the personal freedoms of millions of American citizens without a moment's thought were doing violence to others who could not be like they were? And that this was a danger to the spirit of our democracy?

It never seemed to occur to the evangelicals or the politicians who aligned themselves with the Fundamentalist message that their focus on other people's sexuality — and especially on women's reproductive systems — was obsessive. Or that children should be allowed to develop their own relationship with the unknown and the infinite. Or that their message derived from their own fears, fears that others did not share.

These men and women wrapped their religious teachings in the Scriptures but politically they wanted to exert power over others — power over making choices that were at the core of human existence.

Not all evangelical practitioners were members of the Caucasian Moral Majority. Alan Keyes was a youngish African-American who was even more fervent than most white Christians in his desire to insert God into the political arena. In 1992, he made his first moves to run for President. He had little impact on the race but kept running, and in time he gained a much more visible presence in the election process. Like Falwell, Keyes passionately wanted to help set the United States on a good and moral path. Unlike Falwell, he was exceptionally articulate, one of the most fluent speakers of the English language that our political scene had witnessed in recent decades.

He was very bright, and on certain traditional political or economic issues he was both a perceptive and innovative thinker. Yet when it came to personal behavior he chastised anyone who saw the world differently from himself. He excelled at attacking and demonizing anybody, including people within his own Republican Party, who disagreed with him in the abortion debate. He had all the solutions for every American family.

Unlike many politicians, Keyes made no attempt to hide his real impulses and feelings; because of this, he put the issues right on the table for everyone to see. When he said that abortion was wrong for moral reasons, he was exercising his First Amendment right to state his personal religious beliefs. But when he indicated that God had told him to impose his views on every other American citizen, he'd crossed the line. Now he was preaching outright dictatorship.

This distinction may seem obvious, but in the last decade of the twentieth century, it was completely blurred. In all sorts of ways, public figures in the media, law enforcement, politics, religion, and elsewhere began to assume that what worked for them must work for all — in direct violation of our Constitution's principles. The original intention of the Bill of Rights was not just to protect the populace from the tyranny of government, but also to protect the minority from the power or prejudice of the majority. It was designed to tolerate and accommodate differences.

Curiously, in many of Keyes's public appearances, he spoke with honesty and feeling about the painful legacy of slavery in the African-American experience and the cost of that historical tragedy to his people. Yet simultaneously he implied that he would have no difficulty enforcing a different kind of slavery on the opposite sex. If these contradictions occurred to him, he chose to ignore them.

4

Pat Buchanan had once been a speechwriter for President Nixon before becoming a national media commentator. In the early nineties, he decided that he wanted to run for President. His launching pad was the 1992 Republican Convention, held in Houston that July. Evangelist Pat Robertson also addressed the delegates. In recent years, these two men had become more prominent in their party but had been held at bay by more moderate Republicans who were uncomfortable with the Christian right. Buchanan's political "coming-out" was in Houston that summer, where he was given the chance to deliver a prime-time televised address.

His favorite subject was the "cultural" war. Echoing the words of William Potter Gale, Buchanan spoke passionately about the moral battle that was being waged in the country, and his party's role in that battle. Richard Nixon, of course, had had a famous enemies' list during his stay in the White House, before resigning in 1974. Buchanan had plenty of self-proclaimed enemies, too, and at the top of the list were non-Christians, non-heterosexuals and, by implication, non-Gentiles (in his 1999 book, *A Republic and Not an Empire*, Buchanan implied that letting Hitler have his way in parts of Europe earlier in the century might not have been such a bad thing).

Buchanan's sentiments once may have been seen as little

more than rabble-rousing, but by the summer of 1992, the times had changed. At the Republican convention, one of the country's most visible and respectable political venues, he condemned entire segments of the American population whom he considered fundamentally dangerous. Because of religious or sexual differences, those people deserved harsh treatment and Buchanan was there to deliver it. His ideas no longer floated on the fringes of American society; they had been accepted — normalized — by substantial blocks of his own political party and were now being fed to a national audience. Buchanan's intolerance evoked a myriad of historical images, including the bullet holes in Alan Berg's garage door, and had taken center stage in our political debates.

"During the Republican convention, I was in Philadelphia for some meetings," recalled John Parr, a longtime Democratic activist and former president of the National Civic League in New York. "I remember coming back to my hotel room, turning on the TV, and watching Buchanan speak. He was definitely the lead dog in their parade. The overwhelming sense I had was of this incredibly mean-spirited man who was almost spitting as he made his speech. You could feel the fear-mongering pouring out of him. It was us versus them, in an effort to divide America against itself."

A favorite target of Buchanan and many others was the eventual Democratic nominee: Bill Clinton, the governor of Arkansas.

Clinton's entry into the 1992 presidential race heralded something new at the highest levels of our civic life, something alarming, and something aimed at a specific individual (and his wife). It was unbridled public hatred.

Many Americans had hated Lyndon Johnson — after he became President. They hated him for perpetuating and deepening the Vietnam War while young American men died (and killed) in a futile conflict in Southeast Asia. Many people also had hated Richard Nixon — after his administration had given us the Watergate scandal and posed a serious threat to free elections and democracy. Both Vietnam and Watergate were significant public events, involving foreign policy issues and domestic affairs, and both had huge public consequences.

By contrast, many people hated Bill Clinton the moment he stepped onto the national political scene. They didn't hate his ideas about international trade or the American economy or his legislative record in Arkansas. Their feelings were much more primal and intimate. When it was learned that Clinton had had sex outside of marriage, people hated and feared his sexuality. Whatever else he'd achieved or might be able to accomplish in the future made no difference. He was now defined by his sex life, and forever condemned by those who need to exorcise such demons from our nation.

This perception of Bill Clinton made public the private war that Americans were fighting among themselves, a war that had begun with the neo-Nazis and the hard-core Christian right. The essential combat zone in this war was personal differences, personal choice, and sexual behavior.

This new civil war was not between the Southern and Northern states over slavery, as it had been in the 1860s. It was a war between different psychological and emotional states — different states of being and consciousness — yet it was equally divisive. It was being fought within individual psyches and, as it wore on, within our largest and most important social institutions. It was a war between tolerance and intolerance; between judgment and acceptance (including self-acceptance); between compassion and blame; between discerning the difference between private affairs and public issues; and finally, between hatred and love. It was fitting that it should arrive at the end of an old millennium and the start of a new one. The country had never seen anything like it before.

5

The most striking thing about Bill Clinton was not that he was so different from most men of his class and generation, but that he was so typical of them. He'd dabbled in drugs. He hadn't wanted to go to Vietnam and fight in a war his government was not committed to winning. He'd experimented sexually beyond the boundaries of matrimony. He'd been uncertain about his identity and tried to fashion an adult self around some very real childhood pain. He'd witnessed an abusive relationship between his mother and stepfather and dealt with the shame and misery of parental alcoholism. Like almost every other middle-class American male who'd come of age in the sixties, he'd struggled to figure out who he was. And he was the first presidential candidate who could not hide the reality of that struggle.

He was, in every way imaginable, just one of us. Countless baby boomers had grappled with their identities and had sexual problems or sex outside of marriage (studies suggest that as many as 40 percent of the adult American population has a sexual dysfunction or has been unfaithful in marriage or has decided to stop sleeping with a spouse). Men everywhere had wrestled with their roles as contemporary marriage partners — and had been befuddled by sex.

The American business culture used sexual images twenty-four hours a day to exploit male impulses, not for the end result of erotic satisfaction or a balanced physical, emotional, and spiritual life, but to provoke men to spend money and consume products. Sex permeated innumerable advertising campaigns — you could use it to sell anything — but woe to any public figure who dared to venture slightly off the well-trodden sexual path.

Our society could not have been more conflicted. Many men were so testosterone-ridden because of the barrage of media images and so adrenalin-ridden because of the constant need to compete and make money that they were living in an altered state — and it was not a healthy one. The only thing more common in our society than mass titillation was mass dysfunction in regards to real intimacy. The end result was that a great many Americans were more concerned with other people's sex lives than with establishing their own sexual harmony. What you can't deal with or accept within yourself, went the underlying message, you are free to hate.

Historically, demonizers and witch hunters searched out a group of people to castigate or kill. But in the 1990s, single individuals bore the full brunt of our massive confusion and guilt over entangled social realities. President Clinton was one such figure. He was the perfect target for our blame and scorn and for what we did not want to confront or admit about our culture.

Bill and Hillary Clinton represented something radically new in American politics. Until now, we had viewed the president and first lady the way children viewed their parents — as Super Mom and Dad. We wore what they wore, read what they read, and ate what they ate. We expected them to know what was best for us and to conceal their problems from us. A country as young as the United States needed these kinds of elevated parental public figures to feel secure about itself, but the Clintons could not fit this image. They'd battled through the difficulties of adult married life and had not resolved every issue. But who had? Nearly half the people their age in the United States were divorced. The First Couple was merely experiencing what everyone else was, but the rest of us were able to do it in private.

In earlier times, these intimate issues and psychodramas would not have mattered as much in the political realm. Now, however, they symbolized the emotional evolution — and emotional instability — of our culture. They comprised some of the great questions and challenges we were facing as a country, and were issues of far more urgency than balanced budgets or warfare abroad. They took us to the root questions: Who were we as people? Did we believe in tolerance or only pay lip service to it? Were we able to expand and accommodate the truth behind adult matters or could we only turn away from such things and pretend they did not exist?

Were we children who would be forever disappointed by our parents' imperfections or were we able to grow up at last and realize that they were just like everybody else, muddling through and doing the best they could? Finally, what was important in our public life — the day-to-day managing of a government that represented 260 million people of extremely diverse backgrounds and interests or the inner workings of a marriage that none of us had any real knowledge of?

The Clintons committed the ultimate American sin: They reflected back to us exactly who we were. They held up a mirror to our culture, our nasty, painful, intimate dilemmas, and our sense that things were sliding out of control everywhere and that nobody could stop it. This mirror made us deeply uncomfortable. We wanted to think of ourselves as better than this but we weren't, and it was far easier to hate the couple from Arkansas than to look harder into the glass.

The president and first lady showed us in no uncertain terms that our leaders are no longer our parents. They can't help us deal with many of our deepest contemporary problems. We're on our own psychologically and emotionally, and that is fundamentally frightening. This requires a new way of thinking, a new self-awareness, and a new strategy for living. It takes work, discipline, and commitment, but it's much easier just to attack those whom you perceive to be the enemy.

In these psychologically unsettling times, it was inevitable that a domestic melodrama would surface in our presidential politics. There were few families left in America that had not experienced emotional trauma. With the arrival of the Clintons in Washington, D.C., in early 1993, the challenge became: Could we accept something different in the White House and judge these two people on their merits as public servants? Or would we dwell on their personal matters? Our news media and talk shows were presented with a novel opportunity for change (our political system, on the other hand, had long incorporated and honored many men with shaky marriages, a taste for alcohol, and voracious sexual appetites). How we interacted with the Clintons would say much about our society and ourselves.

It would be misleading to suggest that people disliked the Clintons only because of their private lives. The couple came to office with a definite political agenda, which many Americans also despised. The social struggle that had begun in the sixties revolved around a single question: Were we a nation committed to expanding individual freedom and to making the United States a more fair and inclusive place for all people, or were we committed to the politics of exclusivity that had prevailed throughout much of our country's past? Were we ready to become a true melting pot, or would we remain the white-dominated, male-dominated culture of earlier generations?

The Clinton administration represented inclusivity more forcefully than any administration before it. Bill Clinton put African-Americans, Jews, women, and Hispanics in prominent government roles. He openly supported gay people and their rights. Unlike almost every other first lady, Hillary Clinton wanted to be an equal partner to her husband and play an active role in his presidency (her ambitions opened up her own personality and sex life to savage ridicule and criticism). The Clintons believed in widening the opportunities for all, and they were constantly under attack by those who opposed such ideas. Sex may have been the hot topic of the moment, but a very real political battle swirled around the Clintons and their ideals.

And yet, they were hardly political radicals. They were elected as moderate Democrats who became more moderate as their time in office lengthened. Their achievements in power were conventional ones. By almost every traditional standard used to measure excelling in the White House — peace abroad, a thriving economy, falling unemployment, a lowering of the national debt, getting people off welfare rolls, and cutting major crime rates (although hate crimes grew during the nineties) — they succeeded and affected many social conditions for the better. The cold, clear numbers bear this out.

By May 2000, after nearly eight years of the Clinton administration, *The New York Times* was reporting that even some of the most blighted inner cities in the country, which had once been "frightening wastelands," were now "showing glimmers of renaissance." Ghettos in Chicago, Miami, Boston, and New Orleans were seeing new construction of homes and businesses, new subway and bus lines, a lessening of disorder in schools and a decrease in drug and gang activity. A combination of public policies and good economic conditions had helped even the poorest neighborhoods.

But all that was irrelevant to those who were fighting a cultural war, those who were fixated on the sex lives of others, those who resisted meaningful social change, and those who brutally judged others because it was fun and good for business — namely many of the wealthiest, most famous, and most powerful people in the American media.

6

Alan Berg had been caustic, annoying, obnoxious, aggravating, belligerent, and irascible, but he hadn't been cynical or divisive. He hadn't played favorites or pitted people against one another. He'd offended everyone — Jews and Gentiles, blacks and whites, men and women, gays and heterosexuals, squares and hipsters and everybody in between. He had no prejudice and irritated virtually all his listeners because fundamentally he was independent-minded and on a comic, eccentric search for his own peculiar version of the truth.

A former lawyer from Chicago and an ex-alcoholic, Berg had suffered from epileptic seizures throughout much of his adulthood. It was only after a doctor sawed off the top of his skull, cut out a malignant tumor, and sewed the skull back on that the worst of his illness was behind him. Berg's experience of life had made him edgy and angry, but it had also left him with a keen intelligence, a scathing tongue, and a broad-based compassion for others. He had helped pushed radio toward rudeness, but he never lost his heart. He'd suffered enough to know that everyone else was suffering too.

Since his assassination in mid-1984, no one remotely like him has been heard on Denver radio. That in itself is not significant or revealing, but what is important is the fact that with his death, his kind of broadcasting, which could loosely be called liberal and humanist, ended. People like him were systematically replaced by those who were not distracted by human complexity, contradictions, compassion, skepticism, or humility. In the last decade of the twentieth century, strangely enough, just about the worst thing a talk show host could be labeled was a "liberal."

The night Berg was killed, Ken Hamblin, his colleague at Denver's KOA, the largest radio station between the Mississippi River and Los Angeles, was on the air. Hamblin was an African-American from Brooklyn. Lately, he and Berg had become pals, a pair of big-city guys who'd found a home in the local media. They'd had their spats (Hamblin was neat in the studio and Berg was a notorious slob, occasionally setting fires inside wastebaskets with his cigarette ashes), but they'd also achieved a closeness beyond professional friendship. When a news reporter walked into the KOA studio at 10:10 that evening and told Hamblin that Berg had been shot to death, the host began to cry into his open microphone. It was a remarkably human moment on live radio.

"I guess I'm not network material," Hamblin said, as he sobbed in front of his audience. When he'd regained control of himself, he addressed the killer, whom he was convinced was listening.

"I wish it were a damn hoax," he said. "I wish it was a publicity stunt, but it's not...If Alan Berg was anything before you blew him away, you have made him an immortal. Alan always used to say, 'They're out there but you can't worry about them.

You can never know where the nuts are going to come from, so you live day to day.'"

In 1984 Hamblin had expressed genuine sorrow over Berg's death and genuine caring for many of his own listeners. He'd grown up poor and black in Brooklyn, and he once said that having lived through all of that in his childhood, and having escaped those circumstances, he could not be anything other than compassionate toward his fellow humans. After Berg's murder, he was the only such voice left on Denver radio.

As the 1990s commenced, something happened to Hamblin. He changed dramatically, and his transformation on the air symbolized not just a personal shift but a much larger media phenomenon. It was a shift that would canonize Rush Limbaugh as the master of petty, mean-spirited, hate radio and would make Dr. Laura Schlessinger the queen of judgment (especially against gays). They would become the two most popular figures on the airwaves in the last part of the decade.

Without warning, Hamblin's compassion evaporated, as did his tears, and he began calling himself the "Black Avenger." He became brutally critical of African-Americans who ran (or were accusing of running) afoul of the law. He became spiteful toward minority citizens who were not as successful as he was or as moral as he perceived himself to be. His views were set forth with regularity and absolute predictability on the air, in his newspaper column, in a book, and on national television. It was a simple formula and it worked brilliantly: by verbally abusing people of color, his career advanced apace. What could be more appealing to the white media establishment, always nervous about racial issues and angry over crime, than a talented, intelligent, and articulate black man demonizing his fellow African-Americans?

In Hamblin's eyes, there were few complexities in our criminal justice system — and certainly no racial complexities. There were good people like him and bad people like the others, and the latter deserved whatever treatment they got. It was irrelevant that America's colossally expensive drug war had caused our prison population to triple between 1980 and 2000, so that we now had 400,000 nonviolent drug users in jail and 300,000 mentally ill inmates. Or that by the late nineties there were two million Americans behind bars — the largest number of incarcerated human beings on earth — and that a hugely disproportionate number of them were black or Latino. Nearly half the African-Americans in our nation's capital, to cite only one example, were either in prison, on probation or on parole. According to a 2000 study conducted by Human Rights Watch, black men were more than thirteen times as likely as white men to be imprisoned for a drug crime.

"Black and white drug offenders get radically different treatment in the American justice system," said Ken Roth, executive director of the watchdog organization. "This is not only profoundly unfair to blacks, it also corrodes the American ideal of equal justice for all."

What happened to these hundreds of thousands of people once they entered the criminal justice system or why many of them were released and then busted again and returned to another cell was of no consequence to broadcasters like the "Black Avenger." Punishment was the only answer to these social problems.

Hamblin expressed his contempt for many of our citizens, but he unleashed his rage most vigorously against the African-Americans who rioted for several days and nights in Los Angeles in the spring of 1992, after a suburban jury acquitted white policemen in the beating of a black motorist named Rodney King. The violence left fifty-five people dead. The extraordinarily entangled realities behind this horror show — including ingrained racism inside the LAPD, widespread police corruption, evidence planting, perjury by cops, and institutionalized brutality against minorities — were ignored or dismissed by Hamblin and most of the media. The pattern of official violence perpetrated against L.A.'s minority communities would not emerge in full-blown ways until the end of the 90s, when Los Angeles found itself ensnared in the largest, most damaging, and most expensive police scandal in the history of the nation. Yet when that scandal erupted and threatened to undermine L.A.'s criminal justice system, many in the media would try to ignore the root causes behind it once again... only now it was too big to be denied or ignored.

In the '90's empathy and compassion were out. Hatred was in — and it was the hippest, hottest commodity in the media marketplace. What had earlier infiltrated our religion and politics was now saturating our airwaves.

When Hamblin finished flailing the African-Americans in Los Angeles, he turned to one of his favorite whipping boys: Bill Clinton, the new president of the United States, the only president who'd ever been truly comfortable around minority people. Hamblin was good at chastising both Bill and Hillary Clinton, but he had to take a back seat in this activity to someone far more gifted at broadcasting bile than he was.

Rush Limbaugh was arguably the most successful talk show host in the history of the medium: his tantrums were pure gold. Limbaugh, who was syndicated virtually everywhere and had tens of millions of listeners, was the leader of a pack of hosts on AM radio all over the country who were helping to mainstream verbal and emotional violence. As they did this, physical violence was increasing on the fringes of our society; hate crimes rose early in the decade, up to about eight thousand per year, and, according to the FBI, explosive and incendiary bombings — terrorist acts — doubled during the first four years of the 1990s.

Limbaugh had gained fame and riches by assaulting the president and the first lady on his radio show, his TV show, and in his writing. This was blood sport and Limbaugh would say anything to hurt them. He called Hillary things like "femi-nazi." He called her husband whatever he could think of that was allowed on the air. Each day, he conducted a three-hour whine on the nature of America's political leadership. His per-formance, which may have been intended to be funny in part, was exactly what one would have expected of a horribly spoiled child who could not tolerate the adult world.

Democracies, of course, flourish on conflict and heated debate. They thrive on the loyal opposition keeping those in power on guard and accountable to the citizenry. Dissent is a good and necessary part of our country's political health. Contrary points of view are inevitable and agreement is not necessary. One could disagree with the Clintons on nearly every one of their political positions and still serve the best interests of the nation.

But Limbaugh and his countless callers and imitators in the media were not members of the loyal opposition. They repre-sented something new in mainstream political commentary — mean-spiritedness for its own sake. Their message, available twenty-four hours a day, was deeply personal and deeply emo-tional: The Clintons were despicable as human beings. They were loathed because of who they were and how they lived. They were hated because they were perceived to be different — and that could not be tolerated. So Limbaugh and minions had the right, if not the duty, to go after the chief executive and his wife relentlessly and do everything possible to damage them as individuals, to humiliate them at every turn and destroy their time in office.

The presidential election of 1992 was overthrown not at the polls but in the broadcast studios of Rush Limbaugh, Ken Hamblin, and other pundits. It was a coup via the airwaves, and it didn't matter to the attackers that the voting public had elected Bill Clinton to run the country. The voters had been stupid and wrong. Limbaugh was smarter and right. He knew what was best for all of us and gave a damn for nothing but his own feelings and his ratings. His attitude was hardly uncommon. It was spreading everywhere, digging in and taking hold not just in the media but in the halls of Congress as well, where plenty of people felt the same way about the Clintons as he did. One day these beliefs would even infiltrate the Supreme Court. Such beliefs were becoming more important than the will of the voting public.

Limbaugh's basic purpose on the airwaves was not that far removed from that of the Aryan Nations leaders. Because I disapprove of you as a person, he kept saying into his microphone, I will assault you with my words and encourage others to do the same.

Limbaugh had learned the deep, dark, ugly secret of the 1990s and was acting it out daily on the air as huge, eminently respectable radio stations — starting with KOA in Denver — gave him a nationwide platform where he could practice his hateful craft. And as he did so, hour after hour and show after show, wealthy corporate sponsors such as Dodge, Snapple, American Express, Perkins, Hooked-on-Phonics, a variety of dot.com businesses, and many, many more companies stood behind him and paid the bills. He could sell cars, fruit juice, food, and countless other products because he was only secondarily peddling those things. What he was really selling was anger and fear — and late-twentieth-century America had a bottomless market for these commodities. Regardless of the nation's growing economic health and the population's expanding bank accounts and stock portfolios, citizens everywhere were upset about something, were anxious and uncomfortable inside of themselves, and they didn't know what to do about it.

Rush gave them a human target. He focused their feelings and their unexplored rage — and that was irresistible.

"The technologies being used by the media now are largely not information technologies," said Bob Richards, a communications consultant in Denver, during an interview in 2000. "They only pose as information technologies. They are really emotional-stimulation technologies and people are very hungry for emotional stimulation, especially when it is based on conflict. We're primates, after all, and we naturally react to conflict in our environment. We pay attention to it. That's what the animal self responds to, and if you have someone out there with a microphone encouraging people to see conflict everywhere and to feel conflict and to react to conflict, they're going to do it.

"The mass media understand all this and they exploit it every day. Our information technologies run on over-stimulation, and that can easily escalate the conflict until it pushes some people toward violence. How do you rise above these primal reactions and start to reclaim your humanity? How do you learn to participate with public events and public figures in a different and more balanced way? How do you stop being a slave to this kind of manipulation? These are the questions we are just beginning to pose.

"In the past, a lot of social controls were imposed on people both from inside and from outside. They were restrained from saying or doing many things because of the culture or their own belief system. All that has changed. There are no rules now for this kind of emotional venting. There are not even any guidelines. So the problem and the challenge become personal. As an individual, you have to find a sense of your own self-control and co-operation with the larger society and its principles. But in order to do that, you have to be become more aware of your own behavior. We're not there yet.

"There's a general attitude today of, 'It really doesn't matter what I say or do because I'm not having any effect on the world around me. I might as well shout fire in a crowded theatre because there are no consequences.' Nothing could be further from the truth. The people doing the venting and the demonizing are having a huge effect on us. They just don't perceive that."

Better than most anyone, Limbaugh understood that decent and intelligent people can be manipulated, from their scalps down to their toes, and if you tell them to hate someone enough times, many will do just that. There's comfort in joining the herd when it starts to stampede. Rush was there to cash in on the huge demand for public thrashings. By mid-decade his kind of talk radio had become business as usual on the nation's airwaves, and business was great.

Why should anyone have questioned what he was doing? It was just entertainment, wasn't it? He wasn't harming anyone, was he? He was only exercising his First Amendment right to freedom of speech and he wanted others to do the same. He wanted them to ape his feelings and mirror back his assaults on the enemy. For those who did this, he had a special name, a term of endearment. He called them "dittoheads," which meant that they were shrewd enough and wise enough to second his own views. This was high praise and these listeners were to be commended for spreading the word from Limbaugh's pulpit. That word and the emotions behind it were just as plain as they could be: anyone who thought, felt, acted, looked, or lived differently from Rush Limbaugh was not merely wrong. He was evil and should be stopped.

Limbaugh didn't hurt anybody, didn't hit anyone in the stomach or slap a face. He was against violence, obeyed the law, and tried to stay out of trouble. He never advocated bloodshed. Like the neo-Nazis before him, he just desired to be a hero and do something good for America by cleaning up the stupidity and confusion he saw all around him. He wanted to be a savior. Who would have dared suggest to his radio station outlets or to his corporate sponsors that what he was doing on the air was not just tearing away at the invisible bonds that held our society together but undermining the entire culture? Who would suggest that it wasn't just entertainment but a new and subtler form of domestic terrorism?

Real power is not the power to load and fire a gun at one person or twenty or one hundred. Real power is the ability to shape the feelings and minds of millions.

7

The greatest act of domestic terrorism in the United States during the 1990s appears to have been the blowing up of the Murrah Federal Building in Oklahoma City on April 19, 1995. One hundred and sixty-eight men, women, and children lost their lives in that tragedy, which is America's largest casualty list on one day due to a bomb or gunfire. But another set of events rivals the Oklahoma City disaster for domestic destruction. From the time Bill Clinton was elected president to the end of the decade, 263 kids were killed at schools by other students.

These murders were widely perceived as random acts by evil individuals — not as horrific cries for help from those who could no longer cope in our culture and the emotional environment they found themselves trapped in. When the internal pressure became too much, they, like Bruce Pierce as he pulled the trigger in Alan Berg's driveway, found a way to relieve it. They found an enemy to blame for what they were experiencing.

Like countless other Americans, Rush Limbaugh expressed bewilderment over why our children were killing each other in mass shootings. What could possibly be causing them to lose so much respect for other human beings that they would pick up a weapon and decide that the strange-looking boy with glasses or the tall girl with funny hair did not deserve to live? How could our kids have become so twisted, so mean-spirited, and so downright cruel? Where could they have learned that absolute intolerance was good and funny and great for business? Or that nastiness is a virtue? Or that a total lack of self-control is normal adult behavior? Or that the best way to deal with your own uncomfortable feelings and inner conflict is to attack others? Or that you can have a fabulous career berating other people? Where could they have learned that the public expression of violence against others — verbal and emotional violence — is all right? And since it's okay to harm others in this way, what does it matter if you go ahead and kill them? How could our children have become so hateful?

This was the unsolvable mystery.

A few years ago the comic Al Franken wrote a book called *Rush Limbaugh Is a Big Fat Idiot and Other Observations.* But Limbaugh was much more than that. His impact on the culture was incalculably larger than that of a provincial media personality like Alan Berg. Limbaugh, first and foremost, was a teacher, one of the most celebrated and rewarded teachers of the American present. Through his program on his self-proclaimed "Excellence in Broadcasting" network, he taught everyone about personal narcissism and corporate greed. He made millions of dollars for himself and his advertisers by despising others, and his nationwide electronic classroom reached tens of millions of adult students. They in turn, through direct influence and osmosis, passed his lessons on to their kids.

Limbaugh taught that dividing the world into "us versus them" was a useful thing to do, that needing enemies is a healthy way to live, and that expressing your loathing of people who are different from you is a means of contributing to society, not gutting it from within. He taught that his kind of broadcasting was good for America — just what was necessary to help move us forward as a nation.

In the 1960s, one of the more fashionable political slogans was: "You're either part of the problem or part of the solution." This statement assumed that if you had good intentions (or ones that were good in your own mind), then you were part of the solution to political problems. By the 1990s, the slogan had assumed a more subtle meaning and raised some sticky questions. Regardless of your stated intentions, what were you acting out at the emotional and psychological level? What were you imposing on external events and social processes? What was the effect of that imposition? In the 1990s, many high-minded individuals, especially those in the media, had no compunction whatsoever about trashing the rights and lives of others while they were presumably serving the public interest.

Deep down, they just wanted to be heroes.

8

The 1990s, as it turned out, were not an updated version of the sixties. They much more closely resembled the fifties, an era also identified by an underlying pathology, hysteria, witch hunting, and a great rise in the herd mentality. The key difference between the two decades was that a very real external threat to the country existed in the 1950s. The United States and the Soviet Union were amassing nuclear arsenals as quickly as possible and aiming their missiles at one another. With the push of a few buttons, the destruction of cities and perhaps nations and civilizations was now guaranteed. Institutionalized madness, on a scale never seen before in international politics, had become normalized.

This environment influenced all those living in both countries and outside their borders. The bombs could not be ignored. Any sane person could easily wake up in the morning filled with dread, terrified that he or she could be killed before sunset because of people and circumstances completely beyond his or her control.

No such external threat existed in the nineties. In fact, the decade began with the collapse of the Soviet Union. Since the end of the Second World War, Americans had believed that Kremlin leaders were committed to wiping out the United States and Christianity through subversion and nuclear weapons. Now the Berlin Wall had been torn down, the Soviet Union had disintegrated, and the old enemy had evaporated.

A void had arrived in America's need for demons, but the talk shows, the rising tabloid press, the mainstream media, and eventually the Internet were ready to fill it. Throughout the nineties, the collective media hunted for new faces of evil and found them in two places — both inside our own borders. One was politics and the other was the criminal justice system. As major crime itself was holding steady or even falling, partly as a result of America's healthy economy, its coverage was escalating.

The press began focusing more and more attention on homegrown violence — on high-profile murder cases and their celebrity villains, such as Eric and Lyle Menendez, who killed their parents in Los Angeles, or Susan Smith, who drowned her children in South Carolina. The vast coverage of these events and the pubic condemnation of the perpetrators through the talk media quickly spread. We constantly had the opportunity to give into our inner fears or secret rages, because another sensational murder was always right around the corner. You could be certain that it would dominate the headlines and the evening news shows because those in charge of such shows knew that we could not turn away from the carnage. We were fascinated by our own self-destruction.

"If it bleeds," went the adage in every TV newsroom across the nation, "it leads."

Crime, in many people's minds, was an excellent replacement for the vanished Cold War. Crime fit perfectly into the notion that there were good guys and bad guys in the world, and we knew precisely which was which. People who arrested and prosecuted suspects were good. People who were charged with crimes, or people who defended them or challenged the powers of the state, were bad. Things in this realm were very black and very white. The meaning and value of our legal system, as defined by the media and talk shows, derived from our desire to punish those whom we knew were guilty because the police had locked them up. Anything less than full punishment was a terrible failure of criminal justice, and anyone who participated in that failure was himself a terrible failure and deserving of our ridicule and condemnation.

The overall public good did not enter into this debate. The point was to find someone to blame for what people were feeling — even if our feelings had virtually nothing to do with a particular crime. The Cold War may have ended, but this new war was getting hotter by the day. No longer distracted by the Soviet Union, the impending doom of nuclear war, a recession, or other issues, people anxiously waited to get on the air and tell a talk show host about how the president or his wife or a criminal defendant or some other public figure was driving them crazy and stirring their rage. It was a time to vent.

But it also could have been a time for the country to look at itself in a new way, to explore its emotional landscape and see what effect it was having on our political process, our spiritual life, our media, our legal system, and on the general public. It might have been a time to ask some novel personal and social questions. Would we be able to separate, within ourselves and our institutions, what was a public matter from what was a private concern? Could we discern what belonged to each of us as individuals and needed to be confronted individually, from what belonged to all of us as a whole? Could we lay aside our insistence that we had to be right, and someone else wrong, in order to co-operate with our governing principles and serve the public interest? Or would we ignore these questions and keep searching for targets to blame and people to demonize? The choice was ours, and the decade would reveal with stunning clarity both the decisions we made and their eventual social cost.

Earlier in the century, the pioneering Swiss psychologist Carl Jung had written about the shadow side of human beings — the darkness that emerges in all of us so that we can observe its debilitating effects and attempt to purge it from our psyche. What isn't confronted within, Jung believed, would be projected outward onto other people and events in ways that not only distorted the reality beyond ourselves but ultimately harmed it.

Nations have shadows, too. One of them, exemplified by the Watergate scandal, is the abuse of social institutions by individuals for their own personal reasons or gain. Shadows that are ignored or denied have a way of coming back in larger and uglier forms. The shadow hanging over America in the mid-nineties was about to get darker, thicker, more expensive, and bloodier.

As the mainstream drifted further into "us versus them" and into more psychological and emotional violence, the rage on the fringes deepened. White radicals continued to spread their toxic message via their computerized network and other venues. William Pierce, the author of *The Turner Diaries,* poured out racist tracts and in the nineties he started Resistance Records, the world's largest neo-Nazi music label, which produced cassettes and CDs by bands such as Angry Aryans, Blue-Eyed Devils, Nordic Thunder, and Aggravated Assault. These groups played what was known as "hatecore" — aggressively bigoted and antigovernment music created to reach embittered young white men. Pierce ran this business from 400 magnificent, fenced-off acres near tiny Hillsboro, West Virginia, in the foothills of the Allegheny Mountains. He and nine employees daily sent out writings, videos, recordings, and online messages from their website to white supremacists across the nation and throughout the world, selling around $1 million worth of merchandise a year.

During the nineties' prosperity, Pierce expressed dismay that America's booming economy was making it harder for him to recruit young men to his cause, but he knew that despite the nation's increasing wealth, angry people and emotional disturbances existed beneath the rising stock market and low unemployment figures. Many Americans felt an unspecified anxiety and rage, churning silently within a constant background of fear, just waiting to be unleashed. Pierce and his neo-Nazi organization, the National Alliance, had a message for them.

"My aim," Pierce once told *The Washington Post*, "is to give them a rationale for their alienation, to give them a target for their anger."

Up in northern Idaho, in his own pristine setting in the woods, Richard Butler continued to run Aryan Nations and recruit new minds to influence. In the summer of 1999, his compound would jump back into the headlines when a man named Buford Furrow, who'd once worked at Aryan Nations and dated Bob Mathews's former wife, entered a suburban Los Angeles Jewish community day care center and opened fire. He wounded half a dozen adults and children and then shot to death a postal worker. Like Bruce Pierce, Furrow had a history of mental illness, a condition that in recent months had apparently worsened.

After his arrest in Las Vegas following the rampage, he shouted out what he'd learned from his teachers in the white power movement.

"Kill the Jews!" he said.

A POSTSCRIPT FROM LOS ANGELES

In 1964, sixteen-year-old Ira Erenberg began stocking the shelves and sweeping the floor of a drugstore in the Rampart neighborhood of Los Angeles. He'd grown up in a Jewish family in East L.A., in a tough section known as Boyle Heights, and as a teenager he needed to make money. His father, a cab driver, knew the man who ran the pharmacy and this connection got Ira his first (and perhaps his last) job. He could not possibly have guessed that more than three decades later, he would still be working at this drugstore at the corner of 6th and Union, just west of downtown L.A. Now Ira was the owner of Mi Farmicia, which was located in one of the city's most colorful and important neighborhoods — at least in terms of police work.

Back in the 1920s, during Prohibition, the drugstore's owner built a still on the roof and funneled booze down into the soda fountains at the front counter. When men asked for a soft drink, they were really ordering hard liquor. The cops looked the other way or came in and had a drink themselves. Prostitution was thick in Rampart and so were bookmaking and other forms of vice. The steep rise of land behind the pharmacy was known as Lysol Hill, because the bordellos up there used a lot of this disinfectant and bought it at the drugstore.

During the 1930s, restrictions were even looser. That decade saw the city's most corrupt political and police administrations — until the present era. The head villain was the mayor himself, Frank Shaw, an ex-grocery clerk who'd become a city councilman and then a county supervisor before winning the mayoralty in 1933. Under the infamous

"Shaw's spoils system," bootleggers, gamblers, and madams made payoffs to district attorneys, councilmen, and to Shaw himself. More legitimate industries had to pay $500 a month to stay profitable. From an office at City Hall, Joe Shaw, the mayor's brother, sold LAPD jobs and peddled answers to the department's promotional exams. The highest bidders got the best test scores.

Madams served caviar and champagne to the vice officers who dropped by for visits; in return, the women were given advance warning to clear out well-known civilians and politicians or shut down the business when a raid was coming. The good times rolled on and on until two men — Harry Raymond, a former LAPD detective, and Clifford Clinton, a restaurateur — decided to fight City Hall. In 1937, Clinton filed a grand jury report charging Shaw and his cohorts with various illegal activities, a move that took extreme conviction and real courage.

Clinton's taxes were soon raised by $7,000 and his cafeterias were stink-bombed. The LAPD set off an explosion at Clinton's home and blew up Harry Raymond's car — with him inside. Raymond was badly wounded but lived to testify against the cops and the mayor. Because of the sustained efforts of these two crusaders, Americans saw the first successful recall election ever of a big-city official. Shaw was forced out of power and twenty-four high-ranking LAPD administrators resigned with him. Some of these racketeers went in search of new opportunities, leaving Southern California for a new city in the desert called Las Vegas.

Following Shaw's reign of corruption, Police Chief William Parker was brought in to clean up the department. He succeeded, but he also instituted a totalitarian attitude, which fiercely opposed outside questioning of LAPD tactics and absolutely rejected any civilian oversight of the police. The cops were there to maintain order in their own way — no matter what.

In the summer of 1965, Ira Erenberg was working at the pharmacy when the first major race riots hit L.A. On that occasion, the fires and bullets did not reach the drugstore, stopping several blocks away at 6th and Alvarado. The violence had erupted after a policeman stopped a reckless African-American driver, who resisted arrest and began to argue with the cop. The weather was warm and the streets were soon crowded with people watching this growing altercation.

Neighbors gathered around the driver and began to vent their own frustration about racism and police work in their part of town. The rage could not be contained. For six straight nights it took over, primarily in the Watts neighborhood of South Central L.A., and by the time the rioting ended, there were 4,000 arrests, 1,032 injuries, $40 million in damages, and 34 deaths. A special commission appointed by the governor of California to study the root causes of the violence commenced its analysis with a theme that would be sounded again and again in the city's future. The report described "a deep and long-standing schism between a substantial portion of the Negro community and the Police Department."

Chief Parker ran the LAPD up to the 1965 riots. After his death the next year, he was replaced by Edward Davis, who was in turn supplanted by a brash younger officer named Daryl Gates, who led the department in the 1980s and early 1990s. He deepened the LAPD's "us versus them" mindset, projecting toughness, arrogance, and extreme indifference to public opinion. What did politicians or average citizens know about the dangers and difficulties of being a cop on the streets of L.A.? Who were they to question him or the actions or racial attitudes of his force? If Angelenos wanted protection, they should just stand back and let the police do what was necessary.

Gates conjured up cowboy justice in the old American West (or perhaps cowboy justice as depicted by Hollywood since the inception of the movie business). As head of a police department in one of the most diverse and complex metropolitan areas on earth, he embodied simplicity. He believed in good versus evil and he fostered such thinking in those who worked for him, right down to the officers on the street. Things went along this way for a while, but more resentment and racial violence were boiling in L.A. When it erupted the next time, it would reach farther into the city and hit many different places, including Ira Erenberg's drugstore.

Over the years, Erenberg had become a fixture on the local business scene. He'd sold diapers to grandmothers, mothers, daughters, and granddaughters in the same family. He'd sold countless prescription drugs to those in need of medication. He'd sold many contraceptives. He'd once sold balloons carrying the store's name but that stopped when he feared that a teenager peddling drugs might put heroin in one of the balloons and have to swallow the balloon to hide the dope from the police. If the teenager died and the balloon was found in his stomach, it could mean trouble for the pharmacy.

Erenberg had learned to speak fluent Spanish because most of his customers had some Latin blood. He proudly displayed photographs that he'd taken of his eccentric customers, men with missing teeth and ground-down women who looked as if they'd spent decades living on the street. Erenberg liked something about all of them, even the old fellow who shoplifted, and he regarded them not just as patrons, but as a strange and enriching part of his own life and that of this remarkable neighborhood.

Rampart had one of the richest and most complex ethnic histories of any neighborhood in the United States. After the Second World War, many Midwesterners had moved to Los Angeles and settled in this area. Then came African-Americans and immigrants from Mexico. Then refugees from Latin American countries that had seen major political upheaval: El Salvador, Guatemala, and Cuba. Then Koreans and other Asians arrived. It has been said that every language spoken in the United States has been spoken inside the boundaries of Rampart.

"In many other neighborhoods," Erenberg says, "people like to sit around and talk about the good old days when their part of town was a better place to live in. Rampart never was better. It was always the same. It's always been a transient section where people are struggling to build new lives and to survive."

By the late 1980s, the infiltration of gangs and drugs in the Rampart neighborhood made survival there more difficult. Mexican-American kids were clashing with the newly-arrived Central

American immigrants. More ethnic groups were moving in all the time, and turf battles erupted over graffiti signs and who controlled which street corner. The 18th Street gang, headquartered in Rampart, became known as one of the most potent in the city, along with its other neighborhood rival, the Rockwood gang. The pharmacy was located on the borderline between their territories.

Coke and heroin were sold openly on the sidewalks near the drugstore and the sound of gunfire, even in the daytime, was not uncommon. In the absence of any social strategy for dealing with the growing complexities and problems in Rampart — with the violence and poverty and lack of employment opportunities — the police built a stronger presence in the area, with an anti-gang unit known as CRASH (Community Resources Against Street Hoodlums).

The federal government was also ratcheting up its War on Drugs campaign, which allowed whatever "us versus them" mentality law enforcement already had to deepen. The campaign, after all, wasn't just police work as usual: it was war. And as in any other war, casualties were unavoidable.

The Rampart cops, people in the neighborhood were soon telling one another, were using very strong-armed tactics with the local kids, away from the eyes of the public.

"Sometimes," says Ray Alvarez, who has worked alongside Ira Erenberg at the drugstore for many years, "the police would come in and close off certain areas and use Gestapo tactics."

This development bothered certain Rampart residents but not all of them. Parts of the neighborhood were dangerous, and with teenagers looking for ways to make fast money by selling narcotics, trouble was inevitable.

Erenberg was very aware of the mounting problems between the gangs and the Rampart police. He felt that getting involved with law enforcement personnel and trying to offer them community support would be helpful, but he found out differently.

"They didn't want any help from us," he recalled years later. "They wanted to be left alone to do their jobs and they had a very derogatory attitude toward anyone who was not one of them. I would attend meetings and sit in the Rampart police station and watch local people come in and try to ask the officers questions. They treated them with no respect. After a while, I stopped going to the meetings."

This LAPD approach was not limited to the Rampart division.

In March 1991, in another part of the city, a civilian named George Holliday caught on video several officers savagely beating a black motorist named Rodney King, while twenty-five other cops stood by and did nothing to stop the attack. The videotape of this assault was given to the media, which aired it repeatedly; each time, it appeared more brutal than before. King's two main assailants, Stacey Koon and Laurence Powell, were charged in the beating but in April 1992 were acquitted by a suburban jury in Simi Valley.

For the next three days, with scenes that echoed the 1965 racial violence in Watts, segments of L.A.'s African-American population exploded into mass rioting — burning and looting and sending the fear of uncontrollable chaos throughout the city. This time, fifty-five people died and the atmosphere in L.A. reflected the sense that the destruction might not be able to be contained. As a wealthy resident of the upscale Brentwood neighborhood (the flames did not come close to his home) recalled almost five years later, "The '92 riots scared the hell out of everyone in this town and that fear has never subsided. Los Angeles is still very nervous over racial issues."

During those three days of rampaging, Erenberg left his house early each morning in Pacific Palisades — another upscale west L.A. neighborhood — and drove to work at the pharmacy twenty miles away. He carried with him a cell phone and a loaded handgun. As his wife Dianne waved goodbye to him, she was terrified that she would never see him again.

"She went bonkers," he says.

Erenberg understood her feelings, but he had customers in Rampart who needed his prescription drugs, his medical supplies, his advice, and his help. When he got to the pharmacy one morning, the buildings across the street were ablaze and looting was underway. The police had set up a command post on the fourteenth floor of a nearby apartment building and were trying to manage and contain the violence from there. A store close to Erenberg's was owned by a Korean man, and because the rioters were targeting Korean businesses, Erenberg expected the worst. He loaded his car with items from the drugstore, preparing to run the pharmacy from his vehicle. He was not alone in these endeavors. Longtime customers came in and hauled merchandise home with them, protecting it until they could safely return it to the drugstore — if Mi Farmicia survived.

It did. Erenberg was so well known and well respected in the neighborhood that the looters did not touch his business. There may have been another reason the pharmacy was spared. The store next to his was run by an Iranian who'd worked as a mechanic for Israeli Defense Minister Moshe Dayan during the 1967 Six Day War. This man was prepared for combat. He stationed a few of his friends on the roof of his building and armed them with Uzis, telling them not to hesitate to open fire on the rioters. His business was also spared.

In time the gunfire fell silent, the flames subsided, the dead were hauled away and buried, and Ira's customers brought back his supplies and helped restock the shelves of his store. Things returned to normal, and Erenberg resumed selling Band-Aids, greeting cards, backpacks, and pinatas to the families in the neighborhood. City officials trying to make sense of the riots appointed a civilian body known as the Christopher Commission, headed by the much-respected and soon-to-be new Secretary of State, Warren Christopher, to study the root causes of the violence. The commission focused heavily on police behavior, identifying many problems and problem officers while putting forward numerous ideas for substantive reforms. Later that year, voters passed the recommended reforms, but the LAPD refused to institute them. The department's attitude was the same as it had been for decades: regardless of the recurring bloodshed and the advised reforms, the LAPD would not tolerate any outside monitoring of its affairs, let alone any outside supervision.

Three years later, in 1995, L.A. voters took a further step in their desire to establish a civilian presence at the department, approving the inspector general's post. Headed by a moderate woman named

Katherine Mader, the post was designed to bring about some of the reforms passed in 1992 and to create accountability by the LAPD to an outside body. But once again, the police brass resisted these attempts at change, refusing to divulge internal affairs matters or share many documents with the inspector general's office. The blind eye that had long guided the actions of the police administration remained shut tight and Katherine Mader's office was rendered impotent.

Following the 1992 riots, Daryl Gates was replaced as chief by a black man from Philadelphia named Willie Williams. Williams lived in the suburbs, kept his distance from the rank and file, and did little to confront the attitude or problems that the Christopher Commission had identified. Police investigators eventually discovered that he was taking free hotel suites and meals from Las Vegas casino owners. His actions went beyond the appearance of impropriety, and he was soon out of a job, replaced by another African-American, career officer Bernard Parks.

As the decade moved on and the memory of the riots faded, business in Los Angeles returned to usual, but its citizens waited and wondered about the next riot, racial explosion or police scandal that would rise up from beneath the beautiful city by the ocean and rock its legal foundations, just like the earthquake that hit parts of the metropolitan area in January 1994. They didn't have to wait long.

A NATION WITHOUT SHAME

9

You're never prepared for the phone call that changes your life — the one that brings news of the death of a parent or a different job in a distant city or an extreme challenge to how you see the world. My call came in early August 1994 and I was not ready for the disruption it would cause. I was not prepared to get involved in something that was absolutely unpopular, risky, and potentially dangerous. For two decades I'd been a journalist who'd kept my distance from whatever I was reporting on. I was just an observer of human affairs and nothing more. This attitude fit well within my professional comfort zone, and I wasn't looking to change it, especially not right now.

When the phone rang on that August evening, I was forty-three years old and married, with a one-year-old son. I worked at home and spent a good part of each day taking care of the baby so that my wife could have a break and get out of the house. We were both adjusting to our demanding new existence with an infant and were not looking for strange adventures up blind alleys. But sometimes, they come looking for you.

My wife answered the phone and handed me receiver. I was pleasantly surprised to hear the man's voice on the other end of the line. He and I had met a decade earlier, when I'd begun researching my book about Alan Berg and the neo-Nazis who'd killed him. We spoke only once or twice a year now, but his calls were always welcome and informative. He said that he was staying in Denver for a couple of days and invited me to meet him the following afternoon at his downtown hotel. This request conveyed a sense of seriousness and urgency, but when I asked what he wanted to talk about, he refused to provide any details.

"Just show up at one p.m. with an open mind," he said.

If I liked what he had to say, he added, I had a large task in front of me. If I didn't like it, I could leave with no questions asked.

There are people you instinctively trust and people you don't. From the moment I'd met this individual, I'd believed that his intentions with me were clean and clear. He was patient, intelligent, and had never given me any bad information. I'd felt a connection with him that was difficult to capture in words.

We met the next day in his hotel room and after a few preliminary remarks, he said, "Are you still interested in domestic terrorism?"

My first instinct was to say no. Three years of documenting

and dwelling inside the minds, emotions, and violence of hate-filled white supremacists was enough for me. This process had produced a few personal threats and some recurring nightmares. Ever since the Berg book had been published in 1987, I'd wanted to move away from that subject.

"I don't think so," I said.

"Not every act of terrorism involves a bombing or assassinating someone for ethnic reasons. Many acts don't involve physical violence of any kind."

I made no response, but had a very strange feeling about where our conversation was heading.

"The neo-Nazi attitude you found ten years ago in the Order is getting larger and more pervasive," he said. "It's no longer limited to fringe groups or racist fanatics. Some dangerous people are now wearing very respectable faces."

I nodded uncertainly.

"Some are in police departments around the country. Almost every big-city force has this mindset inside of it, but right now I'm thinking about the LAPD."

He paused and leaned forward. "Have you followed the O.J. Simpson case?"

The odd sensation I'd been feeling just got stronger.

"Sure," I said.

Six weeks earlier, along with 90 million other Americans, I'd watched on live television as Simpson had taken his infamous Ford Bronco ride up the L.A. freeway with police cars tailing him. Inside the vehicle, the ex-football star held a gun to his head and was apparently ready to pull the trigger. Viewing all this, I'd concluded, along with most other viewers, that Simpson was guilty of killing his ex-wife, Nicole Brown Simpson, and her friend, Ron Goldman, both of whom had been knifed to death five nights earlier in front of her Brentwood condo. Since this ride had ended with Simpson's surrender to the police, his guilt had only seemed to deepen, especially after the endless coverage of a frantic October 1993 911 call by Nicole to the police, with O.J. screaming at her in the background.

"What do you think happened in this case?" the man asked.

"A jealous man killed two people."

"Would you like to know more?"

"About what?"

"Many things."

"Is Simpson guilty or not?"

"That's the wrong question."

"It's the only question."

"No, it isn't." He spoke these words calmly, but the gravity in his voice was undeniable.

"What are you saying?"

"For years there have been significant racial and other problems within the LAPD. There have also been some very out-of-control police officers. Some of them are violently disruptive. They hurt people. They break the law and get away with it. They damage the community they work in. They do terrible harm to the legal system. They engage in a different kind of terrorism than murdering a talk show host. They're much closer to the source of power than the Order ever reached. They're operating inside the system now and that's far more dangerous."

"Where's all this going?"

"For weeks people within L.A.'s legal system have been coming forward and telling the authorities about a homicide detective involved in the case against Simpson — a man named Mark Fuhrman. Are you familiar with him?"

"I've heard of him."

"Do you know what Simpson's lawyers are saying about him?"

"That he may have planted evidence by moving a bloody glove found at the crime scene over to O.J.'s home."

"What do you think of that suggestion?"

"It sounds desperate to me. Like a courtroom ploy by lawyers who know their client's guilty. Everyone I talk to thinks it's ridiculous."

He stared at me and said, "Do you want to get off the sidelines, where journalists always believe they are standing, and do something different?"

"Like what?"

"Do you want to get involved in the case and become something more than an observer?"

"What do you mean?"

"I have a simple proposition for you. All you have to do is

take several pieces of information to Simpson's lawyers and they will — "

"Wait," I said, raising my hand and shaking my head.

"There are three or four critical things that his attorneys haven't yet uncovered. Once they do, the case is over."

I laughed out loud, relieving some of the tension that had been gathering within my body. Laughter seemed to be the best response to what I was hearing, which was preposterous.

The man stood up and seemed agitated.

"I'm sorry," he said. "I misjudged you. I thought you were more curious and probing about things."

His words carried some sharpness, a tone he'd never used with me before.

"Everyone is convinced of Simpson's guilt," I said. "That's all the media or the public care about."

"That's right, but larger issues are involved here. This case has gotten enormous publicity and that isn't going to stop. Some things need to be exposed and dealt with by the system or they'll only get worse. Because of all the attention focused on these murders, certain police activities could be forced out into the open during the trial."

"If you have some important information," I said, "why don't you go to the authorities and lay it out for them?"

"You don't understand. That won't do any good. People in law enforcement — both attorneys at the DA's office and police officers — have already come forward and told the authorities to be wary of Fuhrman and the evidence in this case. No one is listening to them. No one will investigate these allegations to find out what really happened. They're doing what they always do — turning away from their own deepest problems. The prosecutors won't do what's necessary, but I think the defense will pay attention to this information if someone can get it to them in time. If you're not interested in pursuing this, I'll find someone else."

I was silent for a few moments.

"You're dropping a bomb on me," I said.

"I know that."

"Before I could even think about doing anything, you have to tell me the absolute truth about this information. Where did it come from and is it solid?"

"The information is real."

"And it comes from?"

"Inside L.A.'s legal system. That's all I'm going to say. Jobs and careers are at stake. You can only test the validity of the information by going to L.A. and passing it along to Simpson's defense team and getting them to investigate it. If the larger truth behind the LAPD could come out now, in a trial that will be watched as much as this one, that might get people to look at some of the abuses. It might even put a stop to the kind of police misconduct and terrorism I'm talking about."

"Even if I went out there, they'd never listen to me — a reporter from Denver. They'd think I was crazy."

"That's the risk you have to take."

I laughed again at the sheer oddness of what I was hearing.

"This will be good for you," he said, smiling at me for the first time since we'd begun talking. "It will be a very educational experience and teach you a lot about your society and yourself."

"Such as?"

"That's what you get to find out."

I frowned and then said it again: "They'll never listen to a reporter from Denver."

"Oh yes, they will."

10

Six days later, I walked into the Los Angeles office of Simpson's lead attorney, Robert Shapiro, for a meeting with three defense investigators. I was accompanied by a pair of aging local lawyers, Jerry Rubin and Stan Handman, both of whom had seen many things in their careers but had never been at this impressive Century City address, the filming locale for Bruce Willis's *Die Hard* motion picture. We stood in the lobby and took in its grandiose size, high ceiling, and fine appointments, awestruck by its pervasive aura of money. To our left was a glass-enclosed conference room with a shiny round table that must have measured twenty-five feet in diameter. It conjured up a royal banquet.

"Geez," Rubin muttered.

"Now *that*," Handman said, "is a conference table."

The place was abuzz with activity. Phones were ringing everywhere. Good-looking young men and women moved through the lobby carrying folders and stacks of paper. They sported fashionable hairdos and chic outfits. They stepped so efficiently and were so uniformly attractive that the whole scene looked choreographed. I didn't know if this office held any substance, but it reeked with style.

I looked around, astounded at finding myself here. My journey to L.A. had started almost immediately after I'd left the man in his Denver hotel room. That afternoon I'd returned home and called Shapiro's office, which had set up an 800 hotline for this case. A recording came on and stated that if you had something useful for the defense team, you could leave a message and somebody from their staff would get back with you. I deposited my message, hung up, and then remembered a recent media report about this hotline receiving a hundred calls an hour. Many, of course, were crank calls. I was positive that nobody from Shapiro's office was going to get back to me, and by the end of the day, nobody had.

That night I went to bed relieved. I'd made a call, nothing had come of it, and now I could put this peculiar little episode behind me. Even attempting to get involved in something this large and complicated struck me as foolish and absurd. What was I thinking about when I'd dialed that 800 number? What had I expected to accomplish? Why was I looking for trouble? Everyone I knew believed that Simpson was utterly guilty and despicable for slitting his wife's throat and killing the mother of their two young children. People simply hated him.

No topic of conversation stirred as much anger and passion as these two murders — in part because of their racial component. A black man, the media had been insisting for the past six weeks, had nearly cut off the head of his beautiful white ex-wife and left her to bleed to death on her front stoop. What story could be more powerful than that? What scenario could unleash more primal fears in the country's majority Caucasian population?

All of the roots of America's endless nightmare over skin color came together right here. The apparent facts of the case were profoundly uncomfortable for a nation still struggling with racial issues and racism. The overwhelming belief in Simpson's guilt lent credence to the ugliest convictions of the most embittered white supremacists across the land: black men were violent and could never be trusted, especially in interracial marriages. This idea had permeated the thinking of Bob Mathews and the Order; it was one of their core racial and political tenets. Now it was running right beneath the surface of what had quickly become the most notorious criminal case in American history, a case that went to the heart of our racial fears and our collective anger over crime and punishment. If Simpson somehow managed to get away with these murders, went the spoken and unspoken mantra throughout the media and the white populace, this would permanently wound our legal system and the public's faith in law and order.

As I lay awake on that August night and mulled all this over, I was glad to have avoided any connection to the Simpson mess. And yet, when sleep did not come and the night grew longer and dawn finally approached, I kept wondering if I'd been told the truth about several key pieces of evidence in the case but was afraid of acting on the information. What if something very disturbing and disruptive — even criminal — was going on inside the LAPD and needed to be exposed? How much was at stake here? What was my real concern? What if I didn't want to give up my observer's role and my reporter's protective shield because that might jerk me out of my comfort zone and expose me to criticism or even anger and scorn? Were my own fears more powerful than my sense of adventure and curiosity?

At 5 a.m. I got out of bed, made coffee, and read the newspaper. While eating breakfast, I decided to make one more call to L.A. and if it went nowhere, I could tell myself that I'd done all I could and move on. At eleven that morning, I phoned the firm of Johnnie Cochran, the lawyer second-in-command on the Simpson team. With the start of jury selection only a few weeks away, in mid-September, Cochran had begun playing a more prominent role for the defense. As I dialed his number, I instinctively felt that I had a better chance of speaking with a live human being at his office than at Robert Shapiro's.

A woman answered. When I told her that I wanted to fax out some material about the Simpson case to her boss she made a weary, impatient sound. How many of these calls had she recently received? How annoyed was she at getting one more?

Cochran wasn't there, she said, but he would be back in several days and I should try again then.

I asked if anyone else was working on the case and she mentioned Cochran's first lieutenant, Carl Douglas. I told her that I was going to fax out a single page of information. Would she please give it to Mr. Douglas?

She balked at the idea, but after more persuasion on my part, she agreed to do it. I sent off the fax and waited the rest of the day. Nothing happened. That night I went to bed more convinced than ever that attempting to convey information to these people was hopeless. I'd done my best and put some things in writing and tried to get them in someone's hands, but...

The next morning, when things didn't seem so bleak, I phoned the woman to see if she'd given the fax to Douglas. She didn't even remember receiving it. She passed me along to Douglas's secretary, Eloise, who also had no knowledge of the fax. Somebody must have lost it. I told Eloise that in five minutes I was going to re-fax the page, so would she please walk over and pick it up at the fax machine, carry it to Mr. Douglas's desk, put it in his hand, and ask him to read it?

"I've got a lot of work to do here," she protested, "and I — "

"Please," I cut her off, and something in my voice must have affected her.

"I'll see what I can do," she said.

Fifteen minutes later Douglas called, demanding to know where I'd gotten the information and if I could tell him anything more. I refused to answer his questions and asked for a face-to-face meeting in L.A.

He said that he was an extremely busy man and that I was just wasting his time. He added that I was probably a kook anyway — a publicity-seeking screwball like so many others who'd contacted him about the case and were only trying to get on TV or confuse him and cause him more trouble than he already had.

"I don't have time to play games with you, man," he told me.

"This isn't a game."

"Then speak to me."

"Not over the phone. No meeting, no more information."

He began to curse me, and he was good at this. As he swore, his voice rose and then rose some more — until it cracked in my ear. When he stopped cursing he said that his investigators would have to attend our meeting, and they were just as busy as he was. He didn't know what their schedules were, but he was certain that they would never agree to something like this.

"Tell me who your source is," he said, "and I'll think about setting up a meeting."

"No."

He swore again, but then he said, "Let me talk to my investigators and call you back."

I hung up, doubting that I would ever hear from him again.

My head was ringing. The man's words and curses had been thrown like punches. His directness and intensity were still palpable in the air around me. I'd just plugged into the wild, vast, electrical socket known as the O.J. Simpson case and the sudden connection had jolted me as no other professional experience had for a long time.

The phone rang and Douglas told me to be at Robert Shapiro's Century City office this coming Monday afternoon at three o'clock sharp.

11

On Monday afternoon a woman led the two lawyers and me up a flight of stairs to a conference room, where Douglas, private investigator Bill Pavelic, and another attorney, Shawn Chapman, were waiting for us. We all shook hands and sat down at a long table. While the lawyers exchanged pleasantries and business cards, I had the chance to look at Douglas. He had big, sad, jumpy, frightened eyes and pockmarked skin. He was as unpolished and rough in appearance as Johnnie Cochran was smooth and handsome. Douglas was around forty, thin and wiry. He seemed volatile. I glanced at his eyes again. They reminded me of the eyes of black jazz musicians back in the 1950s — Miles Davis eyes — huge, dark pools lined with red veins in the white spaces, intelligent and deeply uncomfortable eyes, wet and bottomless eyes.

Studying Douglas, I understood that L.A. was not Denver and things here were more complex than I was accustomed to, more entangled, more expensive, more beautiful, more buried, and more brutal. Some of that brutality had left its stamp on the attorney's face.

Douglas leaned forward and looked at me and said, "We don't know who you are and we need time to check you out. Now what have you got?"

I proceeded to tell them four of the things I'd heard the previous week in Denver. The first was that homicide detective

Mark Fuhrman had not come to Nicole Simpson's condo that night as an investigator committed to pursuing all of the evidence and every reasonable lead. He'd arrived with his mind already made up about the case. The reason for this, it had been explained to me, was that he'd known Nicole prior to the murders. He'd responded to a 1985 family dispute at her home and since then he'd been aware of her ongoing troubles with her ex-husband. Fuhrman, according to the man in Denver, had been Nicole's "cop on the force," her confidant about her personal problems.

I mentioned a bar in West L.A. where police hung out together and where it had been common knowledge that Fuhrman and the dead woman had communicated with each other. While unwinding at this tavern over a beer, the cops liked to tease Fuhrman about his connection to the beautiful and glamorous ex-wife of a celebrity sports star. The detective took his relationship with Nicole very seriously and did not appreciate the ribbing. He saw himself as her protector and felt responsible for her safety.

"I think I might know which bar that is," Pavelic said. His gravelly voice was the kind that can crawl up your spine and scrape against the back of your neck. I wasn't surprised to learn that he had once been a cop with the LAPD.

By early August, the defense team had publicly suggested that Fuhrman had framed Simpson in the early hours of June 13 by moving a bloody glove from Nicole's condo over to his home.

Their contention was that he'd been motivated by racism, but the defense had done nothing to back up its claim of evidence planting. This lack of substantiation had only solidified the media's and the public's mistrust and anger toward O.J. and his lawyers.

While relating the story I'd been told in Denver, I now gave Douglas two very specific pieces of information about the planting of evidence:

At roughly 3 a.m. on June 13, after spending some time at the crime scene, Fuhrman had talked at least one other officer into leaving Nicole's condo and driving over to Simpson's home in another part of Brentwood. The detective was absolutely convinced they would find evidence of the murders there. When that didn't happen, the men got into a loud argument on Simpson's property because they'd left the crime scene, which was an unprofessional thing to do, and they might get reprimanded or something worse. Months later, Rosa Lopez, who lived and worked next door to O.J., testified during the trial that she'd heard an argument between some men on Simpson's grounds at around 3 a.m. on the morning of June 13. For her efforts on the witness stand, she was attacked and ridiculed by the prosecutors and much of the media.

Fuhrman, I'd been told, was embarrassed by the lack of evidence at O.J.'s. After driving back to Nicole's condo empty-handed, he walked around behind her address, found a nearby fence, and broke a long sliver of wood off of it. He used the wood to pick up one of the bloody gloves, and slipped the glove into a blue plastic bag, the kind that homicide investigators carry with them to crime scenes. Fuhrman then hid the stick and the bag, and an hour or so later convinced three other detectives — Ron Phillips, Tom Lange, and Phillip Vannatter — to drive over to O.J.'s and look for evidence. Once they were at the defendant's home, Fuhrman got rid of the other men and put the glove on Simpson's property. A few minutes later, he informed the other officers of his discovery.

Fuhrman had done all this alone, I'd been told, so he could act quickly and make Simpson the only credible suspect. His plan succeeded brilliantly. Right after he showed the glove to Vannatter, the senior detective in the group, the older cop ordered yellow police tape put up around O.J.'s house, making it an official part of the crime scene. It was roughly 6 A.M. on June 13, less than eight hours since the bodies had been found. The murder investigation into the deaths of Nicole Simpson and Ron Goldman was essentially finished, because the cops were certain that they had their man.

Both the broken-off sliver of wood and the blue plastic bag, I said to Douglas, had been recovered from Simpson's address, taken into police custody, and were being stored at an LAPD property room. Douglas and his investigators would find these two items there with the other evidence.

When I finished laying all this out, I looked across the table at the trio.

Pavelic went off, declaring that everything I was telling them was a lie. There was no stick and no bag in evidence. Fuhrman had not known Nicole Simpson, and none of this could have ever happened.

"Why?" I asked him, taken aback by the fierceness of his response.

"Because someone would have seen Fuhrman do all that and someone would have started talking about it. That someone would have talked to someone else. And that someone would have told the story to others. That's how things work in the real world."

"Why," I said, "do you think I'm here?"

He grunted. "Why?"

"Because someone *has* talked about it."

I then offered Douglas the fourth piece of information, which I'd been told was the most significant of all.

Late on the night of June 12, O.J. had flown to Chicago and very early the next morning was informed by a police phone call that his ex-wife had been murdered. He got on the next plane back to L.A. and arrived home around noon. At 1 p.m. he was taken to the police station and interviewed by Detectives Lange and Vannatter, without requesting that his attorney be present. He also voluntarily agreed to have his blood drawn and placed in a small medical vial. This blood would eventually be tested to see if it matched any of the blood drops found at Nicole's condo or his house.

Blood stored in this type of vial contains a preservative located at the bottom of the tube. Once the blood goes into the vial, the preservative spreads upward through it in order to keep the blood from coagulating. It will remain in liquid form and can later be utilized in DNA experiments or other scientific exams.

By early August, the prosecutors were already asserting that a few blood drops found at both the crime scene and Simpson's home came from O.J. — absolutely implicating him in these murders. These drops would soon be sent off to the Cellmark Laboratory in Maryland for DNA testing, and if the tests proved this was his blood, the case against him seemed unassailable.

"The blood they are going to test," I said to Douglas, "is your client's blood. It will have his DNA. But I've been told that a scientific procedure can show that these blood drops did not come out of his body on the night of the crime, but out of the vial his drawn blood was stored in."

Douglas stared at me with such scrutiny that his naturally protuberant eyes looked ready to leap from their sockets.

"How could it show that?" he said.

"Vials like this have a preservative in them. If traces of this preservative are found in his blood drops, that will conclusively demonstrate that blood was planted. That may be the only provable thing in this case."

Pavelic made a loud sarcastic noise.

Douglas gazed at me in silence for a while, before saying,

"Anything else?"

"I was told that after Simpson's blood was drawn and put in the vial, someone took a syringe and extracted some of it and sprinkled it around. I think you'll find that some of that stored blood is missing."

Douglas was vigorously shaking his head. He began to speak more forcefully than at any time since the meeting had started. He said that while he would like to believe what I was telling him, he was certain that I was wrong, because once Simpson's blood had been drawn and put inside a vial, that vial was tightly sealed and checked into evidence at Parker Center, where it was safely kept for future testing. If what I was saying was true, that seal would have been broken and the defense team would know about this. Because they knew that it hadn't been broken, my story fell apart.

I did not respond to his contention and Douglas went on, throwing me a bone of sorts by saying that my theory was intriguing and of the 200,000 tips they'd so far received, no one else had mentioned anything about a blood preservative. But unfortunately, I'd been misinformed about the vial and was being led astray by an anonymous source. The attorney was sorry but he couldn't investigate any of the four things I'd told him because "they have no basis in hard facts."

He could never trust me anyway, he added, because I was a journalist and he didn't like journalists. He hoped that didn't offend me, but that was how he felt.

I was not offended but disappointed. He and Pavelic were dismissing everything I'd brought them.

"You must understand something," Douglas said. "I sue policemen for a living. I know what they're capable of but I just don't believe they would do something like that."

As he spoke these words, his voice conveyed a note of finality. I glanced at my watch. We'd been talking for an hour and fifteen minutes, much longer than I'd anticipated.

"If you don't have anything more than that," Pavelic said, rising from his chair, "I've got a lot of work to do."

I turned to Douglas and asked if he would consider sharing with me a couple of the preliminary hearing transcripts, especially the ones holding the testimony given by Fuhrman and Vannatter. I told him that I wanted to look for holes or contradictions or inconsistencies in their statements.

Douglas shook his head again and said that he would never give something like this to an outsider. He thanked me for meeting with them and wished me a good trip home.

We all stood and shook hands, saying goodbye and walking out into the hallway. Pavelic and Chapman went off by themselves while Douglas drifted over to me and the other two lawyers.

Coming closer, Douglas whispered in my ear, "Get me some more information."

12

I flew back to Denver and continued speaking with my source. He told me some new things but mostly restated his desire that I look at the larger issues surrounding the Simpson case. Issues that went beyond a sliver of wood, a blue plastic bag, some blood preservative, and a connection between Mark Fuhrman and the dead woman — things that would go far beyond the outcome of the approaching trial.

"Why are you doing all this?" I asked again, as I had earlier at the hotel.

"For decades," he said, "I've watched our legal system deteriorate. Now the Simpson trial will reveal everything that's wrong with it. It will be a sideshow of accusations and counter-accusations, and in the end it will just create more confusion. This case is the natural result of what the system has become. I want you to see firsthand how things work — or fail to work. What the public is now viewing on television is a travesty of justice. We have 'evidence' that is not evidence and we have 'journalism' that is absolutely shameless in its disregard for the underlying facts. We have testimony delivered under oath that is filled with lies and we have some very decent, talented, and hard-working police, prosecuting attorneys, and even the District Attorney who have lined up behind all this.

"Manipulation is the key thing. That's what I'm trying to get you to see and explore — how easily we can be manipulated and controlled by a few words or images on television. The things that have happened in the Simpson case have been done many, many times in the past by the LAPD, but they've been covered up. Evidence-planting is not new. Neither is cops perjuring themselves on the witness stand. People don't know this or want to believe it. They have no concept of how widespread the abuse is, especially against minority defendants, or how quickly the media and the public can be made to believe anything. Who wants to challenge the sworn testimony of a police officer?

"The main thing is not the outcome of Simpson trial. That's not why I contacted you. It's the other questions that need to be asked and answered. How easily can our population be taught to turn against others and hate them? How much fear and racism does this generate in our society? How much damage is being done that cannot be undone, and how much violence is all this creating and unleashing?

"This kind of manipulation is having a devastating effect on our cities and on the entire country. It's undermining people's faith in the legal system, in our police departments, and in the rules we live by. If it's not exposed, it will only cause more trouble and more corruption."

Every few days in August, I phoned Carl Douglas and he always called back. During our conversations, I asked him if he were going to test the blood for traces of preservative and he reiterated that the defense team would never do that. In exasperation, I finally said that if his side would not conduct this experiment, I would take the information to the DA's office.

Douglas laughed harshly into the receiver.

"They will never, ever listen to you," he said. "They will think you're crazier than I do. They don't care about anything but winning this case."

"What do you care about?" I said.

"Winning," he said, "just winning."

"What about discovering the truth?"

He laughed again and in a voice filled with cockiness and sarcasm told me that he didn't need me or my information about a blood preservative or a stick and a bag, because the defense team was going to get at least two African-Americans on the jury and that was all that would be necessary. Given the racial history of the LAPD, Douglas explained, Simpson's lawyers would create reasonable doubt in the minds of those two jurors, and they would free O.J. from his prison cell.

I continued to phone Douglas, and he regularly called back (which indicated to me that he wasn't nearly as cocky about winning his case as he pretended to be). In late August he told me that he now believed that there might have been a connection between Fuhrman and Nicole. He also said that the defense team had located pictures of the evidence gathered outside of Simpson's home on June 13. One photo depicted a small piece of blue plastic bag retrieved from just the other side of a wire fence separating the defendant's property from his neighbor's.

Along the fence was a walkway, and it was on this walkway that Fuhrman had testified at the preliminary hearing that he'd found the bloody glove. The defense had also seen a picture of a broken sliver of wood, picked up by the cops from the parkway in front of Simpson's home. The sliver had been lying on the ground, right next to O.J.'s Ford Bronco.

These photos confirmed the existence of two things I'd been told about and passed along to Douglas. Because of these confirmations, the attorney had written up the information I'd given him and sent this memo to his superiors.

"It's time," I told Douglas one day on the phone, "to test the blood."

He repeated what he'd stated earlier. No blood drops could have been taken from the vial holding Simpson's drawn blood because that vial had been sealed on June 13 and then stored at Parker Center and no one could have...

When he'd finished I said, "Two weeks ago, you told me that no stick or blue bag existed, but they do. You've got to test the blood."

"Never," he replied.

13

A few days after this exchange with Douglas, I called a local scientist named Dr. Dan Ambruso, a hematologist at the Bonfils Blood Center in Denver. He tested blood for a living and told me that the particular preservative (or "anti-coagulant") found in the purple-capped vial that had been used to store Simpson's drawn blood was known as EDTA. It was not a soluble compound, he said, meaning that it would still be intact in a blood sample long after it had spread into the liquid. He further explained that one could examine a blood swatch for EDTA either before or after running a DNA test on the same swatch.

Part of Douglas's resistance to looking for the anti-coagulant in Simpson's evidentiary blood samples was the lawyer's belief — emphatically stated to me over and over again — that this test would make a DNA exam on the same swatch impossible. Douglas's worry, Dr. Ambruso said, was unfounded.

A test for EDTA, he told me, was fairly simple for an organic chemist to conduct and could be performed in a matter of hours, but the preparation for this examination would take considerably longer. The best method for finding EDTA in a blood sample was known as gas chromatography, a procedure that separated out the chemical substance from the blood, so that EDTA was not just detectable, but measurable.

Later that week, during a televised hearing on the case, LAPD criminalist Dennis Fung testified that Simpson's blood had been drawn at around 2:30 on June 13, but Detective Vannatter had not handed the vial over to Fung until about 5:30 p.m. that day. For those three hours — before the tube had been sealed and taken to Parker Center — nobody seemed to know precisely where the vial had been or what had been done with its contents. For part of that time it had been riding around in the pocket of the senior detective on the case (two more years would pass before Gary Siglar, a technician in the L.A. County's coroner's office, would testify in a deposition for Simpson's civil trial that in the initial crucial days after the crimes, Vannatter had the blood vials holding Nicole Simpson's and Ron Goldman's blood in his possession as well).

Carl Douglas's absolute belief that blood could not have been extracted from O.J. Simpson's vial before it was sealed had just been shattered by a prosecution witness, Dennis Fung. After watching Fung testify, I called the lawyer and told him these things and about my recent discussion with Dr. Ambruso. I said that it had now become imperative for someone inside the legal system to run a gas chromatography test and find out if EDTA were present in any of the critical blood samples belonging to Simpson, Nicole, or Goldman.

The attorney no longer offered resistance. Within a week, he and Barry Scheck, his head DNA lawyer, called me for Dr. Ambruso's number. I gave it to them, but tried to explain that I should phone the scientist and prepare him for their call. They swept aside this cautionary step. Jury selection was about to start, and they were clearly desperate for any information about their client's blood.

Douglas soon phoned again and said that when I'd visited him in L.A., I'd asked to see copies of two preliminary hearing transcripts. Back then he'd said that he would never share these with me, but now he'd changed his mind.

"Which ones do you want?" he asked.

"Fuhrman's and Vannatter's," I replied.

He made copies of these and mailed them to me in a brown paper wrapper with no return address.

I read Vannatter's testimony and found nothing of significance. He was a crusty old pro, with a flat voice and eyes so cold and blank that they might just melt down lead. Unlike Fuhrman, he had no documented history of speaking openly about police racism and beating people up.

In 1978, according to Fuhrman's official LAPD files, he'd boasted to a police psychiatrist, Dr. Ronald Koegler, about using excessive force to subdue suspects — about choking them or, if necessary, breaking their faces, arms, and legs. When Fuhrman tried to leave his job with a pension, awarded to him because of the stress he claimed that his LAPD employment had caused him, the pension board turned him down.

Their report on him read: "There is some suggestion here that the patient was trying to feign the presence of a severe psychopathology. This suggests a conscious attempt to look bad and an exaggeration of problems which could be a cry for help and/or over-dramatization by a narcissistic, self-indulgent, emotionally unstable person who expects immediate attention and pity."

Narcissism had surfaced here too.

Fuhrman was typical of the problem officers cited in the Christopher Commission's report, put together after the 1992 riots in L.A, but instead of being given psychiatric help or being relieved of duty, he was promoted to the rank of detective.

Back in 1985, Fuhrman had spoken to screenwriter Laura McKinney and given her details about his workplace, the LAPD's 77th Street division, which he said held "the smell of niggers that have been beaten and killed." His words to McKinney, which were recorded on audio tape, revealed his own history of police abuse, of fabricating evidence against suspects, of creating probable cause, and of beating minority citizens in the line of duty until his pants were soaked with their blood.

One of his confessions to McKinney centered on his role in the beating of several Hispanic men back in 1978 in the Boyle Heights neighborhood in East L.A., a beating that led to a brutality suit against the LAPD. Fuhrman told McKinney that he'd lied to the department's Internal Affairs investigators about his part in the violence and that neither he nor the other officers involved in the beating had been punished or even disciplined for their actions.

"They knew damn well I did it," he said, referring to the beating and the Internal Affairs investigators. "But there was nothing they could do about it. Most of the guys [who did the beating] worked 77th together. We were tight. I mean we could have murdered people. We all knew what to say."

Fuhrman, as the tapes made clear, wasn't talking about his life as a rogue officer inside the LAPD. He was speaking about the behavior of his entire division and the things he'd seen his superiors do, especially when it came to dealing with minorities; he was just aping what others had taught him. Fuhrman bragged to McKinney about arbitrarily deciding as a cop who was innocent and who was guilty — regardless of what someone had actually done. His opinion was all that mattered.

But what if he was wrong? McKinney asked.

That was irrelevant, he said, because out on the street, "You're God."

"In almost twelve years on the department," he told the screenwriter, "I never felt guilty for one day...Even if you get the wrong guy, he's done something wrong before, or he's thought about doing something."

Fuhrman did not stop at demonizing blacks and Hispanics. He also railed against homosexuals and women — especially female cops. He talked about a secret society inside the LAPD called Men Against Women, whose purpose was to divide the males in the department against the females and to belittle the females, because women were not equipped for this kind of employment.

In 1985, the same year that he spoke to Laura McKinney, Fuhrman told an L.A. civilian, Kathleen Bell, that he would pull over any black male he spotted driving with a white woman and find something to accuse the man of. He also told her that he would like to see all the African-Americans rounded up and bombed or burned into extinction.

His remarks and police activities, as they were made public during the Simpson trial in the summer of 1995, were an exact parallel to the beliefs and feelings of the men who murdered Alan Berg. Both were obsessed with black men dating or marrying white women. Both were violent and bitterly racist, and both were promoting genocide against minority Americans. It would not be surprising to learn that Fuhrman collected Nazi memorabilia.

After studying Fuhrman's preliminary hearing testimony, I called Douglas and pointed out several things in the transcript. On page 68, the detective had told the court about something that had flashed through his mind in the first hours after the murders: "I would be concerned with the [younger Simpson] children and the ex-husband since they [Nicole and O.J.] still had joint custody of the children."

Was this custody arrangement, I asked Douglas, common knowledge in Los Angeles?

"No," he said.

"Then I doubt," I replied, "that it was common knowledge

within the police department. Only somebody who was familiar with these people and their situation would be aware of this."

"Correct," Douglas replied in the fast, clipped tone of voice he used when he agreed with you.

On page 37, Fuhrman, for no apparent reason, had testified about finding a "freshly broken" piece of wood on Simpson's property — the same stick that Douglas had recently seen in a photo. Neither the prosecutors nor the defense attorneys questioning the detective asked him why he'd brought up the stick. Yet Fuhrman, true to form, could not keep quiet about anything that he was proud of, whether it was hitting people he despised or ripping a scab off his body in order to use his own blood to create probable cause against someone he was certain had committed a crime.

After I pointed out these details to Douglas, things heated up between us. He began calling more often and stopped telling me that I was always wrong. He was getting ready to ask me for a favor and it was a funky one, so funky that it just might have been illegal.

14

One afternoon Douglas phoned and asked me to find out who inside the LAPD crime lab had been exposed to the critical blood swatches picked up at the murder scene. Who'd worked with them after they'd been checked in as evidence? What procedures had this person followed? The lawyer said that he now believed that something had been done to the swatches after they'd arrived at the lab.

A few evenings later, I called Douglas and told him that Andrea Mazzola, the junior employee in the crime lab, had handled the swatches. My information was that she had not done anything illegal or inappropriate herself, but that other unusual things with the blood had gone on around her.

As soon as I said this, Douglas hung up. I thought he was disappointed or upset with what I'd given him, but a few minutes later he called back. On the line with him was his boss, Johnnie Cochran. Douglas told me that I'd just independently verified something important about the crime lab and because of this, it was time to take our relationship to another level.

I asked what that meant.

He and Cochran then offered me $7,500 to fly to L.A., at my own expense, and persuade Mazzola to come into their office and explain what had taken place in the lab. If I could get her to testify to this in court, the men would give me $5,000 more. What they were suggesting was an impossible task and I knew it. Why would this woman tell me anything that could get her or her superiors into serious trouble and perhaps destroy the case against Simpson? I was certain I would never see a dime from Cochran or Douglas and yet... the opportunity to learn more about the case was too good to pass up. I said I would go.

On October 19 I flew to L.A., and the next day I spoke at some length by phone to Mazzola. She was very frightened by my call and my request to speak with her in person about the case. She would not meet with me unless her crime lab superior, Michele Kestler, was present, but I felt this was not a good solution. Nothing more could be arranged.

Three days later, on October 23, I met with Douglas and Cochran in the latter's office on Wilshire Boulevard. Cochran, who was as polite and gracious as Douglas was brusque, thanked me for my efforts and asked several questions about EDTA. In my presence, he also scolded Douglas and said that it had been wrong for Carl to have me approach Mazzola on the defense's behalf under these conditions. It was, he suggested, even potentially illegal for me to do this, unless the woman knew who I was and what I was doing with her and had an attorney present. Cochran was adamant about this. The last thing he said before standing, shaking my hand, and leaving the room was that I had to leave her alone.

I was relieved by his words. My involvement with these men had gone much further than I'd imagined it would, and the situation had become uncomfortable. I certainly wasn't going to break the law to assist them. For the past two and a half months, all I'd really wanted them to do was test Simpson's blood drops and find out if they held EDTA. In my view, this was the single most important issue in the upcoming trial. If the answer turned out to be yes, scientific proof would have shown what had been done with O.J.'s blood sample.

With Cochran out of the room, I expected Douglas to tell me to have a good flight back to Denver, but he had other things in mind. Using a far nastier tone than he'd ever used with me before, the lawyer said that I'd let them down because I hadn't brought Mazzola into their office and gotten her to talk to them about the crime lab. When I countered by saying that his boss had just insisted that we forget about Mazzola because we were in danger of violating the law, Douglas blew up.

He said that Cochran had his way of doing things and that he, Carl, had his own way, and right now we were going to do things his way. He told me to go out and do anything that was necessary to get Mazzola to open up about the lab.

When I resisted, Douglas began swearing and filled the room with expletives. Then he got up from his chair, walked around the table to where I was sitting, pulled a slip of paper from his pocket, held it in front of him, and let it fall near my feet.

Mazzola's address was written across its face. He wanted me to go to her home immediately and get to work on her. When I shook my head, he began swearing again.

At that point, I realized this adventure was coming to an end. The look in Douglas's eyes and the heat in his voice as he commanded me to go after Mazzola made a lasting impression on me. I was no longer merely inside the combat zone of this all-out war within our legal system. I was in the trenches and being ordered to throw a grenade at the enemy.

15

Douglas and I parted company that day and I never saw him again, but we spoke once more by phone. After our talk in Cochran's office, I returned to Denver and to being a reporter. That fall I put together a book proposal detailing what I'd been learning about the case and some of my interactions with the defense team. I submitted it to a publisher and awaited a response. A week later, the phone rang and it was Douglas. Now he was really enraged.

My proposal, which outlined many of the evidentiary issues he and I had been discussing since early last August, had been leaked to District Attorney Gil Garcetti and then subpoenaed by Christopher Darden, who worked for Garcetti and was prosecuting Simpson. Darden read the proposal carefully and in his 1996 *New York Times* best-selling book about the case, *In Contempt*, he wrote this about the pages I'd assembled: "I was basically looking at a blueprint of O.J. Simpson's defense, months before it became operational. Clearly the guy had spent more than a brief moment with Cochran and Douglas. Singular was writing about information that hadn't been made public at the time he wrote his treatment... Later...I would wonder how much Simpson had paid for a defense that really came from a true crime writer..."

Once the prosecutors had the proposal in their hands, they knew for certain that the question of planted blood and EDTA would be factors in the upcoming trial. Because of this, they enlisted one of own their attorneys, Rockne Harmon, to contact the FBI about the anti-coagulant issue. In February 1995, a month into the trial, Harmon said in the courtroom of presiding Judge Lance Ito, and in front of the nation's TV cameras, that the claim of a blood preservative was absolutely false and that his side was willing to submit to the independent testing of two blood samples in order to show that no EDTA was present in them. One sample was of Simpson's blood and had apparently been recovered from the back gate at Nicole's condo, and the other was of her blood and had been lifted from a pair of socks on the floor of her ex-husband's bedroom. The results of this scientific experiment, Harmon implied, would conclusively demonstrate that blood could not have been planted.

Judge Ito agreed to this procedure and the FBI was called in to run the gas chromatography test, the same one that I'd earlier recommended to Douglas. Special agent Roger Martz conducted the examination and soon had the results. Then something very unusual happened. The matter basically died for almost three months — because the prosecutors refused to bring it up.

But the defense did.

In early May of 1995, Barry Scheck told the court that his side had "a bombshell" coming on EDTA. With this revelation hanging in front of the prosecutors, Harmon himself conceded that the defense had a "flicker of hope" on the blood preservative issue.

Even more unusual was that the prosecution, after making a huge public fuss over EDTA the previous February, never called Special Agent Martz to the witness stand. The defense called him instead, and under oath Martz testified that he'd found a substance in these blood samples that was "consistent with" EDTA. The defense also called their own blood specialist, Dr. Frederic Rieders, who'd first analyzed EDTA in 1954 and had begun doing gas chromatography tests in 1959. He testified that the blood under scrutiny had the "strongest possible presence of EDTA."

Something else was revealed that lent credence to what I'd told Douglas at our first face-to-face meeting. One and a half milliliters of O.J. Simpson's drawn blood was missing from the eight milliliters that had originally been placed into the vial — and it could not be accounted for.

Three of the four pieces of information I'd passed along to Douglas the previous August had now been confirmed. The stick and the bag had been found with the other evidence in an LAPD storage room (Cochran introduced both items into the trial on February 22, 1995). The anti-coagulant EDTA had been found in the blood samples tested by the FBI. The fourth piece of information was about to be validated by an Internal Affairs investigation of Mark Fuhrman undertaken by the LAPD. According to their report, which was conducted in the winter of 1995, several police officers had come forward the previous summer and told the authorities that Fuhrman had bragged to them about seeing Nicole Simpson's new "boob job." He'd seen her breast implants, they said, "up close and personal." To some of the cops, this didn't mean that Fuhrman had merely known the dead woman and occasionally been in her presence. It meant that they'd been intimate.

The Internal Affairs investigation, which was not widely publicized, substantiated other things my source had said about what had happened to those within L.A.'s legal system who'd tried to warn the authorities about Detective Fuhrman. At least three deputy DA's, Lucien Coleman, Julie Sergojian, and Ellen Burke, had also come forward in the summer of 1994 with disturbing stories about this officer, but they were uniformly dismissed or ignored by the District Attorney's office. One policeman, Walter Purdy, had told Sergojian and Coleman that Fuhrman had put swastikas inside of his work locker – because Purdy's wife was Jewish and this was Fuhrman's way of taunting a fellow cop who'd married the enemy.

Nothing came of anyone's efforts to tell those in charge at the DA's office about Fuhrman's attitudes or behavior. All of it was swept aside or buried, as was the information gathered during the LAPD's Internal Affairs investigation, which concluded "there was no misconduct involved" and the anecdotes about Fuhrman "had no basis in fact." The LAPD and the District Attorney were committed to not investigating such things – and particularly not during the O.J. Simpson case.

In June of 1994, when the case began, Peter Bozanich was a high-ranking adviser to DA Garcetti. Bozanich was part of Garcetti's inner circle until he made the mistake of suggesting to prosecutors that the glove found at Simpson's estate made no sense and should be approached with great caution.

"There were no answers for me [about the glove]," he once told the *Los Angeles Times,* "and by the time we got to the trial, there were still no answers."

For raising questions and promoting critical thinking, Bozanich was soon transferred out of Garcetti's downtown office and sent to work in the outlying and utterly unglamorous Compton neighborhood.

The pattern in LA could not have been clearer: from top to bottom, legal officials did not want to examine or independently investigate allegations of misbehavior by those who worked in its police force, its crime lab, its DA's office, or anywhere else. They simply did not want to hear about these things — not yet anyway. In another four years or so, the problems would have grown so large and disruptive and expensive that scandal and corruption would threaten to engulf or break the entire system.

16

In early November 1994, my book proposal was also leaked to *The New York Times* and other media outlets. They paid no attention to these pages, which challenged virtually every assumption the mainstream press held about the case. New information, especially uncomfortable or contradictory new information, did not interest the world's foremost news-gathering businesses, even though they were tirelessly reporting on this event every day.

In late April 1995, the proposal surfaced in Judge Ito's courtroom and my name came up in connection with it. The *Los Angeles Times* called me and wrote a story that mentioned the proposal and its curious route through the trial. I was suddenly, and very briefly, a public figure.

During the next two days, nearly every major media organization in the country, including all the networks, the newsweeklies, and several of the nation's largest newspapers, contacted me. The Associated Press, echoing Christopher Darden's remarks from *In Contempt*, wrote that the "book outline reads like a blueprint for the defense case Simpson's lawyers began revealing in court in January."

During those forty-eight hours, I told numerous high-profile reporters that EDTA was going to be an important part of Simpson's upcoming defense strategy. I gave them a synopsis of the facts behind the blood-planting allegations and explained the significance of the FBI conducting blood preservative tests but not being called to testify for the prosecution. I was naively under the impression that these were significant aspects of the most celebrated case in the history of American criminal justice. It seemed possible that, depending on how the trial developed, I might receive a follow-up phone call from at least one of the journalists who was interested in the crucial blood evidence being presented against Simpson. But I was wrong.

After those two days in April, no reporter ever called back — not after Special Agent Martz testified that he'd found something "consistent with" EDTA in the blood samples, not after Simpson was easily acquitted by the mixed-race jury in October 1995, and not after some of the jurors walked out of the courtroom for the last time and told the media how the blood preservative issue had been a factor in their decision-making process. I'd mistakenly believed that someone who was paid to collect and piece together information would try to establish the cause and effect behind these issues, and would lay out for the public the reasons why the blood evidence had fallen apart.

Nor was it relevant to journalists that Andrea Mazzola testified at the trial that she'd signed her initials to the Simpson blood swatches that were later sent off to the Cellmark Lab in Maryland for DNA testing. Yet the swatches that arrived in Maryland and were examined by scientists — the swatches that were found to contain Simpson's blood — did not hold her initials. The stunningly clear implication behind her words was that other swatches had replaced the original ones and been shipped back east.

The ironies were as thick as could be. No trial had ever received the coverage this one had, but the American public was never told the meaning of the shattered evidence. Our free press was never free to investigate this courtroom proceeding or these crimes because they never gave themselves that freedom. When the facts did not fit their assumptions, the facts were ignored.

No event in the 1990s would reflect our ongoing racial division more vividly than the Simpson verdict. And nothing would illustrate more nakedly the "us versus them" mentality that had pervaded our culture. The mainstream media was shocked and outraged that a jury had listened as the State of California spent $9 million while putting on six months of evidence against Simpson — and then walked him out of jail after less than three hours of deliberation. No jurors had ever made such a strong statement about the evidence in a murder case and about those who'd collected it. No jury had so adamantly said that a criminal trial was masking a deeper and pernicious reality. And never had jurors been treated the way this one was after rendering their decision. They were called everything from racist to corrupt to stupid.

It was inconceivable to the American media that a mostly black group of jurors, who were constantly referred to as uneducated and unsophisticated, could see or feel or grasp things that reporters were certain did not exist — things that added up to an important social evil. The press was only interested in identifying evil individuals and punishing them in public ways. It was far easier to generate and hold a mass audience, as Rush Limbaugh and many other entertainers had discovered in recent years, by finding a single target to hate — and then constantly hating him — rather than exploring the fuller context and texture of events and human beings. Surfaces were what sold now, whether you were buying or selling clothes or make-up or cold beer or criminal trials.

My strange mission in the Simpson case, undertaken in August 1994, ended in failure — even though each of the four pieces of information I'd been given at a Denver hotel turned out to be real and significant. The mission failed because no one inside L.A.'s legal system wanted to consider that a neo-Nazi element, similar to the element that had been so successfully prosecuted by the federal government a decade earlier in Seattle, was now being nurtured, protected, coddled, supported, and lied about by law enforcement itself. No one wanted to consider that the nation's second-largest police department could hold ingrained racism, criminality, and violence — what one might call institutionalized domestic terrorism.

What startled me about Mark Fuhrman's taped revelations concerning his job was not that he was a bigot or that he referred to himself as "God" when on duty and made up the

rules for everything and everyone. What was genuinely shocking was what followed these revelations and our society's
response to Fuhrman. I thought that his behavior and his
desires for racial genocide — the very same neo-Nazi desires
that had been so widely condemned in the 1980s — would have
subjected Fuhrman to condemnation or banishment, but once
again I was naïve and wrong.

The overwhelmingly white, middle-class media dismissed
the detective's stories about police corruption as flights of
fancy. Cops would never really do the things Fuhrman had
talked about. He'd merely been entertaining Laura McKinney
by trying to portray himself as a lawman fighting against the
forces of evil, a uniformed hero.

During the Simpson trial, Fuhrman committed perjury and
then left the LAPD in disgrace. Yet he was almost instantly
rehabilitated after writing a book about the case and becoming
just another celebrity talking head. He was a best-selling
author, a famous guest on the talk-show circuit, a matinee idol
for the new America, and, some time later, a "crime scene" consultant for a mini-series about the murder of Nicole Brown
Simpson and Ron Goldman. Fuhrman's appearances included a
1997 stint on the television program hosted by Oprah Winfrey,
no doubt the most powerful and respected black person in the
United States. Neither Oprah nor her audience seemed disturbed by Fuhrman's admissions to Kathleen Bell about his
desires for getting rid of all African-Americans by rounding

them up and burning them. It was all show business now, even for those whose real business was terrorism.

We'd become a nation without shame.

One final irony capped the Simpson case. After leaving the Los Angeles Police Department, Fuhrman moved to Sandpoint, Idaho, a known white supremacist haven and retirement locale for certain LAPD personnel. This area wasn't far from the Aryan Nations compound and had long been one of Richard Butler's recruiting centers in his search for neo-Nazi converts. The murder weapon that had killed Alan Berg was found in the home of Gary Yarbrough, a core member of the Order, who'd lived just outside of Sandpoint. A room in his home held an elaborate shrine to Adolf Hitler.

A POSTSCRIPT FROM LOS ANGELES

Following O.J. Simpson's acquittal, African-Americans cheered and celebrated his release from prison in the streets of downtown L.A., not far from the Rampart Division of the LAPD and Ira Erenberg's drugstore, while a mostly Caucasian crowd gathered in the darkness of West L.A. and repeatedly called O.J. "the butcher of Brentwood."

Down in Rampart, kids gathered on corners and talked about police brutality and evidence planting and perjury from cops who'd testified against them. They claimed that the same kind of allegations against the LAPD that had surfaced during the Simpson trial had also happened to them, but no one had been willing to listen to their stories. They wondered if people would listen now.

In 1997, after Simpson lost a civil suit filed by the parents of the two victims and was faced with a liability of $33 million, he was forced to sell his property in Brentwood. He briefly moved to another upscale West L.A. neighborhood, Pacific Palisades, where Ira and Dianne Erenberg also lived. Simpson's arrival in their part of town filled the Erenbergs with anger and disgust. The people living near them felt the same way. The affluent, mostly white population of Pacific Palisades was enraged that the freed defendant had settled in their community, and they began agitating to get rid of him. Simpson soon left Los Angeles and relocated in Florida.

But the Erenbergs and their neighbors continued to seethe at a legal system that they believed had badly let them down for failing to convict a guilty man.

THE TRIUMPH OF THE VIRTUAL EVENT

17

Between the assassination of Alan Berg and the O.J. Simpson case, something new arrived on the American scene. It was known as the personal computer, and by the mid-nineties, millions of residences had at least one of these machines operating under their roofs. Many of the computers were connected to the Internet, which offered access to information and goods and services from all over the world. Along with this technological leap forward came a new language: computer-speak. People now talked about modems, cyberspace, and a myriad of things "virtual" — occurring in the computer realm of electronic impulses.

This new reality featured virtual travel, virtual shopping, and the virtual cyber-games that kids loved to play. Virtual activities were suddenly everywhere, and as often happens in contemporary society, the change in our technology produced a shift in our consciousness and our behavior. Once the novel technology and its language were in place, a phenomenon showed up that mirrored these new developments back to us.

It first appeared in the Simpson case. The significance of that case was not so much in its surprising verdict as in its legacy regarding our media and our public dialogue about national events. Commentary on this trial became the model for talking about every large public phenomenon to follow. Many of the same people who editorialized about the murders would be recycled for similar performances when new things happened. They would behave exactly as they had before: taking an absolute position and defending it with all their will and emotions. Investigation and open-minded discussion would be replaced by accusation and blame. Meaning would be supplanted by arguing and the demonizing of not just the defendant, but also the prosecutors who'd failed to convict him, the judge, the jury, and the legal system itself. Unexamined hatred would flow.

Back in 1974, three separate elements, all working in relative harmony, produced the Watergate scandal, which culminated with the resignation of President Nixon. These same three elements came together a decade later around the murder of Alan Berg. They were the crime itself, the legal system's response, and the media's coverage. In both cases, clarity and meaning had emerged from that co-operation and harmony. The public interest had been served and dangerous people had been stopped.

Following O.J. Simpson's arrest, a fourth element was added: the virtual event. Like the world of computers itself, the virtual event did not occur in three-dimensional reality but mostly in the growing domain of electronic communications, especially television. It had no boundaries, regulations, or connection to any social institution, and it immediately grew to gigantic proportions. Soon it would overwhelm not only the Simpson case but the criminal justice system itself. The virtual event would triumph at the expense of everything else, including what we valued most in our legal system.

TV talk show host Geraldo Rivera set the new game — the virtual court — in motion. Days after the Brentwood murders, and night after night on his cable television program, he broadcast his conviction that Simpson was guilty. No other thought, no new facts, no complexities of any kind, would penetrate Rivera's mind or cause him a moment of skepticism or doubt. The unfolding evidence, the witnesses who testified in court, the process of cross-examination under oath, the inner workings of a jury, and especially a defendant's right to the presumption of innocence were all instantaneously tossed aside by a talk show host and presented as prime-time entertainment.

When Rivera, in an attempt to be fairer, brought in someone with a different point of view, he orchestrated arguments between the two camps — loud, vitriolic, screaming matches among adults, each insisting that he was right and the other was wrong. This form of discourse, this exercise in shouting and name-calling, this division into "us versus them," would become the dominant mode of public discussion in the media — and would be mimicked by stand-up comics, serious public commentators, lawyers, and reporters, none of whom had studied the evidence. Within a month after the homicides, the dynamics of the virtual court had become by far the most important force in the case — much more significant than the guilt or innocence of the accused. These dynamics threatened to destroy the foundations of our criminal justice system.

The virtual court operates in direct opposition to the principles of American jurisprudence. There is no due process, no jurors, no Constitutional rights, no rules of evidence — in fact, no rules at all. There is no Fifth Amendment right to protection from self-incrimination (in the virtual court, even facial expressions and body language can indicate guilt); no Sixth Amendment right to a swift resolution of your legal difficulties (if you're deemed guilty in the virtual realm, you will remain guilty forever, regardless of the legal verdict); and no Seventh Amendment right of the accused to an impartial jury (not when media personalities proclaim your guilt and national polls quickly follow suit).

The virtual court has no respect for the legal system, which is flawed and makes mistakes, but has one overriding function: to act as a substitute for mob rule and mob violence. It is a thin protective shield over the impulses that made the twentieth century the bloodiest our world has yet seen. By contrast, the virtual court is fueled by a combination of blame, hatred, anger, fear, projection, and prejudice — the very ingredients that feed a dangerous mob psychology.

Virtual justice is just like virtual travel. It creates the impression that you're going somewhere and doing something when you aren't. You aren't interacting with an external, physical reality, just your own imagination, your own emotions, and millions of electronic flashes that are passing before your eyes.

The rest of the nineties played out in the shadow of the Simpson debacle. The same set of dynamics that prevailed in that case would infect every major event throughout the rest of the decade. The media, which had been defied by due process, was now in a very bad mood — and out for revenge. A mob mentality, unseen since the communist witch-hunts led by Senator Joseph McCarthy in the 1950s, was afoot everywhere. You didn't have to be a communist, a communist sympathizer or even a fellow traveler to be demonized now. All you had to do was think, feel, or live differently from the masters of the virtual event.

Many Americans recognized that Joe McCarthy was dangerous and opposed his reign of fear from the start. He was familiar because he resembled demagogues from the past. The events of the 1990s, however, were not at all obvious and did not fit into any neat historical or political context. It was a much subtler war than we were used to, and it was being spearheaded by people who, while trying to do the right thing for the country, were undermining its institutions. By not conveying the same recognizable edge of social danger, this new war was all the more frightening.

18

As the mainstream mood heated up and darkened, the edges of our culture became more disruptive and violent. In April 1995, the Oklahoma City bombing killed 168 people. Timothy McVeigh, who was convicted of this mass murder two years later, was an associate of the people and far-right groups that had formed the Order and killed Alan Berg. McVeigh read their survivalist literature and visited their enclaves around the country. He sold *The Turner Diaries* at white radical fairs or gun shows, and used the book as a blueprint for how to conceive of and carry out domestic terrorism. He followed the novel exactly as Berg's assassins had done back in 1984, but with much deadlier results.

He was only the most extreme of the violent haters. Between 1994 and 1995, hate crimes, which are defined as crimes committed against people for racial, religious, ethnic, or sexual orientation reasons, surged by thirty-three percent. They rose another ten percent in 1996. In the first half of the nineties, incendiary bombings doubled. Most were done by so-called "single-issue terrorists": anti-abortion activists, animal rights activists, and environmental protection activists. Arson and sabotage had become especially prominent in the American West, and in Oregon in particular, with scores of destructive acts that caused tens of million of dollars in damages.

As all this was unfolding, Ted Kaczynski, the man dubbed

the Unabomber by the FBI, waged his lone campaign of domestic terrorism in order to solve, as he once put it, "the technology problem." From May 1978, when his first explosive injured Terry Marker, a public-safety officer at Northwestern University, to April 1995, when he mailed a bomb that killed Gilbert Murray, the president of the California Forestry Association, Kaczynski sent out or delivered sixteen package bombs that injured twenty-three people and killed three others. In 1995, Kaczynski began revealing himself to the public by mailing letters to newspapers, magazines, and to one of his victims. In 1997, *The Washington Post* and *The New York Times* published his 35,000-word essay on "Industrial Society and Its Future." This piece of writing, named The Manifesto by the media, railed against technology and contemporary life. The Harvard-educated Kaczynski, who'd fled academia for rural Montana, was the intellectual domestic terrorist par *excellence* — he was willing to kill, and perhaps even to die, for his ideas.

"The Industrial Revolution and its consequences," he wrote at the beginning of The Manifesto, "have been a disaster for the human race." Our current economic, social, and political orders, he believed, were the root causes of modern evil, irreparably harming nature and limiting human freedom: "The system does not and cannot exist to satisfy human needs. Instead, it is human behavior that has to be modified to fit the needs of the system..."

From a cabin in Lincoln, Montana, Kaczynski made his

bombs and went forth with his one-man revolution, which lasted nearly twenty years. In 1996, his brother David recognized the Unabomber's writings and turned his sibling into the FBI. A government psychiatrist offered a provisional diagnosis of Kaczynski as a paranoid schizophrenic, but he was deemed competent to present himself at his trial. Before it could begin, he pled guilty to thirteen federal bombing offenses and took responsibility for all sixteen bombings from 1978 to 1995. In May 1998 he received a life sentence without possibility of parole.

By far the most intriguing analysis of Kaczynski yet put forward came from Alston Chase in the June 2000 issue of *The Atlantic Monthly*. Chase posited that young Ted, who entered Harvard in 1958 at age sixteen, was profoundly shaped and perhaps even motivated to commit later acts of violence by an experience beginning in his sophomore year. In 1959, he took part in some "disturbing and what would now be seen as ethically indefensible" experiments conducted by Harvard psychologist Henry A. Murray, who in World War Two had been with the Office of Strategic Services, the precursor to the CIA. Murray had helped monitor military experiments in brainwashing. At Harvard after the war, he brought together twenty-two young subjects who were given only code names to protect their anonymity (Kaczynski's was "Lawful"). All were severely verbally and emotionally abused over an extended period of time to see how they would react under stress. What would happen when their "most-cherished ideals and beliefs" were attacked?

How would they cope with the anger and fear generated by these experiments, which were designed to resemble interrogations faced by military personnel?

The answer, from a perspective of four decades later, was that some would cope better than others. Kaczynski was not the only student to be deeply affected, well into the future, by these experiments. Several of his fellow human guinea pigs would also regard these programmed assaults as very bad memories, but Kaczynski's reaction went much further. Chase suggests that the Unabomber developed his anti-technology and anti-science views in part because of his experiences at Harvard, which appeared to loosen or exploit turmoil already within him. The external, artificially-induced stress of the experiments, combined with Kaczynski's own psychological difficulties, helped create a brilliant but unstable man, who would eventually turn murderous.

There were parallels between what had happened to the young student at Harvard in the late fifties in the name of national security and what was happening to American culture as a whole in the 1990s. Institutionalized amorality, or immorality, undertaken to protect the country from a perceived threat, could create long-term social damage.

Because of media hatred of political figures and hysteria surrounding criminal cases, the public was now being fed a constant diet of artificially induced anger and fear. For millions of people, all of this may have been little more than an evening's entertainment, a chance to watch lawyers on television shouting at one another in disregard of due process, but for certain individuals, who were not psychologically healthy and already had trouble coping, this was the daily environment, the background noise, they were now living inside of and being molded by. The highest levels of the media — the Harvards, so to speak — were encouraging them to hate.

Beneath America's pervasive expression of public outrage was a desire for understanding and meaning that our legal system does not, for the most part, offer. People wanted to know where all the violence in our culture was coming from, how to protect themselves from it, and how to achieve justice or peace or forgiveness or acceptance or healing in these circumstances. The answers to these questions were usually not found in the realm of jurisprudence (even though Americans had been trained, by watching endless hours of fictional TV about law and order, to believe that the system did provide instant clarity, fairness, and truth). What the system mostly does is react to a society filled with crime. Through compromise and bureaucratic procedure, the system tries to process a vast number of criminal matters and defendants. About ninety percent of all cases are plea-bargained and never reach trial. Many trials themselves are exceptionally muddy affairs in which both sides hide or obscure portions of reality. People — especially victims or their family members — who try to extract meaning from all this are often left hurt and embittered. They want something more than the system can give them. They want a transcendent understanding of bloodshed, which doesn't come without doing some work.

To get the deeper answers one frequently has to probe complicated social conditions or the sticky issues of criminal mental illness, or find one's way to the heart of one's own violent impulses and examine where they came from. The latter is largely a spiritual search and not something many people want to undertake. It's much easier simply to blame defendants or hate the system itself, but that only generates more anger and more stress.

This stress is just one more thing to cope with in a society that is fast-paced, extremely complex and diverse, very competitive economically, exceedingly well armed, and already prone to violence. America has more gun murders per capita than any country other than El Salvador. Adding an extra dose of rage over legal matters to this mix is only taunting the beast and encouraging it to strike.

As the decade proceeded, it would strike again and again, with "random violence" erupting at workplaces, schools, churches, and other public venues all across the land.

19

By 1996, the stage was set for more virtual events. The press, having exhausted the Simpson case, was anxious to pounce on new villains. The tabloids, long regarded as little more than a journalistic freak show, had gained considerable clout during the O.J. trial. In the absence of any real reporting, the public and the media itself had begun reading and referring to the tabs' coverage of the double homicide. The tabloids were eager to cash in on another prominent murder, and when it came they were fully prepared.

The Internet was now in play, too, in a much larger way. Countless people logged online, eager to serve as detective, judge, and jury for the next publicly displayed criminal event. What was more fun than sitting at home and deciding who was the latest American embodiment of evil? What was more entertaining than relaying that opinion to people all over the country and the world? Wasn't that what Rivera did? Look where it had gotten him.

The virtual court, now more pervasive and overwhelming, had everything necessary to explode into a phenomenon unlike anything the news-gathering industry had ever seen. In the summer of 1996, it got a test run when an unassuming young Atlantan named Richard Jewell was accused throughout the media and society of bombing the Olympic Games being held in his hometown, a terrorist act that left one person dead. TV, radio, and the Internet treated him as they'd earlier treated O.J. Simpson — until it was soon determined that Jewell was a thoroughly innocent man. Mea culpas were forthcoming from media outlets, but Jewell wasn't satisfied with such apologies. He and his Atlanta attorney, Lin Wood, set about successfully instigating legal actions on several different fronts.

The Jewell case was short-lived, but another one was approaching, and it would unleash the full power of the new technology and the mindset of the virtual court. All it took was the right dead body in the right location.

That body was discovered the day after Christmas 1996 in Boulder, Colorado, when six-year-old JonBenet Ramsey was found sexually assaulted and dead in her parents' basement. The girl had been a rising star on the child beauty pageant circuit, her mother was a former Miss America contestant from West Virginia, and her father was a multi-millionaire in the computer business. Within a week, 300 mainstream and tabloid reporters, plus support personnel, had descended on Boulder and were looking for someone to blame. They began by chastising the police department for failing to secure the crime scene. Then they blitzed the District Attorney's office for failing to arrest the parents immediately and charge them with the murder. Next they blamed the town of Boulder for being a little different from other towns — a little more educated, a little more affluent, a little more self-conscious. Because anything that was different was suspect, Boulder was scorned nightly by the talk show hosts, the TV comics, the Internet sleuths, and other creators of the virtual event.

The demonizing of Boulder was light compared to the accusations thrown at JonBenet's parents. At first, the talk shows and tabloids accused the girl's father, John Ramsey, of raping and strangling his daughter with a garotte, leaving semen on her body. When no evidence supported these claims, the collective media shifted its focus — again without evidence — to Patsy Ramsey, who, obviously, had murdered her daughter because she was jealous of her or because the girl wet the bed or because Patsy was having a terrible day.

As time passed without an arrest, tabloid headlines declared that JonBenet's brother, Burke, who was nine years old when his little sister was killed, had garroted her to death because he was envious of her or simply for fun. The authorities eventually cleared Burke, but that made no difference: the accusations against him continued to flow in big black letters splashed across the front pages of the tabloids, which were sold at supermarket checkout counters all over the nation. The words may have hurt the boy in deep and long-term ways, but who cared? This was just entertainment.

Only these three murder suspects — the father, the mother, and the son — were allowed a place in the virtual event. No other discussion or investigation into what might have happened to a child who'd been exposed, through her beauty pageant connections, to a subculture of exploitation and criminal behavior, was considered worthwhile.

Of the three acceptable suspects, by far the most popular was Patsy Ramsey. Newspaper stories, magazine articles, and books were published incriminating her. The Internet seconded this choice. Talk TV and radio programs broadcast the conclusion that Patsy had murdered her daughter with absolute confidence and regularity. Without access to the evidence in the case, Geraldo Rivera "tried" the Ramseys on national television and found them responsible for JonBenet's death, as a studio audience looked on and cheered, thrilled that someone with courage and vision had finally brought the guilty parties to justice. Rivera's employers did not step forward and reprimand him for mocking our legal system or publicly destroying the Ramseys' presumption of innocence. They did not question his actions. Instead, he was rewarded with a reported six-year NBC contract worth $30 million. The most vain and self-serving legal commentator in the TV business had just been given the grandest imaginable stamp of approval by some of the most powerful media executives in the country.

As this was occurring, web sites sprang up that were devoted exclusively to the Ramsey case and to the conviction that Patsy was a child killer. The online crowd made fun of her hair, her weight, her makeup, her voice, her face, her posture, and her wardrobe. They brutally criticized her speech patterns and body language, dismissing the possibility that she was genuinely distraught because she was suffering from the worst experience a parent can endure: the death of a child. Armchair psychologists analyzed her facial expressions and handwriting — then told the world what was in her subconscious mind. TV shows and movies, implying her guilt, were in development. The witch hunt was in full swing.

At best, this behavior toward Patsy was that of a nasty clique of high school students. At worst, it was the compounding of an abysmal tragedy. JonBenet's mother had been tried and found guilty in the court of virtual justice. This court was operating in exactly the same way it had operated in the Simpson case — and with exactly the same results — even though no one had been charged, let alone convicted, of anything.

Those who worked for Boulder's criminal justice system had studied the evidence in the case and the 30,000 pages of investigative documents. One of these people, Dr. Henry Lee, widely regarded as the most astute observer of crime scenes and criminal evidence in the world, seemed genuinely baffled by the homicide. In a comment that reflected the incredible difficulties in solving the murder, Dr. Lee told the public that what was needed was "luck." Forensic experts do not talk about luck, and when they do it means that they haven't been able to make sense of a crime. It also means that breaking real cases and being able to prosecute them successfully has nothing to do with opinion polls or talk shows or kangaroo courts.

Twenty-one months after JonBenet's death, the evidence

was presented to a Boulder grand jury, which spent thirteen more months studying it. Grand juries in murder cases usually hear testimony for a few days and then indict a suspect. This grand jury, which was overseen not by a single district attorney but by half a dozen highly-qualified DAs in the Denver area, did not charge anyone with killing the child. On October 13, 1999, it disbanded, and under the leadership of the Boulder County DA's office, led by Alex Hunter, the investigation continued. (Seven months later, Patsy Ramsey passed a lie detector test administered by some of the most respected polygraphers in the country; the test indicated that she had neither killed her daughter nor written the odd ransom note found inside her home. Strangely her husband wasn't asked about penning the note.)

DA Hunter had learned the hard lesson of the O.J. Simpson trial. He'd resisted the call by some members of Boulder's police force to focus only on the Ramseys and arrest them immediately. He'd learned not to rush to judgment against people with resources, but to wait and see where the evidence led. He'd chosen not to try the girl's parents (not yet anyway) in a fantastically expensive courtroom melodrama that he knew he could not win. He'd tried to broaden the murder probe into other areas and had hired extremely competent people from around the country to help him in this pursuit.

For all these reasons, Hunter became the most attacked and reviled authority figure in the Ramsey case. People who were filled with bloodlust, and those who hated due process and the idea of exploring other scenarios, vented their rage against this man in numerous media outlets. One Denver radio personality, Peter Boyles, led the local pack, making fun of Hunter's nearly three decades of public service in Boulder — as well as his appearance. They ridiculed his height. They compared him to a dwarf. They called him names. They wrote and aired songs about his lack of intelligence, courage, and professionalism. They labeled him corrupt and worse. Boyles was soon promoted to the level of a national commentator on the Ramsey case, an "expert" in legal affairs.

After the Boulder grand jury had finished its work and no indictment was handed down, the criticism of Hunter reached its greatest frenzy. The jurors had taken a very long time, done an extremely complex job, and attempted to serve the public interest. They, along with the DAs who'd overseen the grand jury process, were lambasted by a media that understood little or cared nothing for the criminal justice system and whose only commitment was to the public airing of their views.

Rage and narcissism ruled.

The most vehement commentator on the grand jury's failure to indict the Ramseys was the Fox News Network talk show host Bill O'Reilly. On his program, "The O'Reilly Factor," he unleashed a stream of invective against Hunter and the system itself, both of which had personally let him down. It did not matter that Mr. O'Reilly was completely unfamiliar with, or simply chose to ignore, the results of the examination of evidence—the hair, fiber, blood, and unidentified DNA that had been found on the child's body — none of which could be connected to the Ramseys. The evidence did not establish the parents' guilt (nor did it necessarily confirm their innocence).

What it did indicate, and what Boulder's criminal justice system had been confronting from the start, was a complexity that legal experts could not unravel and that the media simply could not accept. The talk show hosts knew the truth behind this murder — a woman had killed her daughter. Anything that challenged their view was not merely wrong but deserving of their contempt. Things, they kept telling us, were either black or they were white. No other colors were acceptable, and shades of gray were always to be feared or denied. The legal system was there to please them, and if it failed to do so, they had no recourse. They must embrace tabloid justice and blame others without restraint. It did not matter who got hurt in the process. It did not matter that rights and principles were being smashed. What mattered was self-expression — at any cost.

The JonBenet Ramsey case, at least to date, is a true murder mystery. Unfortunately, mysteries, contradictions, complexities, subtleties, twisted ironies, painful secrets of the heart, and other realities that make up the rich and fantastically textured fabric of real life cannot be tolerated in the realm of the virtual, where the object of the game is to find someone to hate and then do so in public. Demonizing has become the fastest career path in the media.

The lessons drawn from the virtual justice surrounding the Boulder murder were not lost on me. A couple of years after her death, I published a book called *Presumed Guilty: An Investigation into the JonBenet Ramsey Case, the Media, and the Culture of Pornography.* Over time, I'd been drawn to this homicide because of the problems it posed for those trying to solve it and because it showed so clearly how our society was now at odds with itself and its social institutions. Legal officials were having more and more difficulty co-operating with one another in order to make systems work and to bring clarity, resolution, and meaning to large events. They were also having difficulty conceiving of alternative explanations — especially social explanations — for those events. We wanted our crimes to be done by individuals with no connections to the rest of us, so we could stand back and howl at their public disgrace.

A well-documented subculture of violence with multiple homicide victims had surrounded the Simpson case, but a self-blinded media and a dysfunctional legal system had shown no interest in investigating such things. Everyone wanted to blame — no one inside the system wanted to look below the surface. Some of the same conditions applied to the JonBenet Ramsey murder.

In the summer of 1999, the United Nations identified 23,000 worldwide web sites devoted exclusively to child abuse, exploitation, and pornography. Child porn, and a broad range of attendant criminal activities, had become growth industries in cyberspace. These crimes involved thousands of people and billions of dollars. Legal experts in Colorado and nationally all agreed that JonBenet, as a winner on the child beauty circuit, was precisely the sort of youngster who could be drawn into this seamy underworld — with or without her parents' knowledge. And the little girl had had known connections to people familiar with this realm. Was it possible, I asked in my book, that she'd been exposed to some part of this violent subculture and something had gone terribly wrong? Should this part of her life be investigated more thoroughly? Could one or both of her parents hold shameful knowledge of such things yet be innocent of any intended crime? Might this explain some parental involvement in the homicide and the physical evidence belonging to someone outside the family?

These were some of the questions I raised, but in the land of the virtual event, new inquiries are not welcome and investigation is shunned. I was widely criticized for suggesting different scenarios for the murder. Chuck Green, a *Denver Post* columnist, threw my book into a trashcan on live national television. No one could have reflected more accurately the behavior and mindset of our mainstream media during the past five years. No one could have shown more clearly what has happened to public discourse about public events. Green was in a position to do what he did because he too had been elevated to the level of national commentator on the case and rewarded for his views. His message to me could not have been blunter: "You will either think like me, feel like me, and write like me or I will condemn you and your work in public."

This, of course, was exactly how unpopular books were treated in Nazi Germany.

20

The truth of the JonBenet Ramsey murder, whatever it was, was insignificant compared to the market forces at work and the larger phenomenon of social anger and blame.

"Each of the big national events of the 1990s," Denver communications consultant Bob Richards told me in the winter of 2000, "was packaged and sold by the media as a brand name for a particular psychological dysfunction — a deeply personal dysfunction. The Simpson case was labeled as domestic violence: a jealous husband killed his ex-wife. The Ramsey case was presented as a mother gone bad and murdering her child in the middle of the night. The Clinton-Lewinsky scandal was a sex-crazed older man taking advantage of a younger woman. The actual complex flesh and blood reality of all of these situations did not matter. It had no meaning.

"The meaning was in the marketing, in what could be packaged and sold to a mass audience. As in all corporate strategies — and the media is now one huge corporation devoted to the merchandising and selling of products — the branding and the advertising are what's most important, not the product itself. That's where you put most of your dollars. The image is what counts, just as it does with tennis shoes or beer or anything else.

"What each of these major stories had in common was that they all centered on the concept of being out of control in some private part of ourselves, either as a spouse or a parent. That's the underlying truth of our times, and that's why these stories have the broadest appeal. They touch our core fears. They bring up what we don't like within ourselves and what we don't want to look at. They reflect back to us our own emotional truths — not necessarily the social truth behind the crimes. What all this means is that we are being deeply manipulated to view things in this way, but many people have no awareness of that manipulation. It's become normal.

"The public latches onto these big stories because our greatest fear is that we're not in control of ourselves and we don't know how to be. So all of this becomes the driving force for the branding of each event. The real importance of these events in our lives becomes totally lost under these circumstances. What matters is what the event triggers within us and then gets amplified by the media."

The separate trials of Timothy McVeigh and Terry Nichols provide a dramatic example of Richards's point. The trials of the two men accused of plotting and carrying out the Oklahoma City bombing were held in Denver in 1997. Both defendants were convicted for their roles in the deaths of 168 people. Their legal proceedings unfolded over a period of months in a downtown federal courtroom. During this time, I did not attend one gathering in Denver in which people discussed this case, which had caused more death and destruction than any single terrorist act in American history. No one seemed to care much about the trials (other than wanting to see the men convicted), or at least nobody could find a doorway into discussing them. People simply could not imagine filling a truck with explosives and detonating it in front of a building filled with strangers. They had no intimate connection to this kind of criminal behavior.

But I could go anywhere in Denver at any time and start a passionate argument about O.J. Simpson, the Ramseys or Bill Clinton. One or two sentences about these cases would send people into paroxysms of outrage. Everyone, it seemed, had known the impulse, if only for an instant, of wanting to obliterate a spouse or a child or a lover who would not behave as he or she desired.

"The primary animal impulse within us," said Richards, "is fear, and the things we are most afraid of are ourselves and one another. The media know that the fastest way to get our attention is to manipulate these fears, to make others seem very different from us and very frightening. That's what they do, but in the process they strip away the more human parts of us which are not controlled only by fear.

"When the animal impulses become primary, you will naturally start to see more aberrations within the population and more violence. Our emotionally-based technologies have not simply entertained us during the past few decades. They have helped de-stabilize the entire environment we live in, by encouraging people to hate others and to act out their personal demons. When the mainstream becomes de-stabilized, the fringes tend to erupt. The at-risk element of the population spins out of control. The question now is: How many people out there are at risk?"

Astute cultural critics have long seen the approach of these problems, but they haven't necessarily predicted their depth or consequences. In 1985, Neil Postman, a professor at New York University, wrote a brilliant and prophetic book called *Amusing Ourselves to Death*. In it, he expanded the ideas of Marshall McCluhan, who in the sixties had put forward the notion that how we receive information is more important than the content of the information itself. The medium, as he put it in his famous phrase, was the message. According to Postman, television was now clearly the dominant medium, presenting nearly all information as entertainment. Because of this, entertainment had become the overwhelming influence in our lives — in politics, religion, education, and public discourse. To Postman, the turning of serious matters into entertainment has a negative impact on all of our social processes, reducing many of them to nothing more than sources of amusement and trivial affairs.

Postman compared the views of George Orwell, as expressed in his futuristic novel *1984*, with those of Aldous Huxley in *Brave New World*. Orwell feared that humans would be defeated by the machines and the power of an external, all-controlling state, which he called "Big Brother." We would be ground down by a totalitarianism imposed from without. In Postman's view, it was Huxley who looked more deeply into the true difficulties that lay ahead for those living in a high-tech society. Huxley felt that the much greater threat to freedom and democracy came from within the populace itself. He feared that we would eventually become so enamored of, and so distracted by, our new technologies that they would enslave us and we would not even realize what had happened.

"In his [Huxley's] vision," Postman wrote, "no Big Brother is required to deprive people of their autonomy, maturity, and history. As he saw it, people will come to love their oppression, to adore the technologies that undo their capacity to think. Orwell feared the truth would be concealed from us. Huxley feared the truth would be drowned in a sea of irrelevance."

Postman believed that the future affirmed many of Huxley's intuitions. He also believed that when everything becomes one vast entertainment, the American population might just sit back and gaze at the TV and laugh ourselves to death. He didn't really focus on the connection between all that laughter and the potential for violence.

Although TV does present everything as entertainment, the core dynamic of that entertainment, especially concerning legal and political issues, is pure conflict and "us versus them." The winning formula is to divide those with different points of view into different factions and encourage them to take absolute positions on the air, while attacking or insulting anyone who disagrees with them. Conflict for its own sake is being packaged and sold to a public addicted by nature to conflict in the wiring of its nerves and the adrenalin secreted from its glands.

The animal part of us makes no conscious choices. It only reacts and pays attention to this kind of stimuli before all others because it senses that its survival may be in doubt. Those who argued about the Simpson case or the Ramsey case argued as if their own lives were at stake. By insisting that they had to be right while someone else had to be wrong, they were turning up the conflict in the environment as a whole.

"You might think of the nineties as a large pool of water that was slowly getting hotter," said Richards. "Imagine a group of frogs sitting in that water as the heat was gradually increasing. The rise in temperature was imperceptible for many of them so that by the time they noticed that they were too hot and couldn't cope any more, it was too late for them to get out of the water. They were already fried."

At best, the kind of public discourse — or arguments — that became business as usual in the nineties did not illuminate the issues. At worst, they added to the de-sensitizing and demonizing that were spreading throughout the entire culture. Early in 1984, Alan Berg could have perhaps made the claim that he really did not understand the effect he was having on disturbed people in his audience. No one following him could make this claim. Berg's death had proven that we are social creatures who produce unpredictable social effects.

21

Many of those who have promoted conflict most intensely — the talk shows, the Internet, the tabloids, and certain sections of the mainstream press — make up what is now loosely called "new media." This term comprises both the novel forms of communication that have been created by recent advances in technology, such as web sites on the Net, and a new interpretation of journalistic principles.

The new wave of commentators does not have to play by the time-honored rules of journalism. They are inventing their game from scratch. They do not have to be objective or restrained or fair-minded. They do not have to have the facts before they make up their minds. They can engage in "yellow radio," as Peter Boyles in Denver likes to refer to his form of broadcasting, with impunity. They answer to no one but the ratings book, and see themselves as performing a beneficial public service, perhaps even as cultural heroes. They can venture into realms far beyond what is acceptable to the legal system and traditional journalism. Because they are free of the past, they can publicly accuse anyone of anything.

In fact, a lot a terrific thinking, writing, and passion has been generated in some areas of the new media, particularly regarding the subject of the Internet. For example, *The Cluetrain Manifesto*, a collection of pieces from emerging voices published at the end of the twentieth century, was filled with a dawning sense of new human possibilities and defiance in the face of a corporate world that was threatening to control and shape every part of American life. The book carried the tone of real rebellion and real hope. It spoke of the Net as the "Promised Land" of opportunity for a thousand or a million new writers, all of whom were shedding the past and moving on to something much better. Weaving together all these voices was a single revolutionary idea: that the old paradigms, the established ways of looking at and doing things, were no longer working.

What was missing from the analysis was the concept that you can't change behavior, or paradigms, until you understand what is fundamentally driving them forward. Machines will only reflect the emotional reality of the people pushing the mechanical buttons. If one has unexamined fear or anger over racial, sexual, or other political issues, those fears and angers will be magnified by the technology. Hatred in, so to speak, hatred out.

Our new technology demands something just as radical and novel as it is: a rejection of "us versus them" as a blueprint for living, and an awareness of the power each person now has by being able to communicate instantly with countless numbers of people. As we would soon discover with the Clinton-Lewinsky scandal, a single individual could easily mold the perceptions of 260 million people, almost paralyzing a government for a year by disseminating certain information on the Internet. The Web makes the point better than anything else: none of us is alone.

All of us are part of a large, interconnected, living creature, joined by electronic and emotional impulses, wired together for better or worse in a new marriage of social and technological forces. The new machines demand a new consciousness that we are not victims of society but participants in it, and we have both the right and the responsibility to understand the nature of our own participation and the effects we create.

This responsibility begins with the awareness that what we impose on external events is very largely what we haven't confronted within ourselves. The media will plug into the deepest and most unconscious parts of us and conduct its business there. Our machines are not neutral. The images they generate collide with our most unruly emotions. If we haven't looked at our own angers and fears, if we haven't begun the long and challenging process of changing our relationship with these feelings, which were handed to us as children and have shaped us as adults, we can be easily controlled and manipulated every time we interact with a social or political event.

Becoming informed about public issues and voting are very important activities for those living in a democracy. But are they any more important than understanding how our intimate feelings interact with our new technology?

22

In the early 1990s, radio commentators like Rush Limbaugh had tried to negate the Clinton presidency daily by attacking the man, his wife, and his administration. On his nationwide network, Limbaugh hammered away at the chief executive and encouraged others to do the same. Although he was very effective at this, he was outside of government and could not directly impact the workings of the Clinton team, only loudly oppose whatever the president tried to do. In the mid-nineties, something happened that carried Limbaugh's get-them-at-any-cost mentality to new levels of conflict and disruption.

A federal prosecutor, Kenneth Starr, was appointed to look into aspects of the Clintons' past, including a confusing real estate deal known as Whitewater, which the couple had been involved in nearly two decades earlier. For the next six years, from 1994-2000, at a public expense estimated at $52 million, Starr and other prosecutors would do everything imaginable to find some wrongdoing to accuse the Clintons of. In the end they would discover nothing of substance, but they would reveal something important: the very same emotional cancer, the blame and hatred that were eating away at parts of our organized religion, our legal system, and our media, had now arrived in our presidential politics.

Starr was given unlimited human resources, time, and money to investigate an event that had no connection whatsoever to the Clintons' current tenure in the White House. He was given an unlimited opportunity to find something to charge the Clintons with, either in the domain of long-past business affairs or allegations of sexual harassment against the president before he took office. Starr was given the absolute freedom to do something unprecedented in American history: find a reason — any reason at all — to undermine a sitting president who'd been freely elected, with all of his well-publicized warts on bold display, by the citizens of his country. He'd been elected not once, but twice, and the second time by a much wider margin.

Starr was not alone in his harrassment of the president. In the mid-90's, during the Paula Jones civil suit against Bill Clinton, the Supreme Court tipped its political hand by allowing a working president to be sued — an unprecedented move by the justices. The court, which had been constitutionally designed to be non-partisan, had now demonstrated its willingness to make a partisan political statement. This decision was the precursor to the far more serious partisan role five of the nine justices would play following the botched 2000 presidential election. The highest court in the land had taken sides in the uncivil war.

What Limbaugh couldn't do, Ken Starr would try to accomplish. As his actions would make clear, he had no other purpose than demeaning, humiliating, and attempting to destroy a man who was his political enemy. The longstanding cultural and political struggle that had begun in America in the sixties was by no means dead. The changes promoted by activists in those years were double-layered: they were about improving social conditions for everyone and exploring personal freedom. Those who opposed such changes naturally opposed anyone who stood for them. Bill Clinton, with all his foibles, weaknesses, and reckless behavior, stood for these things more than anyone who'd ever been elected president. So he had to be derailed or stopped by his opponents. The will of the voting public was secondary to the will of an inquisitor who operated with no social restraints or self-control — or common decency.

After exhaustively researching the president's affair with an intern named Monica Lewinsky, Starr wrote a 445-page document endlessly detailing the most salacious activities between these two people. In effect, he created a publicly-funded pornographic book, which was disturbing enough. Then he sent it out over the Internet to a potential audience of billions, so that people who shared his delight in denigrating the privacy and personal lives of others could join in the demonizing and the fun.

It was hard to say what was more unsettling: the image of a middle-aged man who could not resist sexual temptation in circumstances that were beyond risky; the image of another middle-aged man who could not resist the temptation to wallow in the erotic behavior of others; or the image of the endless numbers of outraged commentators, many of whom had first surfaced during the Simpson case, who now appeared on television expressing unbridled contempt for the president. These commentators talked about Clinton's affair as if nothing like it had ever happened before, when it had happened with at least several other chief executives, from Warren Harding to Franklin Roosevelt to John Kennedy (the August 7, 2000, issue of *The New Yorker* contains a bawdy account from Marlene Dietrich, as told to the late English drama critic Kenneth Tynan, of her brief tryst with JFK in the White House).

The same obsession with people's sexuality, which had infected the Order and had driven men like Jerry Falwell and other Fundamentalists, had now moved away from the edges of our culture and blossomed into a state crisis. This was not a foreign policy crisis, a domestic, economic, or any other recognizable political crisis. It was an emotional and psychological crisis, concerning our most intimate matters, the same crisis that had been building for the past two decades, and it hinted at a deeper crossroads in the life of the nation. What was our relationship going to be with other people and their private choices and sexuality? Could we learn to accept, or at least tolerate, the fundamental differences between human beings, or could we only attack those differences because they seemed to threaten us? Why did they threaten us? Would we be able to confront head on the notion that adults and leaders are flawed, or were we going to behave as children who need to idealize their parents in order to feel secure or loved? Could we grow beyond our limited teenage mindset — or not?

These are very strange political questions indeed, but in the mid- and late nineties they became the burning issues of the day. It was as if we'd elected Bill Clinton for a hidden purpose — so that both the president of the United States and the country itself could awkwardly struggle through adolescence to reach a new level of maturity. This was not a smooth or attractive process, and it conjured up the ghost of Senator Joe McCarthy attempting to destroy Americans in the fifties for their political and sexual preferences.

Ken Starr's efforts against Clinton symbolized in a huge and menacing way a country at war with itself. We were paying some people to run the nation and others to degrade them to such an extent that doing their already-difficult jobs became much more difficult, if not impossible. The uncivil war, which had once existed on the margins of society and grown to include our religions, our politics, our media, and our legal system, was now infiltrating the highest levels of our government.

On one front, this war culminated at the White House in late December 1998 during the impeachment proceedings against the president. The critical moment came when Democratic Congressman and House Minority Leader Richard Gephardt of Missouri stepped forward and publicly reminded the American population that politics is nothing more than a "substitute for violence."

The United States was now dangerously close to crippling itself because of a consensual encounter between its leader and a younger woman. Attacking people's sexuality had taken us to the brink. Yet as it turned out, the president was not removed from office and the matter was resolved politically instead of violently. But at other venues around the country, this would not hold true. At schools and workplaces and churches, there would soon be no substitute for bloodshed and the horror that followed it.

23

Newsweek magazine had gotten the Clinton-Lewinsky scoop first and chosen not to publish it. Carl Bernstein, who with Bob Woodward had broken the Watergate story as a young reporter at *The Washington Post,* would later say that this episode between the president and the young woman was highly questionable newspaper material. It was only after an Internet sleuth named Matt Drudge put the Clinton-Lewinsky details online that it erupted into a full-blown scandal. One person with a computer could now just about bring a government representing 260 million people to a halt.

For the next year, during which mainstream reporters breathlessly chased after the scandal, which dominated the print headlines and TV screens, the great media debate focused almost exclusively on one thing: How should we punish the president? How much punishment did he deserve for being intimate with a younger woman? Were his repeated public apologies for his actions delivered with enough sincerity? Or were they not sincere enough and should he be made to repent some more? How much scorn and hatred should we shower on him? How much suffering on his part would be enough to satisfy those who needed to see him suffer? In a land that endlessly paid lip service to diversity and compassion, charity and forgiveness, open-mindedness and acceptance, the talk show hosts gave in to their profound desire to blame and pass judgment on others.

"He owes me an apology," was the line heard over and over again on the nation's airwaves.

We had personalized everything, and in the process we had killed the public interest.

In a full year of listening to media commentary on the scandal, I heard only one person move beyond the legal hair-splitting and the need to talk about punishing the president. Instead of adding more shame and condemnation to the mix, this individual analyzed our social behavior in relation to the scandal and the effects that behavior was having on the country as a whole. He dared to suggest that a person's social and political morality included other things besides sexual behavior between consenting adults. He spoke as if our *reaction* to the affair was more important than the affair itself.

Michael Lerner was the editor of *Tikkun* magazine in San Francisco. "Tikkun" is a Hebrew word meaning "to heal, to repair, and to transform the world," which was the mission of Lerner's publication. That mission was as much spiritual as it was political. More accurately, it was a combination of the two, with an emphasis on confronting and healing old emotional wounds in order to create a gateway for social and political change. You might say that it was a new paradigm.

Lerner's view of the Clinton-Lewinsky matter was historical and encompassing.

"The scandal," he said in an interview with me in the spring of 2000, "was only the continuation of what I see as a longtime discrediting of the political process. If you demand that your leaders be better than anyone else, the only thing that you will guarantee is that they will be liars.

"What's happened to politics over the past twenty-five years is an assault on and a trivializing of political involvement itself. This came about because of the great upsurge of interest in politics and social change in the late nineteen sixties and early seventies. American corporations were worried about all this interest in movements and environmental issues entering and affecting our economic democracy. They feared that this would place restraints on them. They couldn't directly attack or discredit things like the environmental movement, because that looked bad, so they discredited politics itself.

"They said, in effect, 'This is not the best of all possible worlds, but there's nothing we can do about it.' This kind of cynicism toward the political process was then transferred to a cynicism about the people who get involved in politics and try to change things. And that became a cynicism toward the idea of meaningful change itself.

"It's very easy to be cynical toward politicians. If you grow up in a society with a lot of ethical and moral distortions, as all of us did, then those distortions will be found in each one of us. We're imperfect beings. The media began focusing on those imperfections and saying that since those who want to create change are screwed up in various ways, let's leave the power with those who already have it. That led to an assault on agents of social change and on liberal agents for change.

"This was not, in my view, a conscious conspiracy on anyone's part, but the end result was the same as if it had been. Politics became demeaned and trivialized. When you focus on the personal lives of politicians, you can always find something wrong with them. None of this could have happened without the corporate interests wanting to discredit public discourse and being threatened by political movements. All of this has gradually led us toward an increasingly dominated corporate media that accepts some voices and keeps other out.

"Our population has accepted a despair about involvement in anything larger than oneself. People focus more on their inner selves and on immediate satisfaction and they avoid social issues. Then the same media that has helped foster this phenomenon appear surprised at the narcissism in our culture. We've been driven inward, and that has social consequences. People feel helplessness over all this, and they act that feeling out in increased acts of random violence and all sorts of other abusive and demeaning ways. When the public sphere is destroyed, people give up on it, yet they still need something more. They want meaning and purpose. When that is systematically denied, they will do all sorts of hurtful things to themselves and others.

"The life of the spirit, of awe and wonder, is one of the first casualties of this process and of the materialism and selfishness which the corporate world sees as normal. When people view the accumulation of money and goods as the only goal, then other parts of their lives, such as love and caring for others, are neglected. These areas become privatized, marginalized, and ridiculed — but they don't just go away. They manifest in destructive behaviors. We need a re-thinking of our culture, and an atonement, and to offer serious repentance for many of the events in our past, but instead we're just zooming off to accumulate more things.

"The violence in our society is coming not only from the poor but across the economic spectrum. That's the most revealing thing. The violence is not caused by a deprivation of money but a lack of meaning."

For a year I looked in vain for any social or journalistic meaning in the Clinton-Lewinsky scandal. Scores if not hundreds of big-name reporters, using all of the technological resources now available to them, chased after the story — and told us nothing useful. Their real purpose, stated or unstated, conscious or unconscious, was to titillate us with images of a president fondling a young woman or leaving semen on her dress. The animal part of us could hardly resist such images, while other parts of us could not stop chastising the chief executive. We were living in a state of schizophrenia, not a healthy place to be.

Journalism strives to uncover some sort of truth; that is largely its reason for being. The truth of the Clinton-Lewinsky affair was lodged somewhere in the psyche of the president, the sexual relationship that existed between him and his wife, and the emotional and sexual needs of a young woman. These things, one could assume, held sorrow and considerable pain — a pain shared by countless Americans. It is a pain that shatters marriages, creates domestic violence, hurts children, and damages lives. It is an extremely uncomfortable adult reality and something eminently worth talking about, but that is not what the country did in 1998 and 1999.

After a year of debate and argument, we knew nothing more about these underlying realities than we did the day the story broke. The truth behind the scandal would remain unknowable unless the president and first lady talked about it, and they were no more willing to do that in front of others than the rest of us would have been. It was not a time to talk about intimacy or vulnerability or personal insecurities or the intricacies of the adult mind and the adult heart. It was not a time for understanding or compassion or acceptance or healing. Very briefly during a taped deposition in August 1998, the president tried to speak about the awe and mystery of human sexuality, but he was soon brutally criticized for doing so.

We didn't want to know what it was like to be him. We didn't want to value his inner life or accept him. We wanted to punish him.

The real meaning of this virtual event, the crowning such event of the decade, finally did come to me, and from a most unlikely source. One afternoon in the summer of 1998, at the height of the coverage of the scandal, I was sitting on the couch with my four-year-old son. He'd just returned home from kindergarten. The TV was not on and we were drawing a picture.

"Dad," he said, looking up at me, "I hate the president."

If I could teach my son one thing, it would be not to hate others, especially for their intimate behaviors, yet that is not an easy thing to do at this time. My little boy did not pick up this view of the president from his mother or father because we didn't hate Bill Clinton. Our son had downloaded it from the environment of hatred that he was growing up inside of, a culture that still denies individual differences, desires, and human complexities, a culture that looks for the easy kill.

My son was now exposed to that environment every day, breathing it in and breathing it out. As a parent, I could adamantly oppose what he was saying and feeling, but I couldn't keep him from absorbing what was in the air. Our culture, as other mothers and fathers in Denver were about to find out, had become heartless, deadened — and deadly.

24

For the occasion of Adolf Hitler's 110th birthday — April, 20, 1999 — Eric Harris and Dylan Klebold, two seniors at Columbine High School in suburban Denver, built an arsenal holding ninety-five explosives. These included forty-eight carbon dioxide bombs, known as "crickets," eleven 1-1/2 gallon propane containers, seven incendiary devices with 40-plus gallons of flammable liquids, and two duffel bag bombs with 20-pound liquefied petroleum gas tanks. One of the crickets was attached to a quart of homemade napalm.

Two pipe bombs were placed a few blocks from Columbine, at a street corner in the town of Littleton. The teenagers planned to detonate these explosives first to draw the attention of the police away from the school. Then the boys would set off other bombs, which were planted outside the school, inside the school, and in their cars.

On the morning of April 20, Harris parked his Honda near Klebold's BMW in the Columbine lot. Each car contained enormous firepower: two 20-pound propane tanks, another twenty gallons of gas, pipe bombs, clocks, and combustible liquids. The clocks were face down in the back seats so that no one passing by would know when the bombs were supposed to detonate. At Columbine's west door was a propane tank filled with gas, buckshot, and nails.

At 11 a.m., Harris and Klebold carried several explosives into the school's cafeteria. These bombs were set to blow at 11:17, but as with most of the devices they'd made for the massacre, the ones in the cafeteria failed to go off, throwing a major kink in the boys' battle strategy. They had intended to go back outside, wait for the explosions, then shoot the kids as they exited from the fiery school. At noon, during the height of the chaos, their two cars were also timed to detonate, but that wouldn't happen, either.

"Thank God, these people weren't good bomb makers," Pete Mang, the deputy director of the Colorado Bureau of Investigation, later told the *Denver Post*.

"As bad as this was," added Chuck Burdick, the operations chief of the Littleton Fire Department, "we were so very, very lucky. It could have been so much worse."

Their grandiose plans for destruction foiled, the boys entered Columbine and began shooting in the cafeteria, the library, and the hallways. When they finished, twelve students, one teacher, and themselves were dead, and twenty-three others were wounded. The nation had seen many school shootings in recent years, but this one was different, both in its ambitions and its intent.

"I look at Columbine High School," said Rick Young, an investigator of the crime scene and a bomb technician, "as a true act of domestic terrorism."

Before the dead had been accurately counted, the blame game began. On Denver radio, people blamed the carnage on teachers, administrators, teenage music, video games, movies, atheism, drugs, the availability of guns, the Internet, the suburbs, modern life, a lack of discipline in schools, and an absence of spanking small children at home. But mostly, people blamed the killers' parents, who had gone into deep, deep hiding.

One counselor for the survivors and the victims' families was Dr. Frank Ochberg, a Michigan psychiatrist who specializes in post-traumatic stress. He was brought to Columbine to help those who were suffering from nightmares and flashbacks. Referring to Harris and Klebold and the reasons for their unfathomable actions, Dr. Ochberg used a term employed by law enforcement and mental health experts to identify problem kids before they become murderers.

The term is "leakage," which means that signs of trouble and violence sometimes leak out of teenagers, as warning signals, in advance of bloodshed. Experts have been trained to be on the lookout for leakage. Dr. Ochberg indicated that there may have been some minor examples of leakage in Harris and Klebold before the slaughter, signs that, unfortunately, no one in a position of authority had been astute enough to perceive or act on. In the aftermath of Columbine, Dr. Ochberg and the other experts were very sorry about this.

What no one discussed, however, was the concept of leakage in society as a whole. No one considered how the emotional environment that was reflected in and encouraged by the talk shows, the hate-saturated websites, and the dynamics of demonization could have played a role in the development of these mass executioners. The experts were much more comfortable speculating about genetic defects or subtle brain dysfunctions that may have been undetected. They were looking for an individual organic flaw, not a social one. According to Dr. Ochberg, Eric Harris was simply the "Mozart of psychopaths, the kind of person who comes along only every two or three hundred years."

Dr. Ochberg was merely repeating the things that he'd been trained to say and that others in his field likely would have said. My point here is not to criticize him. It is that he represents, in many ways, the outer edge of sophistication that we have developed at the professional level when trying to comprehend violent behavior in youths. The notion of a hateful social environment colliding with a set of personal emotional disorders, both of which may have contributed to the horrors at Columbine, did not seem to constitute one of Dr. Ochberg's theories.

In April 2000, *The New York Times* published the results of a study of 102 rampage killers who had murdered 425 people over the past several decades. The *Times's* story on the survey, which included the Columbine massacre and was the largest database yet compiled on the subject, began like this: "They are not drunk or high on drugs. They are not racists or Satanists, or addicted to violent video games, movies or music...They give lots of warning and even tell people explicitly what they plan to do...They do not try to get away."

According to the study, one overriding factor often left out of the great debate over the root cause of the rampages was that, in at least half of the cases, the killers were mentally and emotionally ill. Society, the study concluded, was asking law enforcement to prevent these mass murders, instead of addressing the mental health issues that were causing them.

25

The crime scene at Columbine High School conveyed a feeling of profound numbness. Looking at the silent, stone faces or listening to hundreds of people cry at Clement Park, the site adjacent to the school of the huge memorial that had sprung up to honor the dead, was overwhelming. It was as if an entire decade's rage had found a home, and an expression, right here. What had been boiling underneath the surface of America had exploded at this school for all to see. Everybody visiting Columbine was in shock, even the professionals who were there on a working mission.

"People just stood around and sobbed," recalled Joycee Kennedy, a Denver therapist who helped the children, parents of the victims, and others in the community deal with the tragedy. "They kept saying, 'My family moved here to keep us safe. How could this have happened in Littleton?' Kids came up to me and said, 'I walked to school with Eric Harris. He seemed just fine to me.'"

After assisting the survivors for several days, Kennedy, who has spent decades counseling traumatized and abused teenagers through many tragic circumstances, stopped her visits to the school. "Whenever I entered the city limits of Littleton," she explained, "I burst into tears. I had secondary trauma. Finally, I just had to go home for a while and deal with my own emotional state."

It took some time for the events at Columbine to sink in and even longer to grasp why these murders continued to haunt us as no other tragedy ever had. Part of the reason was that not fifteen but hundreds of students and teachers were supposed to have died. If the bombs had detonated on schedule, the school itself could have been leveled. Also, the boys had been extremely conscious of their violent intentions and had meticulously planned the killings, as though all of their un-channeled imagination, energy, and intelligence, which neither the school nor society nor their peers nor the boys themselves had otherwise tapped, had been focused on this one deadly project.

In a videotape made in Harris's bedroom about a month earlier, the two passed back and forth a bottle of whiskey and talked in detail about their upcoming day of infamy. Several aspects of the tape were startling. One was the boys' calmness and lucidity. Another was their lengthy apology to their parents for what they were about to do. Their words revealed a complexity of thinking and feeling that did not fit any prescribed mold. They could have been talking about a fantasy event, but they weren't. Only slowly did a viewer of the tape realize the most stunning thing of all: the boys' absolute madness was expressed as a normal response to their perceptions of the world around them.

"It fucking sucks to do this to them," Harris said of his mother and father. "They're going to be put through hell once we do this. There's nothing you guys could've done to prevent this."

Klebold told his own mom and dad that they've been "great parents" who taught him "self-awareness, self-reliance... I always appreciated that."

Then he paused and said, "I'm sorry I have so much rage."

"My parents are the best fucking parents I have ever known," Harris said. "My dad is great. I wish I was a fucking sociopath so I didn't have any remorse, but I do."

He spoke just as lovingly of his mother, adding, "I really am sorry about all this. But war's war."

The boys expressed their hatred toward many different groups and several individuals at their school. They also mocked the notion that more gun laws would have stopped them from pursuing their deadly game.

"You've given us shit for years," Klebold said of his classmates. "You're fucking going to pay for all the shit. We don't give a shit because we're going to die doing it."

The problem, Klebold indicated, was very widespread. It was, in his eyes, all of "humanity. Look at what you made. You're fucking shit, you humans, and you need to die."

"We need to die too," Harris said.

The boys clearly were intent on making a colossal social statement, and they did precisely that. But as repeatedly has been the case, our culture was equally intent on ignoring the evidence and dismissing the meaning of the event with a handful of words and knee-jerk reactions.

Many people in the Denver area immediately phoned the talk shows and labeled Harris and Klebold "evil" — the catchall term of the moment. The boys were so inherently bad that nothing could have stopped this from happening. They were so evil that we couldn't possibly understand their motives. They'd been born evil or had grown up immersed in the evil of their parents' world, and they stood far outside the moral boundaries of the rest of society.

In the months following the murders, tidbits of information about the killers and their families surfaced and contradicted this point of view. The parents were consistently described as good people who'd tried hard to give their children advantages and raise them well. They were now paralyzed with guilt and shame. Most everyone who'd known Klebold and virtually everyone who'd known Harris — with the exception of Brooks and Judy Brown, a son and mother who'd complained to the authorities about him well before the Columbine shootings — had not seen evil in the boys until the morning of April 20. They were bright kids with a sense of humor and creativity. A year earlier, they'd gotten into some minor trouble for vandalizing, but a lot of teenagers did things like that. The legal system certainly had not pegged them as being serious criminals, let alone mass murderers. They seemed to be, in every sense of the phrase, the kids next door.

But these kids had felt abused at Columbine by bigger or more successful and more popular students. On the videotape they expressed rage at the criticism directed at their hair and clothes. They showed contempt for kids who'd joined groups that they weren't a part of. They spoke with disdain about a school environment that was intolerant of them and did not respect differences. With self-pity and teenage angst, and perhaps more than a dose of exaggeration, they wallowed in the hatred they believed was aimed at them and that justified, for them, what they were about to do. Their feelings were obviously extreme, yet they were not alone in their perception of the emotional climate at Columbine.

"Everyone hates you," Brooks Brown would later say about the school on Oprah Winfrey's TV show, referring to the cliques at Columbine that had tormented him and other kids. "The people who made fun of me my whole life are still on top."

"It was relentless," Debra Sears told the *Denver Rocky Mountain News* when describing the bullying at Columbine. Back in the mid-'90s, Sears had withdrawn her stepsons from the school because of the harassment. "The constant threats walking through the halls. You had a whole legion of people that would tell you that just going to school was unbearable."

"If you don't fit in at Columbine, it gives you no options," Paula Reed, a teacher at the high school, also told Oprah.

Reed was one of the very few adults professionally connected to Columbine who was willing to come forward and make a public statement about the atmosphere inside the school. Nearly every administrator dismissed the claims made by the killers and others about verbal abuse or physical harassment in the hallways by revered athletic heroes and other cliques. They downplayed the notion of "us versus them" at Columbine — of an ongoing battle between the jocks and kids like Harris and Klebold who assumed the attitude of outsiders. This was just the way things were in high school, many people said, the way they had always been. If you couldn't deal with it, that was your problem.

The administrators chose silence or denial or incomprehension when asked about this atmosphere, but not every student was so reticent.

One young man, Evan Todd, a 255-pound defensive lineman on the Columbine football team, was wounded in the shooting. In a December 1999 issue of *Time* magazine, he spoke out about Harris and Klebold. His remarks, as presented in the article, were apparently intended to show that his school was not prejudiced against kids who stood outside the norm and was not abusive toward them.

"Columbine is a clean, good place except for those rejects," Todd said. "Most kids didn't want them there. They were into witchcraft. They were into voodoo dolls. Sure, we teased them. But what do you expect when kids come to school with weird hairdos and horns on their hats? It's not just jocks; the whole school's disgusted with them. They're a bunch of homos, grabbing each other's private parts. If you want to get rid of someone, usually you tease 'em. So the whole school would call them homos, and when they did something sick, we'd tell them, 'You're sick and you're wrong.'"

"You're sick and you're wrong."

No five words could have better summed up the attitude of parts of the nation and its media now toward anyone who had stepped out of line or was publicly accused of doing something bad, regardless of the facts.

If Evan Todd was correct, then the meanness that was shaping our entire society had reached deep into Columbine, too. Bully boys were prominent everywhere and if you weren't one of them, watch out. You might as well be prepared for abuse, because that was the way Americans were now behaving and doing business. It really didn't matter what horrendous, vicious, insane, and unintended consequences this behavior created — or did it?

"You have to understand," says a former student at the school, "where the story really begins. Harris and Klebold felt a deep hatred of self, as so many teenagers do. That's where the rage comes from. They believed that they were being told from every angle that they were flawed and worthless. Our culture demands perfection in so many ways and all they could see and feel was their own imperfections. Kids don't know how to change this. They don't know how to love themselves or how not to be hurt by the insults of others. They don't know how to value themselves for what they are. No one is teaching them that, only how to learn math or chemistry. They need something more. What worked in the past doesn't work now.

"If you feel sick and inadequate inside of yourself and someone is telling you how bad you are, you will eventually accept their point of view. A whole lot of kids feel these things. They just don't act them out in the same way that these two did."

Yet in the immediate aftermath of Columbine, 3,000 other kids made similar threats of violence, and in the next several months that figure would climb to 5,000.

"Boys," this woman continues, "sit around and play those stupid video games because that is the only way they can win at something. The school saw them as losers and failures, and that only reinforces their own worst feelings about themselves. No one wanted to know who they really were or took the time to do that. No one was paying attention to them or wanted to take a risk and get closer to them. So they formed their own group of two. Two against the world. While others were ignoring them, they were making plans to get their attention."

<u>26</u>

Our nation sees roughly 8,000 hate crimes each year, most of them due to differences in race, religion, or sexual orientation. The fundamental issue behind all of this violence and the "random" bloodshed that had emerged across the country was articulated by President Clinton in early October 1999. The United States had witnessed so many recent spectacular murders — twelve office deaths in Atlanta; eleven hate crime shootings over the Fourth of July weekend against Asians, Jews, and African-Americans in Indiana and Illinois; a church shooting that killed seven in Fort Worth; the shooting of Jewish children at a Southern California daycare center and the subsequent murder of a minority postal employee by a neo-Nazi — that the president felt compelled to break his silence about the spreading horror. He was one of the first commentators to recognize that the root cause of the trouble had so unconsciously infected and pervaded our society that it was being overlooked.

What distinguished his comments was not that he offered any solutions or even any hope, but his tone of utter amazement at what Americans were now doing to each other.

"All you think about is the new millennium," he told the crowd at a fundraiser in Los Angeles. "Isn't it ironic that the thing that's holding us back most... is our inability to form a community around our common humanity because of our vulnerability to mankind's most ancient fear — the fear of the other?"

Then he said that the very same dynamics of international terrorism that he'd confronted in office as president had begun appearing inside our own homeland.

"I see people in this so-called modern world," he said, "where we're celebrating all of your modern ideas and your modern achievements and what is the biggest problem...in America? We are dragged down by the most primitive of hatreds. It's bizarre."

Despite our new, global society, we still believed that others were supposed to be like us. The source of our rage was that we were being controlled by what we feared. And instead of confronting the fear, and trying to manage or change it, we were attacking the differences.

In the wake of Columbine, I heard one word repeated over and over again in the media: "Respect." Kids today, people were saying on TV and radio, didn't have any respect for things anymore — no respect for institutions or schools or their parents or their peers or for many other things as well. Kids today weren't like kids in the past, because now they had absolutely no respect for anyone or anything at all.

Like Rush Limbaugh, the mega-star New York talk show host Howard Stern is fundamentally a teacher. He is paid a reported $17 million a year to disrespect the rights of human beings and legal processes, via his radio show, his cable TV program, his book and movie deals, and to do this with no compunction whatsoever. In an effort to be entertaining to his vast audience, which is made up of many kids about the same age as Eric Harris and Dylan Klebold, Stern has said that he would personally like to pull the lever that executes O.J. Simpson in the electric chair. After Columbine, he publicly floated the notion, while searching for laughs, that it was too bad about those young girls killed at the school because some of them were good-looking enough to take to bed.

"Howard Stern," says Denver therapist Joycee Kennedy, "cannot feel the pain of the Littleton community any more than Harris or Klebold could feel the consequences of their actions when they were shooting inside the school. Stern is as shut down and numbed out as they were. Children need a protective shield around them when they're growing up. That's what good parents try to provide. Communities need the same thing, but we've lost that. We've lost that connection and that shield because today anything goes. There are no limits on cruelty now."

Following Columbine, I asked myself two questions: How could our kids possibly have any respect left for our culture, given the way adults have been behaving? And how can we stop the violence if we continue to encourage and reward our public figures for being hateful?

Evil is not a person. It is not a thing or even a force. It is a collective social process that people and nations gradually slide into and normalize, because they're not paying attention to their own behavior and their own destruction of their principles and ideals. Over the past ten years, we've casually thrown away our heritage of being a nation governed by laws, becoming instead a country of unrestrained and unexamined emotional reactions. The social cost of all this is now emerging in a variety of locations, from Los Angeles to Denver to New York. The meaning is there for all to see.

Turning hatred into a national sport and a thriving business is lethal. Virtual events can kill.

27

During my visit to Columbine soon after the shootings, the school grounds were so crowded with other visitors that my wife and I had to park half a mile away and walk through the mud to get to the crime scene. It was late evening and the sun was about to fall below the Rocky Mountains on the western horizon. As we made our trek toward the school, I noticed a huge mound of earth, perhaps a hundred feet in elevation, jutting up in front of us, a natural outcropping from the landscape. A large wooden cross rose above it, put there during the past few days, bold against the sky.

Long lines of people were wending their way up the mound toward the cross, as if drawn there by an invisible hand. The damp, cold wind blew over them, ruffling their hair and stretching out their clothes. They lowered their heads as they marched upward through the dirt and the sticky mud, determined to reach the top. When they arrived at the summit, they raised their fingers and touched the cross, holding onto it and gazing westward at the snow-covered mountains or eastward down onto Columbine High, which was now surrounded by thousands of bouquets of flowers, balloons, and hand-written messages to the dead.

I stopped walking to watch this procession. The wind was high and wild. Dark clouds had appeared overhead. They were churning and shifting in black and gray patterns. Suddenly, they split apart and shafts of light shot down through them, illuminating the mound and the cross and the people climbing toward it. Everything was covered with golden rays.

"Look at that," I said to my wife, as I touched her arm and pointed at the image in front of us. It was stunningly biblical, evoking the hill at Calvary outside of Jerusalem, where Jesus had been crucified.

The pilgrimage up the hill reminded me of other images: the endless streams of devout Muslims who walked into Mecca during the Hadj or the droves of ecstatic Hindus who moved as one as they ran toward the Ganges to bathe in the great and healing river. But this image was different from those and American to the core.

These were not individuals making a joyous pilgrimage to an ancient holy site, but grief-stricken mourners visiting a shrine that hadn't existed until now. It was a shrine to human violence, to our incomprehension of ourselves and of what effect we are having on each other, a shrine to the agony this is causing us.

We made our way closer to the school. Red Cross and Salvation Army trucks were humming in the parking lot. The sun fell behind the Rockies and the wind charged down from the mountains and across our skin, making the air feel much colder than the actual temperature. Despite the weather and the gathering darkness, countless more visitors were arriving to look at the memorial or to climb the mound and touch the cross. Some were staring straight ahead and others were crying. All of them seemed to grasp that something very important had happened at Columbine, something more than just another shooting, and that it was time to feel the magnitude of the event and think about where we were going. For just a few moments, there on the school grounds, standing near where the dead had fallen, blame and hatred appeared to evaporate, and in the midst of the sorrow and the horror came the recognition that we were not total strangers or enemies, and that each of us had been hurt and diminished by what had happened here. It had taken a monumental tragedy to knock down the walls and bring us to this common place.

There was, finally, no "us" and no "them" at Columbine, just a lot of suffering people.

My wife and I turned away from the park and walked slowly past the incoming mourners. We wrapped our coats more tightly around ourselves and leaned into the wind.

THREE BRICKS OF COCAINE

28

A Los Angeles drug dealer had just pulled a handgun on Officer Rafael Perez and was aiming it at his face. As Perez looked into the barrel, he imagined the searing rip of the bullet and his blood flowing onto the ground. He knew he was going to die. His hands were shaking badly. So was the rest of him. With no hope left, the cop began begging for his life.

"Come on, man," he said. "Take it easy."

The dealer jammed the gun in closer.

"I'm just a basehead," Perez pleaded. "Don't shoot."

Perez heard gunfire — four quick shots — and waited for the pain to hit him, but he felt nothing. The dealer collapsed in front of him, instantly dead. Perez whirled around and saw David Mack, his partner in the Rampart Division of the Los Angeles Police Department, holding the gun that he'd just emptied into the dealer. The men exchanged stares and Perez's eyes held unlimited relief and gratitude; this officer had just saved his life. The two had long been friends, but this moment in October 1993 sealed a deeper bond. From now on, they were not just partners on the street but brothers in and out of uniform, two cops who'd experienced death together and who knew each other's personal and professional secrets.

Mack was soon transferred out of Rampart, but he and Perez remained buddies, getting together on Friday nights to drink beer, smoke cigars, and share stories about their wives, children, and girlfriends. They were tough-acting, tough-talking young men who liked to boast about their police exploits, their desire for adventure, and their expensive tastes. They fantasized about having far more money than they could earn as cops — and spending it on luxury.

Both were around thirty and already veterans on the force. Mack had grown up in L.A.'s rough Compton neighborhood but escaped it by winning a track scholarship to the University of Oregon. An injury kept him from competing in college, a source of permanent disappointment. He returned to his hometown and joined the LAPD, where he became successful, getting nominated for a top department honor for gunning down the drug dealer. Mack was involved in the community and often spoke to kids, warning them about the dangers of dope and gangs. After nine years on the force, his salary was $55,000, but he had a wife and two children. Always needing extra cash, he moonlighted at security jobs at L.A.'s nightlife venues.

Perez had been born in Puerto Rico but grew up in

Philadelphia. After high school, he enlisted in the Marines and four years later received an honorable discharge. He went to work as an undercover officer in the LAPD narcotics detail and he, like Mack, was considered to be a very good, intelligent, and resourceful cop.

By the mid-nineties, the two men were still meeting on Friday nights and swapping police stories, but some things had changed. They were smoking much better cigars now and drinking more expensive beer. They'd shed their police uniforms or more casual outfits for designer suits. They drove new cars and booked Caribbean cruises. They were married but had mistresses. In November 1997, Mack, Perez, and a third LAPD officer, Samuel Martin Jr., went to Las Vegas for the weekend and dropped $21,000 at Caesar's Palace. In Vegas, their stogies cost $100 apiece.

Accompanying them on this trip was Perez's girlfriend, Veronica Quesada, whom the cop tended to see as not just his lover, but his savior. He wrote her intimate notes. One of them read, "Just like an angel, you came into my life one unforgettable day and swept me away from the far too tired and busy world, quieting my mind...You'll never know how deeply you have changed me — how sweet it feels just to hold your hand in mine. Le Quiero con todo mi Amor."

Seven months before their Las Vegas fling, Quesada had been arrested for drug dealing. Sheets of paper with the words "Pay/Owe" on them were seized from her home, and one sheet had "R.P." written on it along with Perez's number at the Rampart police station. The investigators paid no attention to these initials or made any connection between the dealer and the cop. Quesada was convicted of the charge, but Perez went in front of the judge and pleaded her case, arguing that she was a good risk to avoid future trouble. The judge attached considerable significance to the words of this respected police officer and made his decision accordingly. On September 15, Quesada received a sentence of only two days in jail and three years probation.

Two months later, Perez and Quesada were partying in Vegas with the other cops. A month after that, on December 16, David Mack was arrested for stealing $722,000 from the Bank of America. The heist had taken place a couple of days before the Vegas trip. Mack's girlfriend, Errolyn Romero, an assistant manager at the bank, helped with the robbery and one other person, believed to be an unidentified policeman, drove the getaway car. Mack was imprisoned and awaited trial, while Rafael Perez, his former partner in law enforcement, went back to work on the street.

On March 2, 1998, LAPD Officer Joel Perez (no relation to Rafael) went to court for a drug case and took with him a key piece of evidence: some rock cocaine. After finishing his courtroom appearance at 2 p.m., he left the building and ran into one of his partners, William Mears. They were both members of the

Community Resources Against Street Hoodlums (or CRASH) unit of the Hollenbeck Division of the LAPD. This was supposed to be Perez's day off, so he asked Mears if he would mind checking the cocaine back into the police property room at the Parker Center in downtown L.A. When Mears agreed, Perez gave him the drugs and went back to the station, got out of his uniform, and drove home. Officer Mears returned the drugs to Parker Center around twenty minutes after two.

At 2:25 p.m., Rafael Perez, who was at Parker Center and closely following all of these developments, used his cellular phone to call the Hollenbeck Division and make certain that Joel Perez worked there. The answer was yes, so he walked into the property room and spoke to the employee on duty that afternoon, Laura Castellanos. He told her that he was assigned to the Hollenbeck Division, but at the moment was on special assignment with another CRASH unit. He said that he needed to check out some evidence for an upcoming court appearance — evidence that had been seized the year before in a drug arrest. In a brusque tone that bordered on rudeness, he asked Castellanos for three brick-sized kilograms of powder cocaine, which weighed a total of 3,167 grams, or about eight pounds, and had a street value of roughly $750,000.

Castellanos was struck not by the request, which was standard operating procedure, but by the officer's belligerent attitude. She went back into the vault and brought the cocaine out for him; the kilos were being stored in a box measuring 12" x 18"

x 8". While she was doing this, Perez called his girlfriend (he would phone Quesada numerous times that day). When he hung up, Castellanos asked if he was the one who'd seized the coke during the bust. No, Perez said abrasively. She gave him the box and he signed it out to Officer Joel Perez, using the other man's name and serial number. On the computer screen that logged in this transaction, only the last name and serial number became a part of the permanent record. First names were ignored.

At 2:48 p.m., Rafael Perez walked out of the property room carrying the bricks of cocaine. He'd done this sort of thing before, checking out a kilo of marijuana and two kilos of coke in the autumn of 1997. In January 1998, he'd checked out $100,000 worth of cocaine using the name of Officer Armando Coronado (Coronado and Perez had earlier clashed over police procedures; Coronado had complained about Perez to his superiors, but his complaints had been dismissed).

On another occasion, Perez had considered using the name of fellow officer Frank Lyga for his scam, perhaps as a way of seeking revenge. Perez was black and Lyga was white and Lyga, like the LAPD itself, had a long history of racial conflict and numerous enemies inside the department, especially among minority cops. Lyga had recently shot and killed a black officer, Kevin Gaines, during a mysterious traffic dispute in Studio City. Gaines had been under investigation by the LAPD's Internal Affairs division for charges of police corruption, but the investigation ended with his death.

In January of 1998, Perez hadn't actually gone down to Parker Center to check out the coke under Armando Coronado's name. He'd simply phoned in the order from the Rampart station and asked if a courier could be sent over with the drugs. He said he needed the cocaine in court. Robin Schaefer, who worked in the property room and recognized his voice, complied with his wishes. By now, Perez's technique for removing dope from LAPD storage was about as complicated as dialing for a pizza.

Perez was running a circular business. He arrested people in Rampart for selling drugs. Their dope was confiscated and held in the Parker Center property room. Then he checked the drugs out under false pretenses and passed them along to dealers who unloaded them on the street and paid him off. These dealers, whom Perez didn't arrest, were in effect working for him. He'd then arrest more dealers and the cycle would begin again — a closed loop of an extremely lucrative enterprise, a foolproof way, it seemed, of boosting his income.

But on March 2, 1998, Perez did not pinch a few grams or even a few hundred. He stole three-quarters of a million dollars worth of cocaine and sooner or later an amount that size was bound to be missed. Within a few weeks of the theft, property room officials noticed that the drugs had not been returned. They passed this information along to the LAPD brass, who began an investigation. The police soon determined that the main suspect was not Joel Perez but Rafael, who had an established habit of taking drugs out of evidence, either in person or over the phone. By April, the cops were conducting surveillance on Rafael Perez, snapping pictures of him in an embrace with Veronica Quesada and throwing gang signs.

The investigators spoke to property room employee Laura Castellanos about the March 2 transaction. Castellanos told them that she remembered the event clearly because an ill-mannered officer named Perez had come in that afternoon and checked out a box full of cocaine for an upcoming courtroom appearance. By June, several other property room employees were being asked to make a photo identification of the person who'd taken the three bricks of cocaine in early March. They were all quite certain that the officer was Rafael Perez, who stood six feet tall, weighed 175 pounds and often wore a smug expression. Throughout the summer the authorities, led by Internal Affairs sergeant Luis Segura, intensified their investigation of Perez. They increased their surveillance and tapped his phone. In October, they began interviewing people close to him, including Veronica Quesada, and tailing him in unmarked cars.

On October 25, 1998, at a few minutes past 9 A.M., detectives watched Perez step into a red Ford Expedition and drive away from his residence on Damask Avenue. Officer Cole Brook followed the Expedition for several blocks before pulling Perez over, arresting him, and taking him into custody. He was charged with the sale of a controlled substance, grand theft of personal property, and forgery of a document. He was placed in L.A. County Jail and bail was set at $550,000.

The LAPD and the L.A. County DA's office were committed to prosecuting fully and punishing severely an officer who'd stolen drugs and brought shame and embarrassment to law enforcement. They had no idea whom they'd arrested.

29

Like his buddy and ex-partner, David Mack, Perez sat in jail and awaited trial. Mack himself would soon be found guilty and receive fourteen years and three months for stealing the $722,000, which had never been located. In prison, where it's considered extremely dangerous for a former cop, he was placed in isolation. Faced with a long sentence, a disgraced reputation, and a broken life, Mack showed no remorse behind bars, maintaining a sullen attitude about his offense. He bragged to other inmates about his street smarts and his badness, saying that he was a member of the Piru Bloods gang so everyone had better leave him alone.

More trouble was looming for Mack. He was about to be named by the *Los Angeles Times* as a possible suspect in the 1997 shooting death of the rap star Notorious B.I.G. Police investigators were working on the theory that Mack had conspired with Marion "Suge" Knight, the founder of Death Row Records, in the contract killing of Notorious B.I.G. A 360-pound rapper whose real name was Christopher Wallace, Notorious B.I.G. was gunned down as his motorcade was leaving a music industry party at the Petersen Automotive Museum in Los Angeles.

Mack was not suspected of being the actual killer, but he may have brought in the alleged gunman, Amir Muhammad. Investigators believed that the murder was caused by a fight between Death Row and another rap label in New York. One of

Death Row's leading artists, Tupac Shakur, was gunned down in Las Vegas, and Knight blamed Wallace and his record company, Bad Boy Entertainment, for that shooting. When detectives searched Mack's house following his bank robbery, they found a shrine, as one cop put it, to Shakur.

"Rumors have swirled for years in law enforcement circles," the *Times* wrote, "about ties between Mack and former LAPD officers and Death Row Records."

In December 1998, Rafael Perez appeared at trial, represented by a Beverly Hills lawyer, Winston McKesson. On the witness stand, he maintained his innocence regarding the cocaine theft but confessed to other things. With his wife, Denise, in the courtroom, he broke down as he testified that he'd been unfaithful to her, crying in front of the jury on two occasions. The prosecutors were appalled at his manipulative skills. He spoke to the jurors with textbook perfection, exactly as the LAPD had taught him to do, staring straight into their eyes and exuding sincerity. The prosecutors knew that he was lying about stealing the drugs, but they also knew that he was a very effective witness. He had, after all, testified on their behalf in many other cases that had brought convictions. Now he was using his best courtroom demeanor to oppose them.

"He was excellent on the stand," LAPD Commander Dan Schatz later told the *Los Angeles Times*. "He was a lying son of a bitch and we were squirming in our seats."

One-third of the jurors believed Perez, so a verdict could not be reached and the proceeding ended in a mistrial. The prosecutors, led by Deputy District Attorney Richard Rosenthal, were confronted with a dilemma. Should they go to the trouble and expense of trying Perez again or should they offer him a plea bargain, which he might just take? If he accepted it and served a relatively short sentence, the DA's office could at least feel they'd gotten him to acknowledge his guilt. Or should they retrench, reload their prosecutorial weapons, and go after him once more, this time with more investigative ammunition and a renewed commitment to make an example of this man whom they regarded as a rogue cop — "a bad apple," in the cliched language of law enforcement? They decided to try him again and not just defeat him at the new trial. They wanted to break and humiliate him.

They appointed a task force to investigate Perez's financial records, which contained tens of thousands of dollars of unreported income, as well as his history of infidelity. They discovered that he'd stolen at least two more pounds of cocaine than he'd been accused of stealing in the first trial. Members of the LAPD also began harassing Perez's wife, a civilian employee within the department, tormenting her at work. Word of all this activity filtered back to Perez, who waited in his cell and tried to make his own decisions about the future.

David Mack had turned into a full-blown gang member in jail, but as Perez sat in prison thinking about what the authorities were going to do to him at his second trial, he underwent a gradual transformation, moving in the opposite direction from the man who'd once saved his life. Some of Perez's toughness and braggadocio fell away. He grew quieter, more introspective. He thought about what the LAPD was doing to his wife. He thought about how many years he might have to serve if convicted. He thought about what could happen to him during that time in prison. He started to pray. He'd never really looked back, but now he had plenty of time for that, and the more he thought about what he'd done and seen as a cop, the more he began to change. Some of this change was purely self-serving, a way of getting himself out of a terrible jam, but parts of it went beyond that.

In the language of the incarcerated, it was "Come to Jesus time" for Rafael Perez — time to take a very hard look at his past, his future, and his options, time to be alone in the quiet of his cell in the middle of the night with just his thoughts and feelings for company. It was time to look into his soul. What he mostly thought about was his behavior as a police officer.

He remembered being on the witness stand and swearing an oath before God to tell the truth, but then going ahead and lying to judges, prosecutors, and members of the jury. He recalled how his lies over the years had torn apart families and sent people to prison for a long time, even decades — innocent people who were now doing what he was doing, which was sitting behind bars with no freedom and no hope. He thought about other things he'd done, which were far worse than lying. And he thought about how beneficial it would be for cops everywhere to spend at least thirty days in jail, locked up just like this, so they could experience the consequences that come with arresting people and putting them in cells.

Perez didn't merely think about all these events and memories. Day after day, as he lay on his bed, looking up at the ceiling or staring at the walls, he allowed himself to feel the pain and suffering his actions had caused others. Once he'd started this process, it was impossible to turn back.

On September 8, 1999, as the jury was being selected for his second trial, Perez announced that he'd reached a critical decision. He hadn't come to this moment quickly or without a great inner struggle; he wondered if he was making a mistake. His lawyer, Winston McKesson, was certain that he was and would later say that because of what Perez had chosen to do, the ex-cop would spend the rest of his life looking over his shoulder and fearing retaliation.

McKesson felt strongly that his client could win the second trial. He urged Perez to change his mind and fight the charges again in front of a jury, but the inmate could not be stopped. He was ready to talk to the authorities and cut a deal. He hoped to be able to knock some time off his sentence, but he had a deeper reason for speaking up: if he kept quiet any longer, he couldn't live with himself. So he was going to spill his secrets. His decision was more than shocking - it was unprecedented.

Nothing like it had ever happened before in the history of the LAPD.

"This experience," he said, when making his announcement, "has opened my eyes to a lot of things...I'm doing it for me and my God."

Then he sat down with members of the DA's office and opened his mouth.

Perez told the authorities that cops in the CRASH unit of the Rampart division near downtown L.A., where he'd worked since the early 1990s, regularly shook down kids on the street, stealing their money or their drugs. The police either used the dope themselves or sold it in the neighborhood. For amusement, Perez said, officers liked to pick up young men who were gang members, or labeled as gang members, demean them with racial insults, physically abuse them, and drive them over to a rival gang's territory. They would take away their shoes or all their clothes and leave them there naked to fend for themselves.

Cops, he said, had taken suspects or potential suspects to the Rampart station and beaten them senseless. The most notorious example of this, as independent information would later confirm, involved Officer Brian Hewitt and a man named Ismael Jimenez. On February 26, 1998, Hewitt had approached Jimenez outside a tattoo shop with his gun drawn. He handcuffed the man and falsely accused him of stealing a car. Then he drove Jimenez to the station, led him into an interview room, and locked his arms behind him.

"I could book you for anything," the officer said.

According to Jimenez, Hewitt grabbed his neck and rammed his head straight into the wall. He punched him in the chest and stomach until Jimenez began vomiting blood. He was told to leave the station, and on his way back to the tattoo shop he threw up twice on the sidewalk.

This story was highly disturbing to some members of the DA's office, but not nearly as disturbing as another one. Perez reported that on October 12, 1996, he and his partner, Nino Durden, had stopped Javier Francisco Ovando, a 19-year-old illegal immigrant from Honduras, for questioning. Ovando did not resist them or try to run. During their conversation, they shot the young man in the head and paralyzed him for life. Later in court, the two officers testified that Ovando had burst in on them with an assault weapon, so they'd had to subdue him with gunfire.

Perez now confessed to the authorities that Ovando, who had had no criminal record, had been unarmed and had done absolutely nothing to provoke the attack. The officers had grabbed him, cuffed him, held him upright, and put a bullet into his skull. As Ovando lay bleeding and crying, Durden, according to Perez, placed at the wounded man's side an assault-type weapon with a banana clip, a gun that had been seized during a gang sweep. This was not a spontaneous gesture in a moment of panic. Well before Durden planted the gun on the paralyzed man, he'd filed off the serial number so it could not be traced.

After he was shot and paralyzed, Ovando was arrested for armed assault on the two policemen. While appearing in court in a wheelchair, unable to move or talk clearly or even follow the proceedings, he was tried and convicted on the basis of the officers' testimony. He was given twenty-three years in the Salinas Valley State Prison. At his sentencing Superior Court Judge Stephen Czuleger became visibly upset with the defendant because he failed to show remorse for his crime. (In March 1997 L.A. Superior Court Judge Jacqueline A. Connor, in a letter of commendation for Officer Perez, wrote that he was "the best that law enforcement offers his community.")

Ovando's pregnant girlfriend, Monique Valenzuela, attended the sentencing and wept throughout the hearing. Her mother, Gloria Romero, sat next to her and stared at Perez and Durden, who were also in the courtroom. As Ovando was receiving his twenty-three years behind bars, the two cops looked at the man in the wheelchair and laughed.

"God will punish you," Romero told Perez when the hearing was finished. "Sooner or later, the truth will come out."

Even though she deeply believed these words, at the moment she felt powerless. "We had no lawyer and no money," she once told a *Los Angeles Times* reporter. "We were all alone. We just had faith in God. We always knew he was innocent."

Three years later, Perez would prove her right.

30

Perez's jailhouse confession about the shooting of Francisco Ovando unleashed tremors inside L.A.'s criminal justice system. What had begun to surface about the LAPD during the Simpson case, with Mark Fuhrman's taped admissions of widespread evidence planting, lying, and police brutality, was now emerging again. But this time, not everyone in authority would shrug and attempt to dismiss Perez's words as fantasy. Deputy District Attorney Richard Rosenthal, a tough prosecutor with incorruptible ethics, was stunned by Perez's statements. He felt that the police's treatment of Ovando was "so egregious" that he set about asking for the young man's immediate release from prison. With that process underway, it fell to Commander Dan Schatz, a veteran of the LAPD brass, to tell Police Chief Bernard Parks what Perez had secretly revealed to District Attorney Gil Garcetti and his staff. On a mid-September morning, Schatz drove from the downtown MTA building, where the task force had been working to prosecute Perez, over to Parker Center, where Parks worked. As he rode the elevator up the six floors to Parks's office, he wondered how to break the news.

Parks had spent more than three decades on the force and his last tour of duty before becoming its chief two years earlier had been as the head of Internal Affairs. His job there had been to investigate problems inside his own department. As much as anyone else connected with the LAPD, Parks knew the strains and difficulties of being an officer in Los Angeles, going to work each day or night and fighting the war on crime out in the streets. This war had intensified in the past few years because of the California legislature's insistence on tougher prosecutions, harsher sentences, and the "three strikes" policy, which was designed to put three-time offenders away for good, regardless of the nature of their crimes. The intent of the Golden State's legislators was to crack down and severely punish those who break the law. They had passed the bills instigating and deepening the war on crime, but the front lines were occupied by the men and women of the LAPD.

While overseeing Internal Affairs, Parks had wanted to focus on two areas in particular that were experienced by cops involved in crime wars: substance abuse and domestic abuse. There were many examples of policemen and policewomen using drugs or alcohol to help them cope with their jobs and of violence at home. To his credit, Parks was aware of these problems and tried to deal with them.

A war, of course, produces casualties on every side.

"You can't seriously discuss the problems with our urban police departments without also seeing the officers as victims of the system," says Los Angeles author and historian Donald Freed. "They have rage because they're put in the impossible position of trying to police and manage what are basically a number of deep social problems associated with racism, poverty, and the violence of our entire culture.

"Instead of working to change these conditions, we create a war against those at the bottom of society and send the police out to fight it. Their stress is off the charts. They are caught in the middle between the underclass of victims living below them and the class that has put them where they are. They can't express their rage to those above them so they show it to those on the streets and to those at home. It's an inevitable consequence of their job."

When Dan Schatz walked into Parks's office, he reported that Rafael Perez had confessed that he and his partner had shot an innocent man and left a gun at his side, in addition to other law enforcement abuses. Parks was taken by surprise and became upset. He told Schatz to use the task force that was helping to prosecute Perez to investigate these allegations made by the ex-officer.

Shortly afterward Parks, fearful of another police scandal (or race riot) in L.A., and concerned about the inevitable media coverage of Perez, held a press conference to announce that his department was on top of the situation. He told reporters about Perez's admissions and informed them that several other officers had just been relieved of duty. The press conference caught the DA's people off guard. Not wanting to appear negligent — and fighting their own public relations battle with the LAPD and the city — the DA's office did something unprecedented: Richard Rosenthal, under the leadership of Gil Garcetti, filed a writ of habeas corpus seeking Ovando's instant release from prison. Ovando was set free with no questions asked.

During his time behind bars, Ovando had not been allowed to see his two-and-a-half-year-old daughter, Destiny, who was born while he was in jail. As father and child were about to be united, a $20 million lawsuit against the city and its police department was filed on Destiny's behalf. Ovando made plans to sue for a similar figure.

Within days of Perez's confessions, Nino Durden was removed from his job, not just for the Ovando shooting but for other charges as well, including planting rock cocaine on a suspect and making false arrests. He would eventually be taken into custody at gunpoint and charged with armed robbery while on duty and the attempted murder of Ovando.

If Perez had decided to stop talking at this point, the tremors could have subsided and the scandal might have begun to fade. But he was just getting started.

31

Perez told investigators about another 1996 shooting, which he called "dirty." It involved nine officers from the Rampart Division, the death of one young man, and the wounding of two others. Perez had been present at this event and told the authorities what had really unfolded that night, which was very different from what the police had reported to Internal Affairs. The DA's office began looking into these allegations and questioning more cops about planting evidence and unprovoked gunfire. By late September, twelve officers had been dismissed from the force and three more had left on their own. Another would soon be let go. Every day brought new accusations of police misconduct.

The authorities brought boxes of case files to Perez to read so he could refresh his memory about past activities. In the middle of the night, DA investigators slipped him out of his cell and transported him to places where he said cops had broken the law. There he re-enacted for the DA's staff what he had seen and done. He told them about an apartment kept by Rampart officers where they had sex with girlfriends or prostitutes — the same prostitutes they sent out on the street to sell the drugs they'd stolen from local kids.

He told them about an unnamed sergeant in Rampart's anti-gang CRASH unit who routinely instructed officers on how to plant guns on unarmed suspects. Perez described a box in his own home marked "Secret and Confidential," which contained six knives and seven handguns to be used to incriminate unarmed people. The box also contained a piece of paper that read, "Look for the lowest person to help you with a crooked deal."

As Perez's allegations grew in number, so did the task force that had been assigned to investigate the shocking confessions. Its nine members grew to thirty. It expanded its probe and was given more money, more computers, and more travel expenses. Its members flew all over the state in official airplanes and helicopters, speaking to inmates about Perez's stories of corruption, staking out other cops, and conducting follow-up interviews to determine Perez's credibility. The results of their legwork provided very strong corroboration. A second prisoner was soon set free, a third was released from parole, a fourth was ordered re-sentenced, and charges were dismissed against two others. The District Attorney's office, in yet another unprecedented move, sent out 200 letters to defense lawyers, explaining that their clients' cases might have to be re-examined and their convictions overturned because of dirty evidence. As the summer turned to fall, seven more police shootings would be called suspect and come under investigation.

A POSTSCRIPT FROM LOS ANGELES

Down in the Rampart neighborhood, where Ira Erenberg was still running the Mi Farmacia drugstore at Sixth and Union, the scandal was met with anger and dismay. Until September 1999, due to ongoing outbursts of violence in the area, the LAPD had placed an injunction against the 18th Street and Rockwood gangs. The cops had enforced strict curfews and used other forms of muscle to keep the streets safer than they'd been before the injunction. Many local people felt the muscle was justified.

"Bullets used to fly here from the top of one apartment building to the top of the other," said Erenberg. "The gangs shot at each other in the night. There was also a lot of activity on Friday afternoons, once the weekend got started. We'd hear the rat-a-tat-tat of drive-by shootings at dusk."

"In the mid-nineties," confirmed Erenberg's employee Ray Alvarez, "they would come out and shoot at one another from one block to the next. Because the pharmacy is right on the dividing line between the Rockwood and 18th Street gangs, we were caught in the middle. Back then, there was also a lot of drug action here, buying and selling right in front of the store, and it was a real happening place."

"It's been safer since the police took over," agreed Erenberg. "The regular citizens in Rampart supported whatever they did to stop this from being a war zone. I don't condone some of what the cops do but it was better in the past three years."

"Sometimes," said Alvarez, "the cops got too heavy-handed. I once

saw them break the crutches of a disabled man for no reason at all. We all got together and replaced them for him. After the Rampart scandal began, people from all over the neighborhood came forward with stories of police abuse."

On September 16, 1999, in the wake of Perez's confessions about himself and other cops, the DA's office announced that the city was lifting its injunction against the Rampart gangs. Gone were the curfews, and the streets were now more open than at any time in recent years. In Rampart, this development was met with apprehension and fear.

"Now," Erenberg said after the injunction had ended, "it's like the street thugs can say to the cops, 'We beat you. We won and you lost because the curfew is gone and you're letting people out of jail. We can do whatever we want and no one can do anything about it.' Now O.J. can say, 'I was right and you were wrong.'

"I would hate to see the area regress to what it was but it could. If that happens, it will be unsafe for me and everyone else in the neighborhood. The good people in Rampart depend on the cops to wear the white hats and to obey the law. If they break it, that's worse than when a criminal commits a crime."

John Mills, a local activist, added, "Everything that's come out about Rampart is bad for our community. Now everyone will question every arrest that's made. The lifting of the injunction on the 18th Street gang has made a big difference around here. The graffiti, which had been way down in recent months, is starting to come back. That's how territories get divided up by gangs and that's where the trouble starts.

*I hate to see the police getting all these bad things reflected on them.
Some of the cops are genuine gems and this makes them look awful."*

32

By early fall, the *Los Angeles Times* was referring to Rampart as the city's largest police corruption scandal in sixty years. But Perez was not finished talking. His revelations would leave a huge hole in the blue wall of silence that had protected the LAPD for decades — from the 1980s under chief Daryl Gates, to the 1992 riots following the acquittal of the cops who'd beaten Rodney King, to the 1994–'95 O.J. Simpson case in which Mark Fuhrman had lied about his racism and revealed on audiotape his own history of violence, creating probable cause against suspects, and manufacturing evidence.

Perez's stories about police corruption were not limited to a couple of rogue cops or "bad apples" who'd done a few terrible things over the years. Many officers — black, white, and Hispanic, in Rampart and other divisions — had systematically abused their power in order to make arrests and win praise from their superiors. Perez reported that 90 percent of the cops in CRASH units, in Rampart and throughout the seventeen other LAPD divisions, had falsified information in their cases. Corruption inside the department was deeply rooted and widespread: "a cancer," he said, "that has gone on a long time without being treated." Perez confirmed the ingrained and institutionalized domestic terrorism within the LAPD that I'd been told about in August 1994 and that Fuhrman had revealed was standard operating procedure.

Gil Garcetti, who had ignored or dismissed Fuhrman's statements as tall tales spun for a screenwriter, now rushed forward to agree with Perez's assessment of the depths of the problem. In December 1999, as the scandal continued to grow, he announced that the probe was "potentially the most important case" his office had handled in his thirty-one years on the job, and that it could be "devastating to the criminal justice system."

It was, he indicated, going to affect at least 3,000 criminal matters, which now had to be reviewed for false police testimony and tainted evidence. No one dared to guess how many other cases might eventually be investigated or overturned. Nor did anyone know how much financial liability the City of Los Angeles would face because of the criminal behavior of its police force. Estimates were already soaring over the $100 million mark.

The hard questions now begged to be asked. What had prosecutors known about the evidence in those 3,000 cases? What had employees in the LAPD crime lab known? What about those who worked in the coroner's office?

Very early in the Simpson case, the man who performed the autopsies on the victims, Dr. Irwin Golden, testified that in his opinion two knives, not one, had been used in these murders — a notion that disputed the prosecution's argument. The powers that be got rid of Dr. Golden and he was never allowed to testify again.

Back in 1995, no one wanted to consider the ramifications of

Fuhrman's taped statements in the Simpson case — despite the officer's many admissions of wrongdoing, his psychological profile in the police records, and the fact that in 1987 he'd been charged by Joseph Britton, an African-American, with using excessive force, making racial slurs, and planting a knife on him. The city had settled Britton's lawsuit and Fuhrman had stayed on the job until committing perjury had forced him out of it.

Now, four years later, Los Angeles officials and local citizens were being forced to pay attention to exactly the same kind of stories that Fuhrman had offered. This time, people listened, and Perez's comments about the unfolding scandal had a phenomenal impact on the metropolitan area. L.A. City Councilwoman Jackie Goldberg called his revelations about the Rampart CRASH unit "horrifying." Police Chief Parks, in welcoming thirty-four LAPD recruits to the department, gave the new officers a very clear warning: any filing of false police reports, moving of evidence closer to a suspect to "make a stronger case," or other illegal activities would not be tolerated. Mayor Richard Riordan, afraid of riots in a city that had exploded and burned over racial incidents in 1965 and 1992, assured the public that the LAPD would rid itself of all malevolent elements.

Then other stories began to surface, which carried the scandal outside of Rampart. There were reports that the Newton Division in the Central Bureau made up T-shirts with the words "Shootin' Newton" printed on them — openly glorifying police gunning down people in that neighborhood.

Nino Durden, Perez's partner during the shooting of Francisco Ovando, had come to Rampart from the 77th Street Division, the same division that Fuhrman had once bragged held the "smell of niggers that have been beaten and killed." When Durden arrived at Rampart, Perez was struck by how the new man did precisely the kinds of things that he'd been doing in another part of town.

"When he [Nino Durden] came up to Rampart CRASH," Perez told members of the task force, "he was talking the talk from the get-go. I mean, he was talking like he knows everything that goes on."

Cops from various divisions around the city, Perez told the investigators, regularly gathered at the Short Stop Bar on Sunset Boulevard or other taverns, where over beer they traded war stories and police secrets. An example was how, in order to justify their actions at one shooting, they would spread ketchup on the ground where they needed the appearance of blood.

"You know," Perez said, "77th CRASH and Rampart CRASH get into a shooting...We talk about how things went down. How they really went down and how they were fixed up...If there's an officer-involved shooting, no one, but absolutely no one — not the lieutenant, not the captain — [is allowed] to come into the scene. You create some kind of diversion, something, 'Sir, we still got suspects running. Stay here for a second...' If we need to add something to the story to make it look a little bit better, that's what we do...And we always say that once we come up with a story, that's the story...You never change it...no matter what."

According to Perez, the police shot a twenty-one-year-old man named Juan Saldana and let him bleed to death while they put a gun next to him and concocted a scenario that justified the killing.

Perez told investigators about the widespread nature of tampering with evidence and crime scenes: "If there was fifteen officers in CRASH," he said, "thirteen of them were putting cases on people."

"When you say 'putting cases on people,'" he was asked by a task force member, "do you mean manufacturing probable cause or do you mean actually...framing somebody who did not do something for a crime?"

"Both," he replied.

Why were so many cops caught up in this activity?

"All that was cared about was the numbers," Perez said. "All they [his superiors in the department] cared about was that at the end of the month...how much total narcotics was brought in, how much money, and how many bodies. That...was the only concern."

What about women officers?

Men didn't want women in the CRASH units, Perez said, because females were "weaker links." Some males were rejected, too. CRASH members voted on new men before letting them into "the loop." A man had to be sponsored by another man already in CRASH, someone who could vouch for his loyalty to their cause of intimidating, controlling, arresting, or hurting whomever they wanted to.

Perez's words echoed what Mark Fuhrman had spelled out for Laura McKinney nearly fifteen years earlier. Fuhrman had talked about a secret group inside the LAPD called "Men against Women," which obviously did not like the idea of working with females. According to Perez, Rampart's CRASH members wore tattoos featuring a nasty-looking insignia — a grinning skull with demonic eyes — in order to make themselves look tougher to gang members (the logo of another controversial LAPD unit, the Special Investigation Section, was a cloaked man with a dagger). CRASH initiation rites resembled those of L.A. gangs. Veteran officers welcomed new members by forming a circle around them and beating them. During this ritual, one CRASH recruit had been permanently injured.

Perez also mentioned a plaque that hung in his home — an award he'd won from fellow officers. It depicted a red heart with two bullets in it. "Sgt. [George] Hoopes gave me that plaque for the Ovando shooting," he said. "We give plaques [of playing cards] out when you get involved in shootings...If the guy dies, the card is a black number two. If he stays alive, it's a red number two."

Was it more prestigious to get one that was black?

"Yeah...The black one signifies that a guy died."

33

Father Gregory Boyle was a Jesuit priest and the director of "Jobs for a Future/Homeboy Industries," located in Boyle Heights in East L.A. Boyle Heights was in the Hollenbeck Division of the LAPD's Central Bureau. It was the same neighborhood where Fuhrman had bragged he'd beaten up people. Father Greg's organization was founded in the late 1980s to provide a job referral service and gang rehabilitation for young people. It got work for hundreds of teenagers each year and helped some of them break away from the influence of gangs and drugs — and police abuse.

Following Perez's confessions, Father Greg conducted an informal survey of the young men who came into his office seeking work. Every one of them had had guns or drugs planted on them or were beaten up by the police. Many described local law enforcement as an occupying army whose activities only made gangs stronger and more cohesive, more criminal and more resistant to change.

Father Greg recognized a step toward a possible solution of the root problem, and he unveiled it in an editorial in the *Los Angeles Times*. Echoing President Clinton's remarks about the spread of homegrown terrorism in America, he wrote that the LAPD had created a "poisonous police culture [that] demonizes 'the other' and holds in stark tension the 'us versus them' dynamism."

"CRASH," he concluded, "is bad policing. You don't try to fix it; you stop it."

But that wasn't easy.

"If you use police only to go after gang members, they will quickly get burned out and become abusive," Cara Gould, the assistant director of Jobs for a Future/Homeboy Industries, said in January 2000, four months after the Rampart scandal was disclosed. "We're still hearing the same stories. A kid just called and told me about an officer accusing him of blocking the sidewalk. The kid wasn't doing anything illegal, but the officer gave him a ticket just for standing on the sidewalk. The ticket costs fifty dollars. Another young man — he was seventeen — came into the office recently and told me about the police putting a gun in his mouth because he wouldn't tell them where his brother was. That's how they treat the people in this community.

"In years past, the cops took kids down to the local factories. People work there in the daytime but it's deserted at night. The police beat kids up there when nobody was watching. Some of the mothers in the neighborhood found out about this and got together and decided to put a stop to it. They went to the factories at night with video cameras and threatened to take videos of the beatings. That scared the police off. The women just wouldn't stand for something like this, but it's still going on in Rampart and South Central. The LAPD will have to do something drastic to change and rebuild its reputation."

"The good officers don't feel supported in their activities so they become complicit with the bad ones," said Celeste Fremon, an L.A. journalist and author of *Father Greg and the Homeboys.* "The problem is leadership. L.A. has never had a police chief who's been the right person to confront this situation and do what's necessary. Gates wasn't. Willie Williams wasn't. Parks isn't. The last three have turned a blind eye to all of this, and I'm not hearing anything now that makes me feel good about the future of the LAPD."

"The entire power structure in L.A. is complicit in all of the corruption," said Joe Domanick, who in the mid-nineties wrote a book about the LAPD called *To Protect and To Serve.* "The Rampart scandal will soon die down and they will try to pass it off as the 'rotten apple' syndrome. Just a few bad cops, they will say. I'm very cynical about there being any real change. Gil Garcetti is the most complicit of anyone in all of this. I mean that in the worst possible way that you can interpret it. At this point, he just wants to keep his job."

The scandal was making that difficult for the district attorney. In the March 2000 primary, Garcetti was challenged by two candidates who won enough votes to force the DA into a November runoff election.

Deputy DA Steve Cooley, who was Garcetti's employee and one of his opponents, said that the scandal would be "*the* issue" in the upcoming election and that Garcetti's office was responsible for prosecuting tainted cases.

Barry Groveman, a corporate lawyer, was even more out-spoken, stating that the activities uncovered at Rampart and elsewhere were "just the latest scandal in a legacy of failure by" the current DA. Garcetti should have looked for problems in police testimony and behavior during the bad prosecutions — not after people had already been tried, convicted, and sent to prison. The DA's office should have been the watchdogs over the entire process instead of protecting the actions of criminal police officers. L.A.'s electorate agreed. In the November runoff, Cooley defeated Garcetti and became the new D.A.

Our legal system, and not just in Los Angeles, had become the primary combat zone in the uncivil war. Every week now brought a new set of troubles or revelations. There were allegations of evidence planting in Kansas City and charges of police stealing from businesses in Chicago. Following a party at the January 2000 Super Bowl in Atlanta, Georgia authorities arrested pro football star Ray Lewis for murder. The media, along with comics and commentators everywhere, immediately proclaimed his guilt just as loudly as they'd done with others in recent years. They condemned not just Lewis but athletes (and particularly black athletes) in general. Nothing had been learned. A few months later, the case against Lewis was dropped. Mea culpas from the press and the comedians were virtually non-existent.

Down in Miami's "Little Havana" unbridled passion and rage

flowed around six-year-old Elian Gonzalez, a Cuban refugee whose mother had drowned off the Florida coast while fleeing the Castro regime with her young son in tow. Elian had made it to Miami and found a home with his relatives in Little Havana. When his father wanted the boy to return to Cuba and live with him, Elian's Miami kin unleashed a custody fight and media blitz in order to keep him in the United States. American jurisprudence clearly ruled in favor of the father, but that only made the crowd in Little Havana more incensed and determined to defy due process. Their emotions and resistance filled the streets of Miami and American television screens, but their strategy ultimately failed. Once again, in a highly visible legal matter, hysteria and bloodlust had run rampant, in total opposition to the law.

A 2000 study conducted by a team of lawyers and criminologists at Columbia University reached a stunning conclusion: two out of three death penalty convictions were overturned on appeal, largely because of serious errors by incompetent defense attorneys or over-zealous prosecutors and police who withheld evidence. The survey covered appeals in all cases from 1973-95 and was the most extensive analysis ever done on this subject. The report heated up the longstanding conflict surrounding the death penalty — a conflict that in March 2000 caused Republican Governor George Ryan of Illinois to declare a moratorium on executions, after thirteen death row inmates in his state were exonerated by new evidence.

Another prominent Republican governor, George W. Bush

of Texas, who would be his party's 2000 presidential nominee, was not dissuaded by the new information emerging about death penalty cases. As the leader of the Lone Star state, Bush had overseen the execution of an astounding 131 people (Colorado, by contrast, has killed one inmate in the past thirty-three years). A *Chicago Tribune* investigation, published in June 2000, reported that dozens of Texas prisoners who'd been put to death under Bush had had cases tainted by unreliable evidence, suspended or disbarred defense attorneys, questionable psychiatric testimony, or false testimony from jailhouse snitches. The governor, undeterred by these considerations, soon condoned several more executions.

34

As 2000 unfolded, one hundred criminal cases in L.A. were overturned, five officers were charged with crimes, a dozen more faced internal misconduct proceedings, several more resigned, and at least seventy remained under investigation for numerous criminal acts. Every Los Angeles defense lawyer in every future case had just been given license to doubt the credibility of the entire department and to present that doubt to jurors.

While the probe spread, a grand jury was empanelled to hear testimony from police witnesses, something that had not happened to the LAPD since the 1930s. L.A.'s legal system was now charged with taking a full, unblinking look at all of the allegations and issuing criminal indictments when necessary. They soon came down against three officers: Michael Buchanan, accused by Perez of planting rock cocaine on suspects; Brian Hewitt, for beating Ismael Jimenez at the Rampart station; and Nino Durden, for various activities perpetrated with Perez.

It was possible that the LAPD's vaunted Code of Silence was not just starting to crack but might crumble. It was just as possible that this investigation, like others before it, would be shut down before richer and deeper truths were revealed. By early 2000, Garcetti was publicly complaining that the police were not turning over documents to him for review because they wanted the probe to cease.

When informed of this lack of co-operation between governmental agencies, L.A. City Councilwoman Laura Chick summed up the situation best. She called it "absolutely insane."

The underlying madness was well illustrated by the case of Ruben Rojas, who'd served two years for a drug conviction based on bad evidence and police perjury. The cops had planted rock cocaine on Rojas and then arrested him for possession. In a letter written to the judge before his case was re-opened, Rojas proclaimed his innocence and revealed the inner workings of a legal system in which producing bottom line numbers of convictions was the most important commodity. He wrote that following his arrest, his defense counsel had given him just five minutes to make a decision about his legal troubles. He could either accept a six-year sentence for a crime he did not commit or go to court and fight the drug charges. If he lost at trial, he faced twenty-five years to life. It was much better, his attorney advised him, to take the six years because "there was no way I could have won my case because I was up against a police officer."

Rojas pled guilty.

Then there was the ongoing issue of money. L.A.'s city council settled one case with a framed drug suspect by giving him $3.7 million. It approved $500,000 for the family of a man who'd been hog-tied by the LAPD and died in its custody. (In

November 1999 the *Los Angeles Times* reported that over the past five years the police department had shot thirty-seven mentally ill people and killed twenty-five of them; investigators who were charged with looking into these shootings also "appeared to falsify information, distort witness statements or ignore damaging facts.")

In addition to the $20 million sought by Destiny Ovando's lawyers in compensation for the maiming and incarcerating of her father, and Francisco Ovando's own suit for a comparable amount, Johnnie Cochran instigated a civil suit on behalf of the late Mario Paz, a sixty-five-year-old Compton man who'd been shot in the back and killed during a SWAT team drug raid. Officers had stormed into his home and murdered him as his wife clung to his pant leg and cried, begging the police not to shoot her husband because he was innocent. The cops, as it turned out, were in the wrong apartment.

The cost of all these police actions to Los Angeles was initially estimated at $100 million, but that figure was soon bumped up to $125 million. When it climbed to $250 million, the DA's office instructed the city council to set aside $300 million for the upcoming civil suits. Some legal observers said even this number was too low, and that the figure could easily reach half a billion dollars.

A few months into the scandal, a great irony surfaced, which had the capacity to bring the story of the spread of domestic terrorism — from America's fringes to the center of power — full circle. L.A. attorney Stephen Yagman filed a $100 million federal civil rights lawsuit on behalf of DeNovel Hunter, alleging that Rafael Perez had planted drugs on him back in 1992. Hunter, who had two previous convictions for drug offenses, was found guilty of the 1992 charge and sentenced to five years in prison. Although such allegations and the resulting lawsuits were becoming almost commonplace in L.A., this one was different.

Hunter charged that Rampart's entire CRASH unit was not being run as a law enforcement agency but as a racketeering enterprise, and that top officials of the police department had condoned its illegal activities. Hunter named fourteen officers as defendants — plus former Police Chief Daryl Gates, Police Chief Bernard Parks, all of the current police commissioners, city council members, and past members of both bodies. Hunter also called for the abolition of CRASH.

Fifteen years earlier, back in 1985, when the white supremacists in the Order had been arrested, prosecuted, and imprisoned for racketeering, the federal government, in its desire to destroy this group of racist revolutionaries, had used the RICO (Racketeer Influenced and Corrupt Organizations) statute to throw the largest net available over them and lock them up for long periods of time. Now Yagman was asking a federal judge to rule that the police and city officials in Los Angeles could be charged under the same statute. The enemy, the lawsuit implied, had moved into the hierarchy of a major metropolitan governmental agency. Many legal observers, while struck by the boldness and creativity of Yagman's request, felt certain that a judge would not allow this case to go forward.

But that belief didn't make things any easier inside the LAPD, where the scandal had caused morale to sink so low that there were stories of officers not even reporting crimes now, for fear of being reprimanded or punished for wrongdoing. As one frustrated cop told the *LA Weekly* in early 2000, "We're spending all our resources looking into ourselves. We're cannibalizing ourselves."

35

The law enforcement corruption scandal in L.A. was only one front in this nationwide war. During the 1990s in New Orleans, ninety-nine officers were charged with felonies. In Pittsburgh, tensions between police and the black community were an ugly and unresolved source of conflict. In Cleveland in 1998, forty-four officers from five different agencies were accused of taking money to protect cocaine trafficking operations in that city and northern Ohio. They were hardly the only cops to be accused of such activity. Between 1994 and 1997, 508 police personnel in forty-seven cities had been arrested for similar offenses.

In Denver at the turn of the millennium, Police Chief Tom Sanchez was driven from office after a no-knock drug raid resulted in the death of a man named Ismael Mena. This assault, like the one in L.A. that had caused Johnnie Cochran to file a suit against the police, had been carried out at the wrong address. In New York, under the leadership of Mayor Rudolph Giuliani, three unarmed black men were shot to death by the police in three separate instances, and a fourth black man, Abner Louima, was sodomized with a broomstick by a cop as another officer looked on, leading to near-riot conditions in the streets. One of the unarmed men, Amadou Diallo, an immigrant from Guinea, had been shot nineteen times while reaching for his wallet. Patrick Dorismond, a security guard and the son of a Haitian singer, was shot to death after an officer conducting a drug sting allegedly asked Dorismond to sell him marijuana. The two got into a scuffle, backup officers arrived, and Dorismond was killed.

Instead of apologizing for the death of this twenty-six-year-old, or offering sympathy to Dorismond's family, the mayor of New York demonized the dead young man and released his juvenile record to the public — a violation of law according to many attorneys. Giuliani's behavior provoked 3,000 citizens to march in protest and demand the mayor's resignation. They tore up an American flag, set it afire, and knocked down police barricades. They displayed a sign for the mayor that read, "If you shoot one of my children, I shoot five of you," and one protester shouted, "Rudy, I'll blow you up to kingdom come, cut you with a chain saw, and feed you to the dogs!"

The mayor was unmoved by such sentiments or felt that his own interests would not be served by showing empathy or compassion or remorse for the suffering of these people in his city. He was at that time running for the U.S. Senate against Hillary Clinton, and the last thing he wanted to focus on in his election campaign was the dirty little war being fought in the streets of urban America between police forces and the minority poor. He wasn't alone in his avoidance. The presidential candidates in the 2000 election, Al Gore and George W. Bush, didn't want to talk about it, either.

The uncivil war, which includes the war on drugs, was spreading apace. In a report published in late 1999 by the respected Milton S. Eisenhower Foundation, a non-profit research group that developed from a commission created in 1968, crime in America in the late 1990s was compared to crime three decades earlier. President Johnson had originally picked Milton Eisenhower, the brother of the former president, to conduct the first study, which was then repeated in the late nineties. The recent survey concluded that the nation had moved backward in dealing with crime and was "a society in deep trouble" because of misguided policies about criminal justice.

Violence in America, the study said, was far more prevalent now than it had been thirty years before. The current decline in crime rates was misleading and had been created by recent prosperity, not by addressing the causes of our social problems. The report's statistics contended that murder, rape, robbery, and assaults had not fallen but actually risen in recent years — from 860 per 100,000 people to 1,218. (In L.A. in 2001, murder rose by 27%).

According to the study, the odds of dying a violent death in the United States remain much higher than in almost every other industrialized society, in part because Americans now own 200 million firearms designed solely to kill other people. A root factor in the widespread violence is the "vast and shameful inequality in income, wealth, and opportunity" in the culture, which raises one-fourth of its children in poverty.

In response to the violence, the nation has embarked on

building more prisons, increasing its war on drugs, and creating a "zero tolerance" attitude or a "three strikes and you're out" mindset toward people in trouble. The emphasis is on these areas instead of drug treatment, job training for youth, or early prevention programs for potential offenders.

"Prisons," the report reads, "have become our nation's substitute for effective policies on crime, drugs, mental illness, housing, poverty, and employment of the hardest to employ."

Both Rafael Perez and Mark Fuhrman had told the bitter truth: Make justice a game and the number of convictions the ultimate measure of success; turn cops into gods on the street and give them the power to abuse without any consequences; encourage silence everywhere; focus on punishment and blame above all else; place angry young men in these circumstances, men who have emotional or behavioral problems to begin with; send these men into combat against those who've been deemed worthless and dangerous — then watch what happens. The violence will not be random, but predictable.

In March 2000, the LAPD released a 362-page document on the Rampart scandal, which basically congratulated the police department for ferreting out the trouble within its ranks and dealing with the perpetrators. The pages were clearly intended to bring an end to the scandal, but most people felt that would not happen and might just cause the opposite reaction. The *Los Angeles Times* now called for an outside investigation of the affair. When Police Chief Parks was asked if the size and nature of the problems uncovered inside the LAPD made it necessary for an outside monitoring of the cops by a civilian agency, he dismissed the idea with one word, the same word that L.A.'s legal officials had been using in the face of such suggestions for the past several decades.

"No," he said.

But in the end Parks would not have his way. Since 1996, in the wake of the Simpson case and other LAPD allegations of evidence tampering, perjury, and violence against suspects, the Justice Department under Attorney General Janet Reno had been investigating the city's police force and looking for a pattern of civil rights violations. By late summer of 2000, the Justice Department had in fact determined that there was such a pattern within the ranks. This finding backed the City of Los Angeles into a corner and presented its law enforcement brass with a hard choice. L.A. officials either had to sign a consent decree — a binding legal agreement — that would allow the federal government to oversee and monitor a series of reforms designed to alleviate or remove the causes of scandal from the police department, or Janet Reno and her lawyers would file suit against the city, suing it for a broad range of civil rights violations. Chief Parks and Mayor Riordan refused to go along with signing the consent decree — despite the knowledge that a majority of city council members would vote to accept it and that legal experts throughout L.A. insisted that the city could not win such a lawsuit. In the process of fighting and ultimately losing this costly battle, they contended, Los Angeles would look even worse than it already did. But the chief and the mayor continued to resist. Their defiance lasted until the eleventh hour, in mid-September, when they finally gave in and decided to co-operate with the federal government and its findings. The city agreed to sign the decree and implement the Feds' recommendations for improved police training, installing some form of civilian leadership to audit and publicly report on the police, and tracking and removing bad cops from the street. The City Council voted 10-2 in favor of this measure and it was done.

This development was not the only shock to L.A.'s legal system. In late August 2000, U.S. District Judge William Rea ruled that the LAPD could be sued by a variety of defendants under federal racketeering (or RICO) laws. Defendants who believed their civil rights had been violated by the police could now bring lawsuits charging that the department had been run as a criminal enterprise.

Under RICO, the statute of limitations for filing cases went back a decade, as opposed to one year for most civil right violation complaints. This opened up L.A.'s legal system to many more potential lawsuits and also made the city vulnerable to three times as much financial liability as before. In addition, the LAPD was confronted with a federal injunction against their department, instituted to stop evidence planting and perjury.

The LAPD's pattern and practice of abusing and violating the rights of citizens had at last been identified and substantiated by the U.S. government itself. The blue wall of silence and denial had finally been punctured.

A POSTSCRIPT FROM LOS ANGELES

On a sunny afternoon near the start of the new millennium, I visited the Rampart neighborhood, a busy family-oriented place. The sidewalks were full of women shopping on foot and pushing baby carriages. Teenagers moved in and out of new storefronts built since the 1992 riots: Home Depot and Rite Aid had moved into the area. Rampart's streets were calm but carried an edge. Parked cars had bullet holes in their bumpers. Tennis shoes were draped over electrical wires, meaning that drugs were for sale nearby. The homeless lived in the alleys with their possessions stuffed in grocery carts, constantly asking visitors for food and money.

Mi Farmacia was crowded with customers buying sundries or sitting in rows of chairs waiting for prescriptions to be filled. Small children looked at the colorful pinatas on the walls, while mothers held babies and whispered or sang soft melodies in their ears. Ira Erenberg and Ray Alvarez spoke on the phone or gave their patrons advice in Spanish. People drifted in off the street and found refuge in the pharmacy.

Ten years earlier, a local man had been released from jail and immediately got drunk. He decided to paint Our Lady of Guadalupe on an exterior side wall of the drug store. The icon would protect the business from harm, the man said, and give Mi Faramcia more respect in the neighborhood. Erenberg did not argue with his reasoning, and the man put up a full image of the Virgin wrapped in a long green shawl. People came by and stared at the artist's work. They crossed them-

selves and kneeled down and put flowers at her feet.

Whenever gang activity picked up in the area, someone would des-ecrate the lower part of the mural with spray paint, as a way of mark-ing one's territory and letting others know that the pharmacy's turf belonged to the Rockwood gang or the 18th Street gang or another upstart group. As soon as the Virgin had been marked, somebody else would come along and remove or paint over the foreign colors, not wanting the Virgin to be defiled or for local rivalries to escalate. More paint would appear on Our Lady's shawl but never on her face — until now. When the gang injunctions had been lifted in Rampart, somebody put a blue slash across her cheek.

"In this neighborhood," said Ray Alvarez, "that is sacrilege."

Graffiti was starting to show up throughout Rampart. Erenberg was worried about the growing signs of conflict but felt there was nothing he could do about it — least of all contact his local police department and look for cooperative ways to prevent violence. The pharmacy had long had an emergency panic button that was wired into the nearby Rampart station, but Erenberg had never used it. Thirty-six years of serving the local community had convinced him that he couldn't ask the cops for anything.

"If I pushed the button," he said, "I don't have much faith that anyone would show up and help me. The LAPD's response to trouble is based on priority. A drug store robbery is not a high priority. They have other things to do."

East of Mi Farmacia, the great metal-and-glass corporate towers of downtown L.A. loom up above the horizon, floating and shimmer-

ing in the diffuse California sunlight like palaces rising from the desert. From Rampart the shiny monoliths seem unreal, insubstantial, and very far off in the distance. Yet in some ways, downtown Los Angeles and Rampart are linked closely together.

L.A.'s criminal courts building is not far from the towers and many Rampart citizens end up inside the walls of its courtrooms, on trial for countless activities. You can spend a whole morning in the rooms and hallways of this structure and never see a white face.

A second connection exists between downtown L.A. and Rampart. Attorneys and other professionals who work in these silver towers have been known to leave the office for lunch and drive over to MacArthur Park in the neighborhood, where you can buy stolen or manufactured social security cards, drivers' licenses, and other forged documents. Sometimes, lawyers purchase cocaine or heroin from the kids who hang at the edge of the park and hide the dope in plastic bags tucked inside their mouths — a little pick-me-up for the rest of the afternoon.

The Rampart police station is near this park and only three blocks from the pharmacy. It's an easy walk from the drugstore to the station, and along the way one hears Latin music coming over the tenement windowsills and smells Latin food being cooked. Youngsters sit on front stoops and talk or dance on the sidewalk to the sounds from the windows. They look warily at strangers, as if they know very well who does and does not belong in the neighborhood.

There are two Rampart stations, but the CRASH unit operates from the one closest to the pharmacy. The division's top brass is at the other, bigger location; they would later claim that they didn't know every-

thing CRASH was doing. Rafael Perez worked out of the smaller sta-tion, and from here he'd ordered cocaine delivered to him by courier from the LAPD property room. By early 2000, Perez had finally stopped talking to the authorities and was now serving a five-year sentence for his drug theft, plea-bargained down from twelve years because of his confessions. Officer Brian Hewitt had also been work-ing here when he'd brought in Ismael Jimenez and beaten him until he vomited.

The inside of the two-story station is clean and tidy and looks like any other administrative building. Spanish and English placards on the wall read: "The Los Angeles Police Department — Quality Service Is Your Right." The outside is beige, surrounded by palm trees and blooming birds of prey.

In the parking lot on this warm afternoon, officers stood in clumps and laughed about a TV show they'd watched last night. They pulled their shotguns from their patrol cars, holding them upright and pol-ishing the barrels until they gleamed in the soft-edged California sun-light. They checked their belts for ammunition.

They were stocky men with crewcuts or slicked-back hair. Muscles bulged from beneath their impeccable blue uniforms. Their shoes shone. They wore dark shades and looked hip in a belligerent sort of way. They didn't walk so much as strut. They wrapped tape around their shotgun butts and chuckled at their own private jokes, cocky in their expressions and movements, as they prepared to go to work in the evening and police the neighborhood. They were the occupying army to the hilt, resting and relaxing, taking a breather in the sun-

shine before going back into combat.

This image more than any other captured the full complexity of Los Angeles during the golden moment of American prosperity. No such army could be found on the west side of L.A. this afternoon, over in Santa Monica or Malibu or Brentwood, where money was abundant and so were drugs. The cops weren't gathered there to mount an assault on the cocaine that flowed into these affluent neighborhoods and was then distributed by the young people — known as mules — who carried the bags from one hand to the next and got the money in return. No cadre of police was aggressively looking into these crimes or the unsolved murders that resulted when people refused to pay their bills.

One cop who spoke up had rattled L.A.'s legal system from top to bottom and set off hundreds of millions of dollars worth of trouble. What would happen if twenty officers under investigation decided to open their mouths?

36

On my trips to Los Angeles, I often stayed in Venice, a beachside community in the southwestern part of the city. I rose very early each morning, drove over to the Washington Street Pier, and in the cool dampness of the California dawn, walked out onto the pier until I was several hundred yards into the Pacific Ocean. I loved the fresh, dank smell of the murky water. I loved the sound of lapping. By the time I arrived at the end of the pier, older Asian immigrants were there fishing in the waves below. The men held the poles while the women handled the bait. They spoke quietly among themselves or were silent, and occasionally they pulled an exotic-looking creature from the deep and excitedly reeled it up onto the pier, a perfectly flat fish or a writhing squid or something I'd never seen anywhere before. They quickly took the hook from the creature's mouth, re-baited their line, and threw it back into the water.

As the sun came up on the pier, I looked out across the ocean and sometimes thought about the country's future. Everywhere there were signs of deepening conflict and pain. A six-year-old boy in Michigan had gone to school one winter morning and shot another six-year-old to death. A black man in Pittsburgh had gunned down two white people (he was fighting a private race war and had made sure that his victims were Caucasian). In Tennessee, a man started a blaze in his home and shot to death firefighters as they came to put it out. A workplace shooting in Texas killed six, and another church shooting in that state left two dead. A high school student in Florida shot a teacher to death. With each new round of bloodshed, President Clinton pled fervently for Congress to pass more stringent gun laws, while actor Charlton Heston, representing the National Rifle Assocation, belittled the chief executive in an ad campaign and spurned his call for change. Heston hardened his pro-gun stance and pledged to raise the NRA's membership from 3.6 million to four million. Amidst the warring factions, there was no common ground and no common sense.

As the first anniversary of the Columbine massacre approached, the suffering intensified in Denver, where several families of the victims, outraged at the loss of their children and determined to lay blame somewhere, sued the local sheriff's department in Jefferson County for not stopping the violence ahead of time or dealing with it differently when it struck. Law enforcement personnel, in the face of these charges, seemed genuinely baffled, hurt, and angry. In what would come to symbolize the legacy of Columbine, three dozen defendants would be sued, including government agencies, teachers, friends of the gunmen, and the killers' parents. Nobody wanted to talk about what had happened at the school before the violence exploded, because everyone was too busy now holding someone else responsible for the carnage.

In New York City, the Reverend Al Sharpton, while protesting another police shooting, led marchers as they shouted, "No justice! No peace!" More shootings erupted in Michigan and other locations. More kids made threats of bloodshed at their schools. Accepting lawlessness was everywhere, from the sidewalks of Rampart to the streets of New York.

Most disturbingly of all, following the chaotic 2000 presidential election, the U.S. Supreme Court, in a 5-4 decision, stopped the counting of votes in Florida and handed the presidency to Republican George W. Bush. The four dissenting justices angrily criticized the majority opinion and hinted at the long-term damage of their actions. No one dared to suggest that we were not living in a democracy where every vote counted equally, yet they did imply that the highest upholder of the law in our nation had just violated the very principles upon which the country was founded. Once again, those principles were sidestepped by those charged with protecting them.

As our nation entered the new millennium, one could find plenty of cause for gloom and plenty of reason to suspect that things could only get worse. But something else — a glint of hope — was also becoming visible, a hint that changes were coming and the 1990s would eventually fade away, as the fifties had once done. There were signs that a fresh new wind might blow in from an unknown direction, knock the clouds sideways, and sweep the country toward something new and unimaginable; signs that people were awakening to the beast at the door, the hatred and numb passivity that had been allowed to grow and expand throughout the nation. Maybe America was frightening itself, as it had back in the fifties, into some new ways of thinking and being. Maybe it was time to reconsider the cost of encouraging adults and teenagers and children to express their loathing of one another whenever they felt like it.

Maybe there were reasons for optimism. In 2000, the electorate had almost completely rejected the bitterly divisive politics of Reform presidential candidate Pat Buchanan. Several conservative governors and even the evangelist Pat Robertson had recently called for a halt to the death penalty in our nation's prisons, because of all of the current evidentiary flaws and problems with our legal system. The *Los Angeles Times,* which had adopted a "See No Evil, Hear No Evil" policy during the Simpson case, had lately stepped forward and done some excellent reporting on the Rampart scandal. Maybe investigative journalism was not yet dead.

Maybe political activism wasn't either. In mid-April, thousands of young people from all over nation and world came together in Washington, D.C., to protest the policies of the World Bank and to share some of their idealism with others. Their gathering may have been largely symbolic and their issues may have been difficult for the mainstream to understand, but they were picking up an old American drum and starting to beat it, and they were willing to go to jail to make their point. They were telling everyone that this was not the best of all possible worlds and if you wanted to change it, get off your assumptions and get involved.

In Denver, radio talk show host Peter Boyles, who'd earned a national reputation by implying on the airwaves that the Ramseys were guilty in the death of their daughter JonBenet, had been trying to extend his thrust into other criminal matters. Following the January 2000 murder of a local white schoolteacher, Emily Johnson, who had dated a black man with a record, Boyles began singing his same old tune: he had a good bead on this case, just as he'd had on some other highly visible homicides in the 1990s. Anyone who took a different view or questioned his version of the truth was wrong and deserved his public contempt.

Except that in the Emily Johnson case, the Denver police actually investigated the crime without corruption and without detectives who were committed to one scenario right from the start. Within days, three teenagers had been arrested for breaking into the teacher's home and killing her. In the wake of this development, for the first time in recent memory, prominent people began raising their voices about what was being done to our legal system, and to our populace, in the name of free speech, high ratings, and unabashed careerism. Maybe it was time to rethink the trashing of the rights and the reputations — of both the living and the dead.

After the teens' arrest, Denver's Mayor, Wellington Webb, who is African-American, came forward and said, "Listening to all the presumptions and moving to pre-judgement on talk shows and other places, I think we have to be careful. We have to be careful raising issues about the deceased and her lifestyle, who she dates and interracial couples. Making pre-judgement serves no purpose."

The mayor was being cautious and polite, but his spokesman, Andrew Hudson, took off his gloves, set them down, and responded in a way that virtually no one in an authoritative position had done throughout the past decade. He got righteously indignant about the fact that people were being paid and promoted to violate and destroy the presumption of innocence — being rewarded to undermine the foundations of our legal system. Hudson went on a rant, and in an e-mail sent to various media outlets in January 2000, he wrote:

"This murder is a tragedy, plain and simple. It has been made more so by the mean-spirited and outrageous comments made by Peter Boyles, who has not only tarnished the memory of Emily Johnson, but also [made] outrageous statements and theories about who was responsible for this murder...We have to look at what this says about us as a community. Are we going to allow people like Peter Boyles to define us? Are we going to raise legitimate speculations or are we just going to play junior detective? Because that's what he was doing. Peter struck pay dirt with JonBenet Ramsey, and he saw this as the way to get back on the national shows."

A month later some even more remarkable words appeared. Robert Scheer, a columnist for the *Los Angeles Times*, offered belated kudos to the most maligned set of jurors in American history — those in the Simpson criminal trial. For almost five years they'd been publicly attacked and ridiculed without pause, enduring everything from charges of racism to assaults on their character and intelligence. In an editorial on the Rampart scandal and policing in L.A., Scheer did something courageous and long overdue by entitling his article "O.J. Jury Knew the Score."

Geraldo Rivera, after originally downplaying the Rampart scandal, changed his mind and did some fine TV work on the corruption inside the LAPD. And in March 2000, the employees of ABC-TV, and more particularly those who worked for "Good Morning America," revolted when the network tried to hire Mark Fuhrman as a legal consultant for the upcoming Martha Moxley trial. A united group of people finally said enough and chose not to reward and protect and pander to a confessed racist, convicted liar, beater, and brutalizer of minority Americans. The revolt worked and the employees won. ABC refused to hire Fuhrman.

There was more good news in the West. In early September 2000, a jury in Idaho awarded Victoria and Jason Keenan a $6.3 million judgment against the Aryan Nations compound and its leader, Richard Butler, after he was found negligent in the selection, training, and supervision of security guards, who had assaulted and shot at the Keenans in front of the compound in 1998. Defense lawyer Edgar Steele tried to blame the guards alone for their actions and to represent Butler as innocent of all wrongdoing, but the jurors did not agree. In order for Butler to satisfy the judgment against him, he was forced to give up the 20-acre Aryan Nations headquarters that had been his home and the location for his hate group for nearly three decades. He deeded the property to the Keenans, who were free to do with this beautiful piece of Idaho land whatever they wanted.

While it was much too early to draw any conclusions, there was a pulse from coast to coast, a rising belief that action matters, that political awareness and political movements could accomplish good things, and that one had alternatives to being a quiet victim of savagery (across the country, 800,000 women took part in the May 2000 Mother's Day march, standing together against violence and for better gun control laws). There was a sense of waking up from the long, bloody, intoxicating sleep of the previous decade with its mass murders and its gathering madness. Maybe there was more to the American dream than just the accumulation of dollars and cents. Maybe the cynical dragon could be challenged and the haters could go elsewhere in search of jobs and places to live.

The seeds of growth and change were emerging not only inside the United States. In early 2000, in a different way and in a different venue, another kind of hope sprang up when Pope John Paul II came before the world and apologized to everyone for past transgressions of the Catholic Church. It was a sea change in the history of his religion, and a signal that many people across the globe were searching for a new way of living with themselves and their neighbors. This elderly man, approaching death and sharing his wisdom with his one billion followers, had witnessed a great deal of carnage in the twentieth century. Now he was telling his fellow worshippers, not just Catholics but followers of all denominations, that the healing process can best begin by acknowledging your own involvement in the life and the death around you. The Church, he acknowledged, was not detached from these social processes. Nobody was. And everyone needed acceptance and love and forgiveness — even the Holy Father. In his own way, John Paul was offering a starting place for making our horribly wounded and fragmented world whole. He was humbling himself for a greater good.

Out on the pier on those early mornings, as I turned away from the ocean and walked back toward the land, I watched the sun come up on L.A., pink and orange and golden streaks breaking across the horizon and lighting up the city and its rolling hills. Palm trees shook in the breeze and the eucalyptus held that faint smell of good health. In the sky, silver airplanes took off in every direction, catching the sun's rays on their wings. Sea gulls tossed and dove above the shoreline or sat on the pier's railings and called sharply to one another. Joggers were out on the beach now, leaving their footprints in the sand. People were strolling together in conversation or carrying papers or cups of coffee and enjoying their solitude.

The air was rich with life and the day held the hope of every dawn. I looked at the wondrous city in front of me and knew there were good people in every corner of it and in every corner of every place in America. Maybe they'd become tired of the hatred and the racism, sick of the petty emotional politics of our time, disgusted with the chatter that had no meaning, and ready for something new. Like the Pope, maybe they would act toward a better future and try to stop the flow of blood that could always reach them and their own children. Maybe all it would take to remind them of that buried desire for something better, or to stir them from the numbness and deadness of the heart that had created so much violence, was a sound riding on the wind, like the cry of a seagull or a single trumpet's blast.

IT WAS IN THE CARDS

37

And then the blast came. Once again it was triggered by America's legal system, only this time it did not involve an out-of-control cop on the street who'd decided to play God or a prosecutor who'd chosen to ignore contradictory evidence. This time it did not concern the taking away of the rights or freedoms of a group of poor, minority teenagers in inner cities. Now the dark edge that had been growing on the underbelly of our society was much bigger and much harder to ignore. Now it was trampling on the rights of 50,000,000 Americans, and these actions were being taken by those who sat at the very top of our judicial system. The disregard for the fairness and principles of law would at last became so obvious that the general population itself began to perceive the dangers in this process — and to fight back.

Throughout the '90s, the difficulty had been to see any of the major legal events being played out on out television screens in social or political terms. The Simpson case was only about domestic violence, the Ramsey case only about a homicidal mother, Columbine only about some very, very bad teenagers, and the Clinton-Lewinsky scandal only about a president with too many erotic impulses. All of them were merely entertainment for a mass audience always hungry for more emotional and sensual stimulation. The meaning of each event was too easily lost in the constant desire to identify and punish new villains. The uncivil war, which was unfolding behind and within all of these dramas, remained for the most part buried. A populace that had been trained to view everything as amusement, even the gradual erosion of its rights and values, had been able to maintain its conviction that none of these situations had anything to do with the average citizen.

But what occurred in the fall of 2000 forced the deeper reality into the open and laid it out in front of everyone. The divisions in our society, which had been so rawly exposed and so violently acted out in the 1960s, had never been bridged or healed. There were still two Americas, one struggling to hold onto power and the other trying to emerge from a new coalition of groups and interests. At the end of 2000, the old issues of racism, sexism, the separation of church and state, the sanctity of individual rights, and letting others besides (for the most part) aging, white males run the government were thrust into the headlines again.

The uncivil war, as people used to say in the 60s during

protests over Vietnam, had finally come home.

On the night of November 7, 2000, a very peculiar thing happened on American television. That evening, some networks — ABC, in particular — began broadcasting that Democratic presidential candidate Al Gore had won the critical state of Florida and its twenty-five electoral votes. By implication, this meant that he now had more than the 270 electoral votes needed for victory and had just become the 43rd President of the United States. ABC made its prediction after employing the same polling techniques it and other news organizations had long used to determine election outcomes before every ballot had been counted. It had interviewed people exiting the voting booths in Florida. Based upon what these people were saying, ABC could confidently tell viewers that Al Gore had defeated Republican candidate George W. Bush, the son of former President George Bush.

With nearly fifty million votes nationwide, Gore was ahead in the popular vote (he would eventually win it by more than 500,000 ballots). Now the White House was his. In a sense, the Clinton administration and much of what it had accomplished would be extended for a minimum of four more years. All of the relentless efforts by the media and other interests to derail or destroy it had fallen short. Despite his scandals, President Clinton had finished out his second term, and by a narrow margin the majority of the voting public had elected his vice-president to be his successor. The choice in this presidential race had been clear-cut, and now the country had chosen a Democratic Clinton ally over the born-again Christian son of an old-guard Republican. The vote had been close, but the will of the people was the final say.

Peter Jennings, the longtime ABC anchor, made the announcement about Gore's victory in his calm, business-as-usual style well before midnight. He conveyed just a trace of superiority because he was able to call the election right then. He and his network were obviously pleased to be breaking a huge of piece of news and felt they had nothing to worry about in doing so, even though all the Florida votes had not been tallied. Exit polls had worked in the past and they would work tonight. A simple statistical extrapolation allowed the numbers crunchers to figure out the larger voting patterns, once they'd gathered enough data from those who'd cast ballots for president. Polls were remarkably accurate — but not tonight.

Jennings soon came back on the air looking flustered. In an awkward and embarrassed manner, he said that ABC was withdrawing its prediction about Gore's win because Florida was now too close to call. The unflappable anchorman with the soothing voice was clearly confused. His credibility, and that of his entire news operation, could be thrown into doubt by this turn of events; ABC was supposed to know what it was doing before it broadcast to the nation such an important piece of information. Backtracking in this manner was unprofessional —

or worse. The news reports were now indicating that based upon the actual machine-counting of votes in Florida, Bush and Gore were essentially tied. No winner could yet be declared. Something had occurred that did not quite add up, and nobody seemed to know what it was. Throughout the rest of the night, ABC would hold to its position that the victor in the crucial Florida race remained unknown. On November 7, several networks did this kind of flip-flopping.

But it was a very different story at Fox TV, where John Ellis, a cousin of George W. Bush, played a key role in Fox's election night decision to give Florida to the Republicans. A consultant hired by Fox, Ellis ran the team that analyzed election data and recommended when news executives should project a winner in each state. The Ellis decision to name Bush triumphant in Florida came at 2:16 a.m. on Wednesday, November 8, and during the next four minutes, other networks hurried to follow Fox's lead and hand the presidency to Bush. Some time later, *The New Yorker* magazine reported that Ellis was on the phone with George W. Bush and his brother, Florida governor Jeb Bush, that evening, providing them with internal network information and election data. In a letter to *The New Yorker*, Ellis would strongly deny being the source of any improper leaks, but the disclosure of these connections between his employer and the Bushes raised questions of impropriety at Fox. The chairman of Fox News, Roger Ailes, had been a strategist in George Bush senior's 1988 and 1992 presidential campaigns.

In the weeks following the election, ABC and other networks, including CBS, which had made early predictions about Gore winning Florida, took a beating from many sides. The blame game that had become so popular in America was now unleashed on them. Media critics howled out their judgments. How could the networks have made such a stupid mistake at such an important moment? Why had they been so irresponsible? Why would they rely on an unreliable thing like exit polls? Who should pay for this error and what should the punishment be? CBS in particular absorbed this scorn and then publicly delivered a mea culpa, while vowing not to repeat this mishap.

The networks wanted to put this incident behind them, yet unsettling questions lingered around what had taken place on November 7 (of course, as the days and then weeks passed in November and still no winner had been determined in Florida, the most unsettling issue of all was who would become the next President of the United States). Unfortunately, a lot of questions were buried under this assault on TV newsrooms themselves. The most important thing, as had happened so often in recent years in the country, was to find someone to flail for an apparent miscue and then to keep on flailing.

In the days following the closing of the polls, the public learned that some strange things had occurred in Florida on election night. Approximately 60,000 ballots, which were used in conjunction with the punch card voting system found in more than a third of the state's counties, had not registered a selection for anyone for president. These were known as "undervotes." Other cards had shown voters choosing more than one person for president. These were called "overvotes." In both cases, the machines counting these punch cards rejected them as invalid. Three counties alone in South Florida — Miami-Dade, Broward and Palm Beach — had nearly 45,000 overvotes and 28,000 undervotes, all of which had been thrown out of the final machine count.

The problem in many cases was that the little perforations on the punch cards, known as chads, which were supposed to be punched cleanly out after a voter had made his or her selection and pushed them through with a stylus, had not fallen off. They'd either folded back into their slots, which indicated to the vote-counting machine that the voter had chosen no one, or they were left hanging by one, two or three corners. The latter condition also registered as a non-vote. The term "hanging chad," which was completely foreign to the general public until now, suddenly became the most notorious phrase in the nation. Tens of million of people were now asking the same thing. What did a hanging chad mean, in terms of the will of a voter? Did it show that the person casting the ballot had intended to vote for someone but failed to push the perforation all the way out? Or did it mean that the voter had been confused and not really selected anyone at all? Should the cards with hanging chads be hand-counted now and included in the final totals, or should these ballots be discarded altogether? What effect would including them or getting rid of them have on such a close race for the White House? And who got to make these historic decisions?

This set of circumstances had never happened before in a presidential election, and the country was at a crossroads — a crisis of principle. Would we as a society make an attempt to count every reasonable vote and hold to our democratic convictions or would we not? Would we take the time to discover the will of the voters, or would we rush to a conclusion and a judgment as quickly as possible? Would we, in the most basic sense, do what was fair by preserving every individual's right to vote — or do what was expedient? Was there a special need to be fair now because one candidate had clearly won the popular vote? The core issue of the value of one-person, one-vote was squarely in front of the whole nation.

In November 2000, most Americans, or at least most non-minority Americans, believed that regardless of how our legal system treated some people, it was deeply committed to fairness and objectivity. It was not a political tool or weapon to be used for one group and against another. It played by the rules. Now these assumptions were open to question and debate. Now the system would be exposed and tested at a level unseen before in modern times. How the country addressed this crisis would not only shape America's political and social future, but say much about where we stood as a nation.

Amazingly, almost four per cent of Florida's six million ballots cast in the 2000 presidential election had not functioned properly (the state employed a variety of voting systems, but the bulk of the problems centered around the punch cards used in 24 of its 67 counties, where the majority of Florida's 8.7 million registered voters reside). Several weeks after these disturbing facts began to emerge, former President Jimmy Carter was asked to comment about them. President Carter, who in recent years had overseen election processes in Third World countries, said that based upon what he'd seen in Florida, he would not certify such a vote. In his opinion, voting conditions in the Sunshine State did not meet the standards that applied in what many Americans regarded as backwards or corrupt societies.

But Carter's views did not apply in the Florida government itself. That state was now being run by Jeb Bush, George W. Bush's brother. Their father had been defeated in the 1992 presidential race by Bill Clinton. In the wake of that election, George W. had gone on to become the governor of Texas, while in 1998 Jeb had won Florida's top office (a third son, Neil, had been tainted by his connection to the savings and loan scandal that erupted in Denver a decade earlier, and he'd disappeared from the public stage). By the late '90s, both George W. and Jeb were positioned to play hugely significant roles in the next presidential election. Opinion polls had already determined that if George W. Bush ran against Vice-President Gore, the almost-certain Democratic candidate, it would be a tight race, and Florida's twenty-five electoral votes would be a must for the victor. The state might even decide the winner.

When Jeb Bush assumed power in Tallahassee, a new secretary of state had come with him. Her name was Katherine Harris, and she was the wealthy granddaughter of Ben Hill Griffin Jr., a Florida citrus and cattle magnate. Her net worth was reportedly in the range of $7 million, nearly all of it stock in her family's firm, B.H.G. Inc. A Key West native, she later moved to Sarasota, a Republican bastion on the west central coast. In 1994, when Harris was entering her late thirties, she won a seat as the Republican State Senator from Sarasota. She quickly established a strong pro-business voting record, chairing the Commerce and Economic Opportunities Committee and promoting international trade.

During her Senate campaign, she'd come under attack for accepting $20,600 in illegal contributions from an insurance company known as Riscorp. The corporation's officers later pled guilty to violating state election law, but Harris maintained that she hadn't known the contributions were illegal. Her campaign difficulties did not prevent her from running for and winning the secretary of state's office in 1998. Her job description now included being the top elections official in Florida; she oversaw the entire voting system and had the capacity to make recommendations for changes in the process. Interestingly, 1998 was the final year that Florida would elect a secretary of state. In

2002, the job was being eliminated by a Cabinet reorganization that had been approved by the voters.

As secretary of state, Harris won praise for encouraging trade with Latin America, but she also gained notoriety for her tendency to book pricey hotels when she left Tallahassee on business. According to the *Tampa Tribune*, between January 1999 and November 2000 she spent more than $100,000 on travel, including $400-a-night stays at the Willard Inter-Continental in Washington, D.C. Harris was always quick to defend her spending habits by saying that she was "working my heart out for the state of Florida."

She was known to be a hard worker and fiercely loyal to the Republican party. Because of this, while carrying out her duties as secretary of state, she became a co-chairperson for George W. Bush's Florida election campaign. If this raised the question of conflict of interest, or even of impropriety, the issue remained more or less dormant until the 2000 election. So did the issue of Harris, who was married to a man named Anders Ebbeson, being a close confidante of Governor Jeb Bush. Both Harris and Governor Bush were relatively minor players on the national scene — until November 7, when the presidential election went awry in their state.

As a campaign chair for George W. Bush, Harris had made a real commitment to his capturing the White House. During the primary season, she'd braved ice, snow, and sub-freezing New Hampshire temperatures to travel north and work for her candidate. In her home state of Florida, she'd toured the Panhandle in a motor home, asking voters to put a Republican in the Oval Office and urging Democrats to switch parties. No attempt was made to hide her sympathies: Al Gore and his ilk had to be defeated come November. This would not only be best for the country's future, but there was a lot of talk around Florida that it might also ensure her political future as well. Months before the election, she'd indicated to a newspaper reporter that if she were to take a job with the Bush administration, it would have to be something she was genuinely interested in. The scuttlebutt floating around Tallahassee was that if Bush succeeded in besting Gore, she was most likely in line for an ambassadorship.

None of this seemed of much significance until several days after the 2000 election, when the question of who would be the next American president moved into a bizarre state of irresolution. A quick machine count of the votes had given the race to Bush by only about 300 ballots, but there were tens of thousands of other ballots, many from heavily Democratic areas, that the machines had discarded. What should be done with these votes? Would hand counting them turn the election in Gore's favor? By mid-November, as had happened in so many other large events in the country's recent past, teams of lawyers on both sides flew down to Florida, charged into court, and began arguing two diametrically opposite points of view.

The Democratic position was that the hanging chads on the

rejected punch cards clearly established voter intent, so these cards had to be added to the final count. If they were counted, the Gore attorneys believed, the election would go to their man. Their logic was based on a simple numbers game. Punch cards had been used in the overwhelmingly Democratic Broward County, which had voted more than two-to-one for Gore and had had about 6,600 undervotes. The cards had also been employed in the largely black areas of Miami-Dade County; African-Americans had voted for Gore at about a ten-to-one ratio, and this county had had around 9,000 undervotes. If these same figures held up in the uncounted ballots, Gore's attorneys argued, the vice-president would become the obvious winner.

The Republican viewpoint was that no one could adequately decide a voter's intent by simply looking at the cards, therefore all of these ballots had to be left out of the election results. From the very beginning of this discussion, Bush's people did not want the cards handled or closely examined. Their argument implied that the cards were quite delicate and that further contact with them could change the way the voters had left them, perhaps even knock out more chads. It was unfortunate, their lawyers indicated, that so many people in Florida had mistakenly marked or ruined their ballots, but human error was a factor in all events and just had to be accepted. What they didn't say — but implied — was that more minority voters and Democrats had bungled their ballots than Republicans because the latter were better educated and more sophisticated at the polls.

At stake in this great legal debate were two things. The first was a fair resolution of the election conflict. Whoever got the most votes in Florida should be declared the winner. The second issue, which was just as important, was that the situation be dealt with in an even-handed fashion and that the rule of law prevailed. In recent years, many Americans had felt that the law had been demeaned and devalued, if not trampled upon. This was a chance to rectify that perception on a very grand scale. The matter was no longer the fate of a few criminal defendants but the value and meaning behind the 100 million votes that had been cast for president.

As the attorneys rushed into court and began launching their extremely entangled legal arguments, something more reassuring was going on in South Florida. The citizenry was actually looking at the evidence in this case. Local efforts were already underway to hand count the disputed ballots in Miami-Dade, Broward, and Palm Beach counties. Through this tedious, time-consuming process, average folks were working overtime at the ground level of democracy, studying the cards and groping toward a solution. They were painstakingly trying to discern who voters had cast their ballots for and who'd really won the most significant election in the United States this past November. There was something very comforting about turning on one's television and watching people, who were not being paid large sums of money to take up absolute positions in court-rooms, engage in an activity that was much more real. They were gently handling and carefully eyeing the punch cards — the thin, rectangular pieces of paper that were supposed to allow Americans to transfer power peacefully and fairly from one group of politicians to the next.

The cards stood as an alternative to bloodshed and violent coups. They symbolized the social contract between a country's right to choose its leadership and the leaders' obligation to honor that choice. They made all people, at least when in the voting booth, equal. Their function was crucial to how our system of government functioned. Violate or disregard these pieces of paper and the foundations of the nation could begin to shift. The agreements made more than two centuries ago by the Founding Fathers could suddenly be called into question.

Questions this large were being talked about everywhere as the citizens of Florida sat side-by-side at tables counting these machine-rejected ballots. The meaning of our democracy was, in some sense, in these cards.

Now it was up to Katherine Harris to make the next move. As Florida's secretary of state, she had a choice. She could either follow the absolute letter of the law and demand that all Florida counties deliver their final vote tallies by Tuesday, November 14, at 5 p.m. Or she could play a non-partisan role and wait until another solution could be found. Because of the time required to hand count the cards, it was not possible to do a full tabulation of them by this deadline. If Harris chose to meet that deadline anyway, she would have to disregard the work being done by those examining the hanging chads and counting the ballots. She would have to dismiss all the evidence in those stacks of cards and go with the machine count. If she did that, she would, in effect, give the election to George W. Bush and certify him as the next President. What would Harris do now? Would she act as a co-chair for the Bush campaign in Florida or see herself and her job as part of a much larger and more complicated national dilemma, which would take some time to resolve?

She plowed ahead and ordered the counties to turn in their vote tallies by the Tuesday deadline or risk being ignored. Her statement justifying this action read: "I have decided it is my duty under Florida law to exercise my discretion in denying these requested amendments [for hand recounts]. The reasons given in their requests are insufficient to warrant waiver of the unambiguous filing deadline imposed by the Florida legislature.

"I have communicated this decision with these counties, in letters detailing the criteria I used in making my judgments and the application of these criteria to the stated circumstances...

"Because it is my determination that no amendments to the official returns now on file at the Department of State are warranted, the state Elections Canvassing Commission, acting in its normal and usual manner, has certified the results of Tuesday's election in Florida, including the presidential election...

"As I've previously indicated, I expect that after the receipt, tabulation and certification of the overseas ballots by the counties, the state Elections Canvassing Commission will finally certify the presidential election in Florida on Saturday...."

Harris's decision set the flame to what was already an extremely volatile mix. A figurehead in the George W. Bush election machine and a political and personal associate of Jeb Bush had now decided whose ballot counted and whose did not. Hanging chads and voter intent were non-issues to the secretary of state, the chief elections official in Florida. If she had her way, it would not be the hundred million Americans freely casting their ballots who'd chosen the next President of the United States, but Katherine Harris from Sarasota.

38

Harris's orders immediately raised the stakes and the tension, not just in Florida but all across the nation. Former U.S. Secretary of State Warren Christopher, who'd come to South Florida to monitor the recount for Al Gore, now accused Harris of blatant partisanship. While spelling out her obvious political ties and declaring that she'd long been a supporter of Gov. Jeb Bush and "quite active" in the Bush presidential campaign, Christopher underlined what had become clear to many people: her decisions appeared not to "ensure that the voices of the voters will be heard" but to create a particular election result.

"I don't see her working with her counties to resolve this," Florida Democratic Party spokesman Tony Welch told the *Miami Herald*. "I see her working with the Bush people to resolve this."

Harris's actions also heightened the legal conflict, which very quickly made its way to the Florida Supreme Court. On Wednesday, November 15, the court overruled Harris and ordered that the hand recount continue. At the time, this appeared to be a defining moment in terms of how the matter would play itself out. Elections disputes were generally regarded as state, not federal issues, and Florida's highest court had just ruled in favor of keeping its citizens busy counting the voting cards.

But Harris and the Republican attorneys held to their fundamental strategy, which appeared to have been in place right from the start. They did not want the cards tabulated, because releasing the results of a manual counting and sharing this information with the voters "will neither advance the process nor serve the interests of public policy." In other words, voters did not have a right to know what these cards revealed. The Republican side, which in many instances promoted states' rights over the intrusion of the U.S. government, was also quick to escalate the legal fight to the federal level. While trying to stop the hand counting, George W. Bush's lawyers told a federal judge that "If Defendants' threatened manual recount occurs . . . and a changed result happens to occur (however unlikely), the tainted result will be broadcast to the nation. Any such taint...will interfere with the orderly transition of constitutional government."

It was a very curious argument — both paternalistic and condescending. It was also strangely reminiscent of the behavior of the media and certain legal jurisdictions in some recent high-profile criminal cases. In effect the Republicans were saying: "We know what happened and what the truth is and we don't want to hear or explore anything else."

U.S. District Judge Donald Middlebrooks denied the Bush request and ruled that the count could continue.

"The mere possibility," the judge wrote, "that the eventual result of the challenged manual recounts will be to envelop the president-elect in a cloud of illegitimacy does not justify enjoining the current manual recount processes. Central to our democratic process as well as our Constitution is the belief that open and transparent government, whenever possible, best serves the public interest. Nowhere can the public dissemination of truth be more vital than in the election procedures for determining the next presidency."

Judge Middlebrooks laid bare the struggle around the election. Were votes to be counted or not? Were we a democracy in name only or a democracy that could rise to the challenge during a time of confusion and doubt? Would we let the process resolve itself peacefully and patiently or force it to an ugly conclusion?

In Palm Beach and Broward counties, the hand counting went forward by the local canvassing boards. Katherine Harris was now in the potentially embarrassing position of having a manual count of the voter cards directly contradict the numbers that she'd claimed were final in her certification of George W. Bush as the winner in Florida. On the other side of legal debate, Al Gore's people felt that with the overturning of Harris's actions, the biggest hurdle to a Democratic victory had just been removed. It was simply a matter of examining the cards, Gore's advisers believed, and adding up the numbers. The most complex election in U.S. history, they were confident, was about to be decided in their favor. What they didn't realize was that a new kind of American history was about to be made.

As the hand counting continued, the Republican Party stepped up its attacks on this process on every front. In Florida, they unleashed relentless criticism of the recount procedures being used in Fort Lauderdale and West Palm Beach. While ballot counters worked long hours and labored under court orders and extreme pressure to determine who'd won the election, GOP spokespeople accused them of excessively handling the voting cards, of dropping and stepping on them, and even of using them as fans, causing more chads to dislodge and fall out (the cards were far more flexible, resilient, and stronger than these accusations indicated they were; in many cases, the difficulty was not that the chads came out too easily but that they didn't come out at all). The manual counters were hardly in a position to attempt anything suspect with the cards. They were not only doing their work in front of observers, reporters, and uniformed sheriff's deputies with guns, but the whole world, via television, was watching them handle the ballots and looking for any reason to find them at fault.

In the Miami-Dade Government Center, where hand counting was being conducted, Republican supporters staged a protest following the county elections' officials decision to move the recount operation to a closed-off area on the nineteenth floor of County Hall. Republicans held a sit-in, while chanting and banging on windows and doors. During the protest, according to Democratic observers, several people were threatened, kicked or punched. The manual counting soon stopped. What state and federal courts had insisted should go forward had now apparently been interrupted by an unruly gang. Half a dozen Democratic members of Congress now called for an investigation into allegations of intimidation of the Miami-Dade canvassing board. Joseph Lieberman, the Democratic vice-presidential candidate, made the strongest charge of all, saying that "orchestrated demonstrations" in Miami had resulted in a halt to the hand count.

"This is a time," he said, "to honor the rule of law, not surrender to the rule of the mob."

But each day, in scenes that conjured up the hysteria surrounding the recent furor in Miami over Elian Gonzalez, the conflict intensified. A brick connected to a sign proclaiming "We will not tolerate any illegal government" was thrown through a window of the Broward County Democratic Party headquarters. Then reports surfaced that the Republican National Committee had paid for protesters to travel to Florida as partisan observers but asked them to stay on as demonstrators.

At a news conference, Democratic Congressmen Alcee Hastings of South Florida and Jerrold Nadler of New York contended that the Miami canvassing board had stopped their hand counting after caving in to the Republican protesters. Nadler read from a column in the *Wall Street Journal* by Paul Gigot, which suggested that the demonstration at the Miami-Dade Government Center had not been completely spontaneous but may have been sponsored by Republican congressman John Sweeney from New York. Republican leaders insisted that the protests were unplanned, but the *Journal* column pointed out that the demonstrators themselves had said that 1,000 Cuban-American Republicans had been bused to County Hall as an implied threat to two board members, who were non-Hispanic judges.

"Ladies and gentlemen," Nadler said at the news conference, "I have never called anything this before, but the whiff of fascism is in the air. We have a Republican rent-a-gang led by a Republican from New York who says, `Shut it down,' not by a writ, not by a legal decision, but by intimidation. That is intolerable."

A few days later, with anger still very high in South Florida and recounts taking place around the state, Bush appeared on national television claiming victory for himself, although the Democrats continued to challenge this outcome in court. Bush now asked Gore to give up his election battle and concede defeat.

"This has been a hard-fought election, a healthy contest for American democracy," the Texas governor said from Austin. "But now that the votes are counted, it is time for the votes to count...

"Until Florida's votes were certified, the vice president was working to represent the interests of those who supported him. I didn't agree with his call for additional recounts, but I respected his decision to fight until the votes were finally certified. Now that they are certified, we enter a different phase. If the vice president chooses to go forward he is filing a contest to the outcome of the election, and that is not the best route for America."

The best route for America, in Bush's opinion, was not to listen to the rulings of the Florida Supreme Court or to that of a federal court, but to follow the orders of Katherine Harris. The best route was to ignore the disputed ballots, the hand counting, and the exhausting work being done by those studying the punch cards and their hanging chads. Bush went on to tell the country that his running mate, Dick Cheney, who'd just suffered a mild heart attack, would be leading his transition team now that he was taking over the White House, while Andrew Card would serve as his chief of staff. Both men had been Cabinet secretaries in his father's administration.

"The last nineteen days," George W. Bush announced to the nation without a sliver of irony, "have been extraordinary ones. As our nation watched, we were all reminded on a daily basis of the importance of each and every vote."

Despite Bush's proclamations, there was still the sticky legal matter of the Florida Supreme Court's decision to let the hand-counting continue until the process was complete and the cards themselves determined who'd won the state. These things were of no consequence to the Bush public relations team. Led by James Baker, who'd been Secretary of State in George Bush senior's administration, that team had since early November scorned the notion of more vote counting as a completely unnecessary exercise. But neither Baker's patrician attitude nor his opinions had prevented the courts from moving the hand count forward. The hard fact remained: by late November, no one had yet won the election.

Faced with this reality, Bush's attorneys took the next inevitable step. They appealed to the U. S. Supreme Court, asking it, in effect, to intervene and stop the manual counting of ballots so that George W. Bush could be named the winner. The Republicans felt certain that although they'd failed with Florida's highest court, they would succeed in Washington, D.C. For one thing, a few years earlier they'd seen the U.S. Supreme court's willingness to rule against Democrat Bill Clinton in his civil suit with Paula Jones. For another, the GOP had friends on this particular bench, and some people who were closer than friends. As President, George Bush senior had appointed Clarence Thomas to the U.S. Supreme Court. Justice Thomas's wife worked at the conservative Heritage Foundation, and in that capacity she'd lately been vetting the resumes of those seeking positions in a new George W. Bush administration. Justice Antonin Scalia, who would prove to be Gore's strongest opponent in the legal war set off by the election, had two sons employed at law firms that were helping the Bush team in its post-election struggle. *The Wall Street Journal* reported that Justice Sandra Day O'Connor's husband had said at an election night party that his wife, who was a breast cancer survivor, wanted to retire from the Court but would be hesitant to leave if a Democrat became the next president and was able to choose her successor. O'Connor had been vetted for her current position on the Court by none other than the man now leading the Republican charge to end the re-counting and hand the White House to Bush: James Baker.

The Founding Fathers had given the nine Supreme Court justices their jobs for life, precisely because they'd wanted them to be as non-partisan as possible when important issues were in front of them, and the nation. The most significant one in a long time now came before the court on Monday, December 4, when it began considering arguments for both sides, and then clearly tilted in the Republican direction. Nearly four weeks after the election, the Court ruled that it found "considerable uncertainty as to the precise grounds for the [Florida Supreme Court] decision...It is fundamental that state courts be left free and unfettered by us in interpreting their state constitutions. But it is equally important that ambiguous or obscure adjudications by state courts do not stand as barriers to a determination by this Court...The judgment of the Supreme Court of Florida is therefore vacated..."

As this order came down, the hand counting was again halted and precious days evaporated. While more legal arguments flew back and forth in a variety of jurisdictions, the Republicans continued to insist that there simply wasn't enough time left for the dispute to be resolved in any reasonable manner, except for the Democrats to surrender. December 12 was the next deadline looming for all the electoral votes to be submitted for a final count. On December 8, the Florida Supreme Court stood its ground and ruled for more manual counting of the cards in an effort to try to meet this deadline. Following its decision, the Florida justices released this statement:

"By a vote of 4-3, the majority of the court has reversed the decision of the trial court in part. It has further ordered that the Circuit Court of the 2nd Judicial Circuit here in Tallahassee shall immediately begin a manual recount of the approximately 9,000 Miami-Dade ballots that registered undervotes.

"In addition, the Circuit Court shall enter orders ensuring the inclusion of the additional 215 legal votes for Vice President Gore in Palm Beach County and the 168 additional legal votes from Miami-Dade County.

"In addition, the Circuit Court shall order a manual recount of all undervotes in any Florida county where such a recount has not yet occurred.

"Because time is of the essence, the recount shall commence immediately. In tabulating what constitutes a legal vote, the standard to be used is the one provided by the Legislature, 'a vote shall be counted where there is a clear indication of the intent of the voter.'"

As the legal battles unfolded and George W. Bush named himself the next president, the *Miami Herald* analyzed the "intent of the voter" to the largest and deepest degree possible thus far. The paper uncovered not only some very intriguing statistics, but found a remarkable consistency in where the bulk of the voting troubles had occurred. On December 3, the paper began its report by describing how it had commissioned a study of the voting patterns in each of the state's 5,885 precincts. The results of this survey "suggests that Florida likely would have gone to Al Gore — by a slim 23,000 votes — rather than George W. Bush, the officially certified victor by the wispy margin of 537."

The *Herald* examined precinct results from each of the state's 67 counties, where at least 185,000 ballots had been discarded either as undervotes or overvotes. Historically, the number of rejected Florida votes was around two percent, but in 2000 that figure may almost have doubled. In the *Herald's* study, these uncounted ballots were assigned to the candidates in the same proportion that they'd received in each precinct. Under this system, Bush would have received about 78,000, or 42 percent, of the uncounted votes, while Gore would have received around 103,000 or 56 percent. The other 4,000 would have gone to the minor candidates.

More important than the *Herald's* projection about the Florida winner were the hard numbers the paper turned up. For example, voters in Democratic precincts had had a much greater chance of having their ballots rejected by vote-counting machines. In precincts won by Bush, one of every 40 ballots was invalidated, but in those won by Gore, one of every 27 ballots was tossed aside. In the 51 precincts in which more than 20 percent of the ballots were rejected, 45 of them (or 88 per cent)

used punch cards. Of the 336 precincts in which more than 10 percent were rejected, 277 (or 78 per cent) used punch cards.

For the 43 counties using optical voting systems, the overall rejection rate was 1.4 percent. For the 24 punch-card counties, the overall rejection rate was 3.9 percent. This meant that voters in the punch-card counties, which included heavily Democratic areas like Broward and Palm Beach, were almost three times as likely to have their ballots rejected as those in optical counties.

In response to this report, a Bush spokesman named Tucker Eskew called the *Herald's* analysis "hocus-pocus" and "statistical voodoo."

What wasn't statistical voodoo was that the biggest problems with discarded ballots came in mostly-minority, low-income precincts statewide — precincts that voted Democratic and tended to use the punch card system. The numbers bore all this out. The perforated cards had played a key role in the 2000 election.

The great bulk of the punch cards employed in Miami-Dade and Broward counties had come from a company called Election Systems and Software, based in Omaha, Nebraska. As the world's largest election management company, ES&S designed, developed, manufactured, and sold integrated hardware, software, and "service solutions" to all phases of the election/voting process. These services included the management

299

of ballot production, voter registration, election programming, counting and tabulation of votes, warehousing and delivery, plus reporting election results. In 2000 alone, ES&S managed over 5,700 elections. With thirty-five years in the business, the company promoted itself as the most experienced in the industry.

In one incarnation or another, the punch card manufacturing side of ES&S had been around for a long time, but under different names and different leadership. In November 1997, the company known as ES&S had come into existence through the combining of two other big election outfits: Business Records Corporation and American Information Systems. The newly-formed ES&S was a privately-held enterprise with nine satellite offices around the nation. It sold products in forty-nine states and to more than 2,200 of the 3,156 local U.S. jurisdictions. It also sold voter registration systems to 350 American locales and punch card systems to many major U.S. metropolitan areas, including Los Angeles, Houston, Kansas City, St. Louis, and San Diego. It had an international presence in Guam, the Republic of Venezuela, Canada, the Republic of Palau, and parts of the Philippines. Its systems counted around 100 million votes a year and its overall impact on the market in recent years had led some state elections officials to describe ES&S (not always favorably) as a "monopoly."

In its literature, ES&S said that its products met the most rigorous guidelines for excellence. Those products were tested by Wyle Laboratories in Huntsville, Alabama, "an Independent Testing Authority, certified to meet or exceed the standards of the U.S. Federal Election Commission (FEC) with respect to accuracy and security, and proven through use in thousands of actual elections."

Despite its enormous reach and clout both nationally and abroad, immediately following the November 2000 election ES&S was quick to point out that it had had little involvement in the problems that were surfacing in Florida. On November 9, two days after the polls closed, the ES&S website posted a press release stating that the corporation "is proud to have 23 of 67 counties in Florida as clients. These clients represent approximately 15% of the precincts statewide. Palm Beach and Miami-Dade counties are not users of ES&S systems."

This last sentence, which remained up on the site for months, was not quite accurate. According to John Clouser, an administrative officer in the elections department of Miami-Dade County, his supervisor, David Leahy, had in fact ordered about four million voter cards from ES&S for the 2000 general election. These cards were used throughout the county, which held one of the largest minority populations in Florida. As the *Miami Herald* had uncovered in its recent post-election analysis, people voting in Democratic strongholds had stood a far greater chance of seeing their ballots rejected than those voting in predominantly Republican areas.

Miami-Dade's hanging chad problem was at the heart of

the disputed election battle. So were Broward County's thousands of hanging or dimpled chads, which were also commonplace on the voter cards; the dimpled perforations had been poked but they'd stretched under pressure instead of breaking through. In addition to selling Miami-Dade four million voter cards, ES&S had sold 1.5 million cards to Broward County. While Florida counties ordered cards separately from ES&S, I'd been told by Broward officials that the relevant counties dealt with the company via what was known as a SPOC — a Single Point of Contact, who passed election information back and forth from the state to the plant in Texas. In Florida, the SPOC was Larry Rose, based in Sarasota, the Republican-dominated home turf of Secretary of State Katherine Harris.

For years, Jane Carroll, Broward County's elections supervisor, had been trying to get rid of the punch card system, convinced that it was mistake-prone and no longer the best available alternative. Because newer systems cost more money, Broward had repeatedly refused to replace the old way of doing things. In mid-1999, Mary Womack, who worked under Carroll, had sent out a purchase order for the million and a half ES&S cards to a plant in Addison, Texas, a suburb of Dallas. ES&S had significantly underbid its primary competitor, Sequoia Pacific of Exeter, California, for this job, by about five dollars per thousand ordered. Sequoia Pacific had earlier sold the county some cards and these leftovers were being called into action in the 2000 races (a push to bring out black voters in Florida would cause a surge in African-Americans going to the polls that November; estimates said that the black vote in Florida rose by five per cent over what it had been in 1996, and nine out of ten of these voters selected Gore over Bush).

Since 1977, the ES&S factory in Addison, under various owners, had been producing punch cards. The manufacturing site, a low gray building in an industrial park, held about fifty employees. This was the only such plant operated by ES&S and in fiscal 2000 it had churned out about 78 million cards to be utilized in elections across the country and around the world. ES&S had by now captured roughly three-fourths of the punch card market while Sequoia Pacific sold to much of the other one-fourth. A smaller company named Global was a third competitor.

The Addison plant was run by a man named Hank Foster who'd been in this field for decades. Workers hauled big rolls of paper into the plant and stored them in a warehouse-like waiting area. Then the rolls were brought onto the floor of the plant and long strips of paper, called "cheese," were unraveled from them and fed into an assembly line process. Machines cut the paper into rectangular voting cards, printed them with the dark ink that designated each perforation, and then a fast-revolving stamping wheel made tiny indentations (or scores) into the face of each card. Broward county cards, for example, held 228 perforations. The cards for Miami-Dade offered more election choices — 312. The stamping wheel was calibrated very precisely for making the scores.

As Hank Foster once put it when referring to his plant, "We live in a one/five-thousandths-inch world."

This remark suggested that a change of only one/five-thousandths of an inch in the manufacturing process could affect the cards.

A number of individuals who worked at this location ran tests on the cards to see if they met industry specifications. Strain gages were employed to measure the chads' "bursting density" (the pressure needed to pop out the perforations). In the 1960s, IBM had held the patents on these kinds of punch cards and established standards for how they were supposed to operate. The acceptable range for bursting density was between 120 grams (according to a company spokesman for ES&S) or 150 grams (according to another spokesman for Sequoia Pacific) and 350 grams. A pound had 454 grams, so the normal working parameters fell in between roughly one-third to three-quarters of a pound. These figures had also been accepted by the American National Standards Institute.

ES&S literature stated that its products were tested at a lab in Alabama for quality control, but Hank Foster has said that the punch card tests were done on site at his plant. His people examined them throughout the day, keeping records of the manufacturing details for each batch of cards sent to every locale around the nation, right down to the precinct.

The *Miami Herald*'s analysis of the Florida vote and the concept that Al Gore would win the election if all the votes were counted was published and on the record before the U.S. Supreme Court ruled that the Florida counties had to stop their examination of the ballots. But the Court, as the nation would learn soon enough, had its own agenda, and that did not include taking these numbers into account.

39

On Thursday, December 7, the federal judiciary sent down another ruling giving the Florida courts the power to settle their own election disputes. The 11th U.S. Circuit Court of Appeals rejected George W. Bush's request to halt the hand recounts already sanctioned by the Florida Supreme Court. Bush, the judges asserted, had failed to prove that he was imminently harmed by recounts. Then the following day, in what was widely called a "bombshell decision," the Florida Supreme Court ordered a last-minute hand count of thousands of ballots from every county in the state. After further ordering that 168 votes from Miami-Dade County and 215 votes from Palm Beach County be added to Gore's total, Bush's lead in Florida fell to only 154 votes.

In making this decision, the Florida justices' majority opinion cited state law, the U.S. Constitution, legislative intent, and judicial precedent, all of which they felt forced a mandatory hand count of the contested ballots. The opinion went on to say that "although the time constraints are limited, we must do everything required by law to ensure that legal votes that have not been counted are included in the final election results...This presidential election has demonstrated the vulnerability of what we believe to be a bedrock principle of democracy: that every vote counts."

Realizing that larger questions were at stake in Florida, the majority's opinion cited a 1997 state House of Representatives election reform committee that had studied election contests and recounts. The citation read, "If the voter cannot be assured of an accurate vote count, or an election unspoiled by fraud, they will not have faith in other parts of the political process...Only by examining the contested ballots, which are evidence in the election contest, can a meaningful and final determination in this election contest be made."

"Bedrock principle" was the key phrase. In taking these actions, the court had decided to stand on principle and the rights of individual voters. As a result, about 60,000 "under-votes" would now be subject to re-examination. Yet all of the vote recounting and court challenges still had to end by December 12, when Florida's electors were due to be chosen. The hand count was to commence at once and to proceed at a furious pace.

Before the process could get started, Bush's lawyers appealed the ruling to the U.S. Supreme Court and petitioned Atlanta's Circuit Court of Appeals, asking that the counting be stopped. The Bush team had now made its ultimate maneuver and revealed its full strategy. It would do everything possible to prevent the scrutinizing and tallying of these voting cards, while insisting that the nation's highest court decide the legal issue once and for all. Neither the election numbers nor the Florida Supreme Court were moving in the Republicans' direction, but they were convinced that when it mattered most, the justices of the U.S. Supreme Court, or at least a majority of them, would find for the Bush cause.

They were right. The nation's highest court now stayed Florida's manual recount, ending it as the Bush lead was dropping to 193 votes. The Court's announcement sent waves of anger and dismay — or waves of joy and celebration — throughout Florida and across the nation. In Tampa, pandemonium broke out at election headquarters, where GOP partisans stood together in groups and grinned at the news on the TV screens. "Bush! Bush! Bush!" they shouted while clapping their hands in unison. Gore supporters knew that the final showdown was coming soon.

Two days later, on Monday, December 11, both sides presented their last arguments to the U.S. Supreme Court. While these were being heard in Washington, D.C., in Tallahassee a Republican-dominated House committee essentially defied its own state Supreme Court and voted 5-2 for a resolution giving Florida's twenty-five electors to George W. Bush. In the nation's capitol, the arguments went on, with the high court spending 90 minutes questioning the lawyers for both Bush and Gore. The justices had inquiries about determining voter intent by looking at the discarded ballots, about using uniform standards for counting the votes, and, if uniform standards could not be found, about the possibility of equal protection violations. Justice Ruth Bader Ginsburg, who was on the record as opposing the recount suspension, wondered aloud why the nation's highest court should overrule the Florida Supreme Court's interpretation of state law and "say what the Florida law is."

As the justices asked questions, protesters gathered at the base of the Supreme Court steps, some of them chanting "count the votes," while others tried to shout them down. When the high court session ended, the demonstrators continued to wave signs and yell, but the justices quietly left the bench without offering a timetable for reaching their decision. All of the appeals were now finished and all of the briefs had been filed. The arguing was done. The hand counting had ceased for the moment. The choice for the next American president was now in the hands of nine people instead of 100 million.

The Court's decision came the following evening at about ten p.m. Eastern Standard Time. By a 5-4 margin, the justices reversed the Florida ruling, gave the victory to George W. Bush, and ended Al Gore's long fight for the White House. With no acceptable options left, the vice-president quickly conceded. He'd been defeated not at the polls but by the bench. The Court's majority opinion said that the Florida recount violated constitutional guarantees of equal protection and that not enough time remained to conduct a new recount (it did not address how much time had been wasted by the legal moves that kept starting and stopping the hand counting process). The decision was released on Tuesday, December 12, exactly five weeks after the voting booths had closed. The election was finally over.

"It is obvious," the court's majority wrote, "that the recount cannot be conducted in compliance with the requirements of equal protection and due process without substantial additional work."

"Substantial additional work" was no longer an alternative in deciding who would be the next American president. Embracing a theory put forward by Bush's lawyers, Chief Justice William Rehnquist, along with Justice Scalia and Justice Thomas, said that voters using punch-card ballots were instructed to punch clearly through the cards and should be required to follow those instructions. Reduced to its ultimate simplicity, this meant that the widespread voter problems in Florida, which had negated around four per cent of the ballots, were caused by the voters themselves. About 200,000 Florida voters had made irreversible mistakes. Case closed. Justices Sandra Day O'Connor and Anthony Kennedy had joined Justices Rehnquist, Scalia, and Thomas in forming the majority opinion. For the first time since 1888, when Benjamin Harrison had lost the national popular vote but won the state electoral contest, a president would not be chosen by the majority will of the people. Reaction to the Supreme Court's decision was swift and harsh.

Rep. Jesse Jackson Jr., D-Ill., while telling fellow Democrats to accept the Court's ruling, added that he disagreed with it "with every bone in my body and every ounce of moral strength in my soul." He then used language virtually unheard of from a sitting United States Representative. He called the high court "a willing tool of the Bush campaign" and said that it had "orchestrated a questionable 'velvet legal coup.'" Other commentators studied the ruling and would soon second Rep. Jackson's opinion.

George W. Bush's attorneys had been very savvy in their hunches and their legal maneuvers, by making the discarded Florida votes not a matter of state law, but of national judicial review. A man who'd lost the popular vote by more than half a million ballots and likely would have lost Florida after a full recount of its votes had now been given the Oval Office by five justices. The other four justices were not at all pleased with this outcome. The Court always tried to maintain a balanced and polite tone, but that slipped away with the resolution of the 2000 election. The division and rancor that had infected so much of the media, the legal system and the entire country in recent years now flowed down from the highest bench and out into the nation's periodicals and airwaves. The uncivil war had infiltrated the last bastion of decorum and fairness in the nation.

The four justices who'd voted to continue the hand counting could not hide their anger and bitterness at what the five others had done. In his bitingly-worded dissent, Justice John Paul Stevens, who had been appointed by a Republican President, Gerald Ford, called the Bush legal appeal a "federal assault" on Florida's state laws.

"Time," he wrote in an opinion that was joined by Justices Ginsburg and Stephen Breyer, "will one day heal the wound to [the electoral] confidence that will be inflicted by today's decision... One thing, however, is certain. Although we may never know with complete certainty the identity of the winner of this year's presidential election, the identity of the loser is perfectly clear. It is the nation's confidence in the judge as an impartial guardian of the rule of law."

Justice Stevens went on to say that the Court's decision "can only lend credence to the most cynical appraisal of the work of judges throughout the land."

The fourth dissenter, Justice David Souter, stated that "there is no justification for denying the State the opportunity to try to count all the disputed ballots now."

In her opinion, Justice Ginsburg wrote, "I dissent," and she did not soften her voice by adding the customary "respectfully." She noted that a majority opinion in this case, written by Chief Justice Rehnquist and joined by Justices Scalia and Thomas, had cited Supreme Court decisions involving equal protection issues from America's civil rights era. Those decisions had once overturned state court rulings in the South and helped minority citizens gain their rights — including the right to vote. In commenting on how the Court had used these same decisions to act in this case and shut down the counting of votes, Justice Ginsburg scathingly wrote, "The Florida Supreme Court concluded that counting every legal vote was the overriding concern of the Florida Legislature when it enacted the State's Election Code. The court surely should not be bracketed with state high courts of the Jim Crow South."

Justice Stevens added that the December 12 deadline to end the vote-counting, which the Court's majority had relied upon to stop the recount, was not an absolute deadline. Following the 1960 presidential election, he pointed out, a contested slate of voters from Hawaii had not been appointed until January 4, 1961.

"In the interest of finality, however," he wrote, "the majority effectively orders the disenfranchisement of an unknown number of voters whose ballots reveal their intent — and are therefore legal votes under state law — but were for some reason rejected by ballot-counting machines."

Yet it was Justice Breyer who put it most simply and succinctly: "The court was wrong to take this case. It was wrong to grant a stay. It should now vacate that stay and permit the Florida Supreme Court to decide whether the recount should resume."

The fallout from the ruling had just begun. The wounds were only starting to open and fester. People who had not been motivated to take any political action or have any social involvement for years or even decades were suddenly mobilized to protest the resolution of the election and the disregarding of the Florida votes. Some wrote letters to papers and magazines. Some marched in the streets. Some planned to travel to Washington, D.C., to demonstrate against the inauguration of George W. Bush on January 20. Many sent e-mails encouraging others to work against the new administration and to fight some of its Cabinet nominees. Countless citizens were now trying to organize online, as the Million Mom March leaders had successfully done the previous spring in their rallies supporting gun control.

The Internet, which had been used so often in recent times to denigrate individuals or to fume about criminal cases and personal sexual choices, was now filled with people and groups ready to protest the Supreme Court decision and the incoming Bush team, which they regarded as illegitimate. A tone and a passion that had been missing from American life for a long time — widespread indignation over real political matters — was back in play. The country's majority population had seen its votes tossed aside by the decision of five people with unlimited power. There was no recourse but to protest. The underlying battle was at last coming to the surface. A pulse had been generated and there was no predicting where it might lead.

40

Two days after the Supreme Court's decision, the U.S. Commission on Civil Rights, a bipartisan investigative agency, decided to hold hearings in Florida on allegations of voter irregularities in the just-completed election. Mary Frances Berry, chairwoman of the Washington, D.C.-based panel, said that the inquiry would try to determine if eligible persons were denied the right to vote and if their votes were properly counted. As this agency announced its mission, civil rights leaders lambasted the high court's decision, echoing Justice Ginsburg in her dissent. They decried the Court's use of the U.S. Constitution's equal protection clause, designed to protect African-Americans against discrimination, to secure George W. Bush's victory. They saw this as not only a bad legal precedent but an historical slap to the thousands of blacks who had died for the right to vote.

The Court's decision, instead of putting the conflict to rest, was an instant catalyst for deepening it. Long-dormant coalitions of liberals and progressives, including women's groups, environmentalists, gays, and civil rights organizations, were now coming together to fight back. Some very old issues — race, voting rights, and the disenfranchisement of minority Americans — were back in the headlines. In Tallahassee, hundreds of Democrats, union members, and other activists protested the Supreme Court ruling, while promising rallies around the nation. On January 10, 2001, the NAACP and five other groups went to U.S. District Court in Miami in order to end certain voting practices in Florida. Their lawsuit asked a federal judge to get rid of all punch card systems in all the counties, to fix the state's method of purging voter lists, and to monitor elections in Florida for the next decade. It also named as defendants Katherine Harris and Clay Roberts, the state's elections chief, as well as election supervisors from Broward and Miami-Dade counties.

"The nation...and the civil rights community," said Dennis Hayes, the NAACP general counsel, "was appalled at what appeared to be an absolute disrespect of the right to vote of persons of color."

Perhaps the most penetrating analysis of the 2000 election came from an old-line liberal from the Kennedy White House days, John Kenneth Galbraith, writing in the *Texas Observer*. The Supreme Court's decision to give the highest office in America to George W. Bush, he contended, had not merely changed the political direction of the country, but had in fact altered our form of government. Until now, Galbraith said, that form had been correctly known as "constitutional republicanism." He dubbed our new government "corporate democracy," in which a Board of Directors (in this case, the U.S. Supreme Court) selected the Chief Executive Officer (or President). Under this system, the company's shareholders (or 100 million voters)

had only symbolic power because management held a majority of the proxies. While the new situation may appear somewhat democratic, Galbraith wrote, it really isn't, because the CEO and the Board would never allow themselves to lose on any important issue.

"The Supreme Court," he went on, "clarified this in a way that the Florida courts could not have. The media have accepted it, for it is the form of government to which they are already professionally accustomed. And the shameless attitude of the George W. Bush high command merely illustrates, in unusually visible fashion, the prevalent ethical system of corporate life."

Don't forget what happened here, was Galbraith's explicit message, and he sent it forth with a commitment that had not been heard on the American left since well before Rush Limbaugh had ascended in the national media and set the political tone that greeted the Clinton administration.

For the past eight years the politics of meanness had been sniping at Bill Clinton and those who worked for him, including his vice-president, Al Gore. During those eight years, Clinton's enemies had refused to accept his leadership or his role as the head of the country or his many achievements in office. Beginning with the Ken Starr investigation of the Clintons in the mid-'90s, and culminating with the 1998 impeachment of the president, the Republicans had unsuccessfully tried to wrest power from the Democrats through ways other than the ballot box. Now they had done so, and with the support of the most august body of men and women in the United States. Like U.S. Representative Jesse Jackson Jr., Galbraith also implied that the Supreme Court decision had effectively supported a coup.

Some commentators went even further, hinting that a kind of social crime had been committed, and not just against African-Americans, other minorities, and the Democratic voters who lost, but against all of us.

"Nevertheless," Hendrik Hertzberg wrote in a column in *The New Yorker,* "the election of 2000 was not stolen. Stealing, after all, is illegal, and, by definition, nothing the Justices of the Supreme Court do can be outside the law. They are the law. The election was not stolen. It was expropriated."

No one wanted to suggest that what had taken place in Florida and Washington, D.C. following the election was one more subtle form of domestic terrorism — a devaluing and a ripping away of the fundamental rights of individuals, not much different from stealing their right to the presumption of innocence or their right to be protected by the police instead of abused by them. The terrible question would not go away. If there was no law for the law enforcers and no law for the lawmakers, then to whom did one appeal when trouble came?

We'd seen a stunningly clear answer to that question at Columbine High School, and it was not a reassuring one.

On Sunday, December 17, 2000, a few days after the Supreme

Court issued its final ruling, the *Miami Herald* ran a story predicting a new political run for the latest Republican "hero." The paper was referring, of course, to Katherine Harris who was touted as having a "rosy future in state or national politics dominated by the Bush brothers." The speculation was that she could run for U.S. Congress from Sarasota or get rewarded soon with a high-level post in the Bush administration, although many observers felt that in the current angry climate in Washington, she would never be able to pass Senate confirmation. The joke making its way around Florida was that she might become an ambassador to a foreign land.

"Maybe Chad," went the punch line.

Others believed that Gov. Jeb Bush would help Harris by naming her Florida's secretary of state when that office stopped being elective in two more years. In early 2001, as all this conjecture swirled around her, Harris began touting electoral reforms and making the network talk show circuit, describing to ABC's Diane Sawyer and CNN's Larry King how many wonderful people had supported her actions after the election and not only thanked her personally, but sent her cards and flowers. She did let it be known that the Bush brothers, and especially George W., had been very distant and quiet toward her recently. With the election over, the two men seemed to be withdrawing their public support of Harris, who'd lately been skewered by comics and made fun of on a "Saturday Night Live" skit for her closeness to the Bushes. If nothing else, Harris appeared quite resilient and resourceful.

While the election lawsuits piled up and the comedians got their laughs, George W. Bush was busy selecting his Cabinet. He'd run for the White House as a healer and a conciliator. His primary campaign theme, delivered in nearly every speech he made, was that he could bring people together to work for the common good. He'd done this in Texas, he said, and he could do it on a larger scale in Washington, D.C. He was a peacemaker, he insisted, not a divider of the nation he was going to serve, and he would prove this if given the chance in office. Now he had that opportunity, and in mid-January, 2001, with the inauguration only days away, he did something that left all of his promises sounding hollow. And in the process, he once again heightened the conflict surrounding his victory.

He nominated John Ashcroft, the former Missouri governor and just-defeated U.S. Senator from that state, to be the country's next Attorney General. Of all the possible qualified candidates, Ashcroft was perhaps the most divisive person Bush could have selected for what many regarded as the single most important cabinet post. This nomination ensured that many more old wounds would be torn open and exposed in all their rawness. Ashcroft, like Pat Buchanan, Jerry Falwell and other prominent names on the religious right, was a cultural warrior from way back.

He was also exactly what his political opponents needed to keep organizing and mobilizing. As soon as Bush named him, the National Organization of Women, gay groups, greens, civil rights activists, anti-gun proponents, and those Americans who believed in a distinct separation of church and state all vowed to fight his nomination. The botched presidential election had brought these factions together and galvanized them into action. The Supreme Court ruling for Bush had strengthened their resolve, and the Ashcroft nomination now gave them a focal point and rallying cry. They began pouring out petitions and messages, via the Internet and other media outlets, for building strategies to oppose Ashcroft and the entire Bush administration.

If the 1990s had wound up looking something like the 1950s, there was a possibility that the first decade of the new millennium might bear a resemblance to the activist '60s. With the Bush inauguration approaching, protesters came to Washington with signs that read "Hail to the Thief" and "Selected, Not Elected." On January 20, they would generate the largest demonstration against an incoming president since the beginning of Richard Nixon's second term in 1973. Thus far, the new president was not proving to be a conciliator, but someone fundamentally beholden to the religious and right wing of the GOP.

The battle over John Ashcroft would not only open a new front in the uncivil war, but raise themes that carried back to the O.J. Simpson case and issues that reflected the ongoing struggle for African-American voting rights. These matters were no longer being discussed in relation to a tiny gathering of far-right radicals building a stash of weapons in the woods and selecting Jewish assassination targets. Nor were they focused around what the criminal justice system liked to characterize as a few "rogue cops" in Los Angeles or other big cities (as President-elect Bush prepared to take office, lawyers in L.A. were about to deliver another huge blow to the LAPD and reveal just how deep and pervasive its troubles were: in January 2001, 200 former and current police officers filed a class action lawsuit charging that while working for the LAPD they were systematically retaliated against for attempting to come forward and report cases of police misconduct to their superiors; when trying to do the right thing, they claimed, their information was brushed aside and they themselves were punished).

The uncivil war was no longer being played out on the fringes of American society or even inside the police department of one of its largest cities. Disturbing questions about race, criminal justice, abortion, and religious bigotry were now being directed at the man whom the new president wanted to become the top legal official in the United States.

41

After undergraduate school at Yale and law school at the University of Chicago, Ashcroft taught law for five years in his hometown of Springfield, Missouri. Springfield had voted Republican since the days of the Civil War, and the Ashcroft family carried on that tradition. John's father, the Reverend J. Robert Ashcroft, was much admired inside the Pentecostal Assemblies of God denomination, and he'd raised his son in that faith (on the day in 1995 that John was sworn into the U.S. Senate, Rev. Ashcroft annointed his head with Crisco cooking oil, a nod back to how King Saul and King David were annointed in the Bible). Pentecostal Christians are widely known for vigorous public praying, speaking in tongues, and other charismatic displays of fervor. As Ashcroft prepared to enter a life in mainstream politics, he avoided such rituals but stayed close to his evangelical roots and continued writing gospel songs.

In 1972, he ran for a local Republican congressional seat and lost, but three years later he was named an assistant state attorney general under John Danforth. Ashcroft soon found himself working in a small office in Jefferson City next to Clarence Thomas, the future Supreme Court Justice who would vote to give Bush the presidency in 2000. By 1977, Ashcroft was Missouri's Attorney General and was building a reputation and

power base by strongly opposing court-ordered school desegre-
gation in St. Louis and Kansas City. In 1983, he fought against a
voluntary plan for 12,000 inner-city St. Louis kids to be bused to
the suburbs — despite the fact that the twenty-two school dis-
tricts in the affected white neighborhoods had already
approved of the move. When Ashcroft appealed the federal ruling that backed this plan all the way to the U.S. Supreme Court,
it refused to hear the case.

After Ashcroft was elected Governor of Missouri, there were
allegations that he had tried to lower black voter turnout in St.
Louis, which is half African-American and broadly Democratic.
Twice, he vetoed laws promoting voter-registration efforts in
the city, perhaps to help the GOP. The percentage of registered
voters in St. Louis was the lowest in the state, and Democrats
believed that Ashcroft's vetoes were part of a deliberate
Republican strategy to help them win elections. Unlike other
Missouri election boards, the Ashcroft-appointed St. Louis
board did not deputize groups such as the League of Women
Voters to help increase voter registration. Bills ordering the St.
Louis board to confront these problems and change the situation came across Governor Ashcroft's desk, but he vetoed them.

When he reached the U.S. Senate in 1995, his elevation to
this office did not temper his views but seemed to harden them.
In a 1998 interview with *Southern Partisan* magazine, Ashcroft
praised this periodical, which had long trumpeted the notion
that slavery had been beneficial to blacks. The following year,

during a speech at Bob Jones University, which had a ban on inter-racial dating, Senator Ashcroft made a point of saying that the school honored the principle that all men were created equal. Those who ran Bob Jones, like those who'd started the Order in the American Northwest in 1983 and those who'd supported and embodied racism inside the Los Angeles Police Department for decades, were frightened by many things, but by nothing as much as the thought of people of different ethnic backgrounds becoming intimate. For white separatists and white supremacists, race-mixing had always been the cardinal sin that needed to be quashed. John Ashcroft received an honorary degree from Bob Jones University.

He wanted to dictate women's behavior as well. Ashcroft opposed all abortions except, as he once wrote, "those medically necessary to save the life of the mother." In his role as a U.S. Senator, he voted against safety locks on guns, voted against the assault-weapons ban, and voted against making it harder to buy firearms at gun shows. Among his biggest financial backers was the National Rifle Association.

Ashcroft gained more notoriety in the Senate in 1999, when he bitterly fought the nomination of Missouri Supreme Court Justice Ronnie White — the first African-American ever to achieve this position in the "Show Me" state — to a federal judgeship. Initially, Achcroft held up White's appointment to Missouri's high court for almost two years (he'd also blocked the nominations of openly gay ambassadorial nominee James

Hormel and Susan Oki Mollway, the first American woman to serve on the bench in Hawaii). But it was on the Bill Clinton-appointed Ronnie White, who had a stellar reputation and whom the American Bar Association had given a unanimous rating, that Ashcroft made his public stand.

During Judge White's confirmation hearing, the Senator focused on a single death penalty case in which White had dissented from the other Missouri Supreme Court justices because he felt the state may have presented faulty evidence. He did not contend that the defendant was innocent or should be released from prison, but to ensure due process, White felt that a new trial was in order. On the Senate floor, Ashcroft replayed the circumstances and called Judge White "pro-criminal," a characterization that was as inflammatory as it was false. In forty-one of fifty-nine death penalty cases, White had voted to uphold executions, while four of Ashcroft's own judicial nominees had chosen to overturn death sentences more often than that. In capital punishment cases, White had sided with the Ashcroft appointees 95 per cent of the time.

These numbers and the judge's public service record were irrelevant to the Missouri Senator and, ultimately, to the United States Senate itself, which decided to vote along party lines and defeat the judge, the first such nominee to be rejected by the Senate in twelve years.

By mid-January of 2001, as Ashcroft prepared to face many of the same Senators in his bid to become attorney general, these wounds were by no means closed. His confirmation hearings were conducted in a large, packed room holding the Senate Judiciary committee, media representatives, lobbyists, and TV cameras. As they began, women's groups opposing Ashcroft put on street demonstrations and a news conference outside the Capitol. They did not believe that a man who'd spent his entire political career fighting against the laws that gave women the right to make their own reproductive decisions could be trusted to enforce and uphold those laws once he became the nation's chief attorney. Many people felt that Ashcroft's private views on issues such as sex or race had always overridden his commitment to legal principles.

At the news conference, Patricia Ireland, the president of the National Organization for Women, said that a vote for this nominee "could mean a rude awakening to Senators in their next elections... We're counting on a mobilized, experienced, angry group of constituents across the country to bring pressure on every Senator."

On the opening day of the hearings, Massachusetts Senator Ted Kennedy strenuously questioned Ashcroft about his past moves to block voter registration in St. Louis. Inevitably, this confrontation brought up murmurs about the recent election fiasco. After the polls had closed in Florida, allegations of voter registration problems for blacks had surfaced throughout the state, as well as reports that police officers had set up roadblocks in African-American neighborhoods and stopped people on the way to the voting booths. Ashcroft's past work against inner-city voter registration in St. Louis exacerbated the feelings of many black Democrats who were convinced they'd been disenfranchised by the Florida vote count. Some saw a direct link between that disenfranchisement, the U.S. Supreme Court's decision to aid Bush in his quest for the White House, and Bush's desire to have Ashcroft as his attorney general. "If the African-American vote had been counted rather than hijacked in Florida," Yvonne Scruggs-Leftwich, executive director of the Black Leadership Forum, told the *Los Angeles Times*, "there would be no Bush presidency and no John Ashcroft."

The sparring between Senator Kennedy and Ashcroft was charged, but the higher drama came when Judge White appeared before the committee on January 18. He began his testimony by describing how he'd been raised poor and grown up in a dwelling with no kitchen or bathroom. He'd gone to work at eleven, selling papers and fast food, and while in grade school, he'd been attacked by bullies who'd regularly pelted with him things that were meant to be eaten. None of this, he said, had deterred him from getting an education and becoming first a lawyer and then a judge; the abuse had only left him more determined to have a legal career. He told the Senate and the nation that as a child he'd learned to stand up to the bullies and not be defeated by their cruelty. As a Missouri supreme court justice he'd now traveled to Washington to defend his record on the bench, but he didn't tell the Senate Judiciary

Committee that he still found himself in the position of warding off bullies.

"After decades of public service," he said, "I come to you today...committed to the rule of law."

"What's happened to you," Senator Kennedy told White, when referring to his treatment by Ashcroft during the judge's 1999 nomination process, "is one of the ugliest things that's happened to any candidate in recent years."

As White offered his story and answered questions from the committee, a sense of shame gradually began to filter into the room and to come through the TV cameras that were covering the event. It was the same kind of shame that had attended the O. J. Simpson trial when the racist tape recordings of Mark Fuhrman were played for the courtroom and the entire nation to hear. Fuhrman's words did not reflect someone's opinion about how certain police officers felt and operated; they were direct evidence of racial hatred and racial brutality. Five years later, White's appearance before the judiciary committee was again dredging up America's historical — and ongoing — racial divide and racial tragedy. It showed just how easily the combined issues of race and crime could be employed to damage (or destroy) anyone, regardless of the facts and whether one had attained the title of State Supreme Court Justice. The game was still the same. If one was made guilty in the public eye until proven innocent, then one was likely to remain guilty for a very long time.

White's statements to the committee moved California Senator Dianne Feinstein to offer a formal apology to the judge and caused Illinois Senator Dick Durbin to become outspokenly indignant over Ashcroft's attacks on the judge. The shame in the room deepened.

It was the twenty-first century, a new millennium, and a distinguished black man who'd spent his life serving the legal system and the community was still fighting the most basic battle of all: for his truth and his dignity. One well-chosen phrase — "pro criminal" — delivered at just the right moment and designed to smear and cripple was all it took to devalue everything one man had overcome and worked for and built. Two words could tar you for the rest of your career.

This was how President George W. Bush had decided to start bridging the racial divide in America.

While re-living his nomination struggle in front of the judiciary committee, Judge White did not become angry. He remained soft-spoken, gracious, and calm. He did not launch a counter-attack against Ashcroft and refused to call him a racist or to use any other label, saying only that the Missouri Senator had "seriously distorted" his legal record. He did not pass judgment or tell those who were weighing the Ashcroft nomination how they should vote on the matter. In a remark that went to the very core of the cultural and political battles being waged by Ashcroft and his allies over personal issues, like sexual preference or abortion, White explained to the committee that it was not for him to deliver final judgments on John Ashcroft. And the reason for this was because he did not know what was in another man's heart.

The most puzzling question generated by the Ashcroft hearings was why, of all the people President-elect Bush could have chosen to become America's next Attorney General, he'd picked this individual. Ashcroft's selection above all others was guaranteed to reinforce the divisions in a Senate that held exactly fifty Republicans and fifty Democrats — a legislative body that in recent times, and especially during Bill Clinton's impeachment process, had been nearly totally uncooperative and utterly partisan. Perhaps Bush was fulfilling a family promise or carrying on his father's work (he'd surrounded himself, after all, with Dick Cheney, Colin Powell, James Baker, and other former associates of George Bush senior). As early as 1991, President Bush had considered bringing Ashcroft in as *his* Attorney General. Then in 1998, a full year before George W. Bush officially announced his upcoming run for the White House, he let it be known that he liked Ashcroft's conservative, evangelical background and was thinking of him for this post, if not for a Supreme Court appointment. Perhaps he wanted Ashcroft to be a kind of mouthpiece for himself, because the Missourian was unafraid to voice the sort of politically incorrect views that virtually any president would now shy away from saying. Whatever the reason, Bush felt that Ashcroft was worth the trouble his nomination was causing.

Now the Senate had to decide whether or not he would serve as Attorney General. In late January, after Ashcroft narrowly won confirmation in the judiciary committee by a 10-8 vote, his nomination passed to the full Senate. For several days, they debated the issues and delayed taking a vote. The Republicans were ready to approve him, but the Democrats were in a difficult position. While many of them wanted to show a new spirit of co-operation inside their own legislative chamber and to develop a more friendly and bipartisan relationship with the new administration, they found Ashcroft objectionable. Some would strictly vote their conscience and others would not.

The Democrats put up a fight, but in the end a few defected and it took only a majority of Senators to clear the nomination. On February 1, after nearly three weeks of consideration, Ashcroft was approved and took office. It was another huge win for President Bush. He was in the White House and his man was now the Attorney General of the United States. Bush appeared to have won everything.

Or had he?

EPILOGUE

In January of 2001, as Bill Clinton's two terms in office came to an end and he and his wife prepared to move out of the White House, a poignancy was felt across the nation, and many political observers commented on it. The lingering sense of illegitimacy hanging over the recent presidential election accounted for parts of this sentiment but not all of it. The Clinton years, one now heard regularly, were going to be missed. We'd gone through eight years with this couple, and those years had been like nothing in previous American history. Our experience with the Clintons had been ragged and real, like the emotional experience inside of most families. We'd seen through the veil of a presidential marriage and been forced to look at this imperfect union — and at some uncomfortable pieces of ourselves. Not only had everyone survived this psychic jolt, we were somehow better for it.

There was more to life than public relations and play-acting for the media. There was the sting and the grace and the binding, bittersweet love of real people in motion. There were layers of feeling and rivers of tender and contradictory impulses. There was the full fragrant odor of human struggle for understanding and acceptance, the very same drama that all of us were caught in.

If President Clinton had grown up a little bit in office, so had his country. We did not have to fear adult reality quite as much as we'd once thought, nor did we need as much protection as we'd once believed. We did not have to deny all of our complexity and humanity in order to play a useful social role. We were stronger than we'd realized, more flexible and adaptable. We weren't children, after all, but capable of something more as adults.

Not every problem we'd encountered with the Clintons offered up an easy solution. Not every personality could be grasped in an instant or a twenty-second political TV ad. We were far more interesting creatures than that, if we only let ourselves be. Twice, President Clinton had tested his ideas, as well as his public demeanor and some of his private demons, in the great marketplace of American democracy. Twice, the citizens of his country had freely elected him to serve in our highest office. In a nation where the ideal was that every person's vote counted as much as every other person's, he had won the ultimate test on two occasions. Despite his flaws and his unvarnished behavior, the population had chosen him to lead.

By contrast, George W. Bush, who had now replaced Clinton and his administration, projected no problems and no messes. When he spoke in public, he hinted at no inner conflicts or intriguing twists of personality. He conveyed no real experience of his own and no identity, except to be pleasant on every occasion. If the goal was to create a sense of unreality, he was a master at this. He gave no clue of who he was, except a son following his father's path, and perhaps not even wanting to do so. He mostly seemed to be listening to the orders of others, but where they came from one could only guess. In his first weeks in office, he invited all manner of ethnic, religious, and political groups to the White House in an effort to be inclusive and to build some connections with the African-American community and others who'd felt disenfranchised by the election just past. With Ashcroft's confirmation as Attorney General, Bush had his work cut out for him.

One did not know what sort of president he might become, and in the end that was not really the issue. What had happened in Florida last November went deeper than party politics or race. It was not a black versus white issue or a Republican versus Democrat issue or an issue that could be settled by attorneys arguing fine points of law, but a matter of freedom and choice and equality — the very same issues that had driven the uncivil war in America during the past few decades. The majority of the populace had not freely elected Bush to office or given him our consent to be President. We had not entrusted him with power or made a social agreement to be governed by him. He had been imposed on the voting public, and that action had diminished all of us, making us less equal to our leaders and making our principles less than what they'd been. One could only hope that this had not permanently shifted the way the United States was constructed and functioned. But who knew what the future offered?

Oppression could come in the back door as well as the front, and it could be wearing the most respectable clothing and face in the land. It could wear a soft grin just as easily as a hard glare. It was a time to be diligent and vigilant toward those in high office and to keep them under scrutiny. It was a time to recognize that the governed have clout too, if they choose to use it. And if they don't, they can passively agree to all kinds of regrettable things.

As Bill Clinton left town and the new President began conducting business in Washington, D.C., down in Florida election officials were trying to figure out what to do with their much-criticized punch card voting system. By late January 2001, it appeared that that system was headed for the scrap heap. Governor Jeb Bush had recently sat on a commission that was moving toward accepting the fact that it might be worth the $20 million or so it would cost to replace the old punch cards and Votomatic machines with something more efficient. And in Miami-Dade County, elections supervisor David Leahy, under the sanction of the Secretary of State's office headed by Katherine Harris, was in charge of using up all the remaining punch cards from the 2000 debacle. Pretty soon, no evidence of that event would be left behind as a reminder.

ACKNOWLEDGEMENTS

Twenty-five years ago, a literary agent in New York told me that writing must be a process of self-discovery. At the time, this seemed like a simple and self-evident statement, but over the decades I've found that it holds layers of meaning and revelation. As a young man, when I started to write a book, I believed that I already knew what I wanted to say and that I was working alone. Much later, I realized that the real challenge was uncovering the subject as I went along and trusting that others could assist me with this process.

When this book was ready to be written, a space opened up to make room for it and certain people arrived to help. Among them were Michael Viner and Deborah Raffin, who own and run New Millennium Press. They have consistently encouraged me to follow my instincts, which is the best thing a writer can hope for, and they've also provided some instinctual direction of their own. I'm very grateful for their support.

In addition, some of the usual suspects lined up to offer their knowledge, insight, and intuitions about the social disorders I was trying to understand and describe. Bob Richards, Donald

Freed, Lee Hill, Nancy Singular, Reid Boates, Mark Daily, and Joyce Jacques all made significant contributions. Each was thinking some of what I was thinking — or what I wasn't yet thinking and couldn't yet articulate. They were there to fill in the blanks.

Finally, Shelly Kale and Julie McCarron, my editors at New Millennium, lent their intelligence, sensibilities, and enthusiasm to these pages in ways that made what I was doing clearer and better. Their thoughts expanded my own, their critical eyes and ears were invaluable in shaping the book. They widened and deepened the discovery process.

HN 90 .V5 S48 2001
Singular, Stephen.
The uncivil war

DATE DUE

#47-0108 Peel Off Pressure Sensitive